The Master Musicians Series

PURCELL

Series edited by
Sir Jack Westrup, M.A., Hon. D.Mus.(Oxon), F.R.C.O.
Professor Emeritus of Music, Oxford University

THE MASTER MUSICIANS SERIES

PURCELL

by

J. A. Westrup

*With eight pages of plates
and music examples in the text*

London
J. M. DENT & SONS LTD

To
G. K. C. R.
in friendship and gratitude

. . . ὁσσάκις ἀμφότεροι
ἥλιον ἐν λέσχῃ κατεδύσαμεν.

Not mood in him nor meaning, proud fire or sacred fear,
Or love or pity or all that sweet notes not his might nursle:
It is the forgèd feature finds me; it is the rehearsal
Of own, of abrupt self there so thrusts on, so throngs the ear.

GERARD MANLEY HOPKINS.

PREFACE TO THE FIRST EDITION

I HAVE to thank His Majesty the King for permission to reproduce a page of Purcell's autograph manuscript in the Royal Music Library; Mr. B. Campbell Cooke for valuable assistance in investigating the genealogy of Purcell's family; Mr. Gerald Cooper, secretary of the Purcell Society, for providing me with materials for the catalogue of works; Professor Edward J. Dent for reading through the book in proof and making a number of helpful suggestions; Mr. Rupert Erlebach, secretary of the Royal Musical Association; the dean and chapter of Exeter, for allowing me to publish a photograph of Purcell's autograph letter; Mr. C. B. Oldman, of the British Museum; Dr. Percy Scholes, who generously placed the whole of his 'Purcell' file at my disposal; and Mr. Lawrence Tanner and the staff of the Westminster Abbey Chapter Library.

The presence of so many footnotes in a book intended primarily for the general reader may cause surprise. I should have been glad to dispense with them if I could have referred throughout to some comprehensive and authoritative work on the subject. But for want of any fully documented study of Purcell or any complete account of Restoration music as a whole I had no other course but to give all the sources of my information. There is, after all, a satisfaction in knowing the authority for even the most familiar statements; and no one is likely to feel regret if familiar statements are sometimes shown to rest on very flimsy foundations. In discussing particular aspects of Purcell's work and period I have had the advantage of several scholarly works which I have been content to quote as sufficient authority. My debt to the late Mr. Godfrey Arkwright, the late William Barclay Squire, Professor Dent, Professor Nicoll and others will be sufficiently apparent from the following pages. Most of the abbreviations in the footnotes will easily be understood by reference to the bibliography; any that might be obscure are explained in a note on page 302.

The musical examples presented a problem. A good many of them are for voice and continuo only in the original text. I had the choice between printing this bare skeleton or having recourse to the elaborations provided by the editors of the Purcell Society. The first course, however, might have proved embarrassing to the reader unskilled in the mysteries of thoroughbass, and the second would have taken up too much space. I have therefore compromised by sketching in on the bass stave an outline of the complementary harmony. This does not pretend in all cases to be a complete realization and certainly makes no claim to be a finished artistic product, which would be impossible within the limits of a single stave; it is intended merely as a rough guide to the basic harmonic structure. I have made an exception to this rule where obbligato instruments accompany the voice and in the examples from *Dido and Æneas,* where I have used Professor Dent's edition as an illustration of what an imaginative scholar can do with the bare bones of an antique score.

LONDON,   J.A.W.
   December 1936.

NOTE ON THE SEVENTH EDITION

IN addition to various minor adjustments in the text I have extended Appendix E to include further information about Purcell's family. This has involved the omission of the 'Suggested Genealogical Tree' printed in earlier editions; but since the relationships within the family are complex and sometimes appear to be contradictory, that is not a disadvantage.

November 1974.   J.A.W.

CONTENTS

ILLUSTRATIONS

Between pages 84 and 85

CHAPTER I

FAMILY AND BOYHOOD

A LIFE of Henry Purcell is of necessity a slender record. His contemporaries have left us abundant evidence of the esteem and admiration in which he was held as a composer. Tudway, who knew him well, says that he was 'confessedly the greatest Genius we ever had.'[1] When he died he was hailed as 'one of the most Celebrated Masters of the Science of Musick in the Kingdom, and scarce Inferiour to any in Europe.'[2] To Roger North he was 'the divine Purcell.'[3] But these generous tributes, illuminating as they are, tell us little about the man. Nor are the diarists any help. Pepys, who was a passionate lover of music, must almost certainly have come across Purcell at some time during his life; but the diary unfortunately stops at 1669, when the composer was only ten years old. Evelyn, as a cultivated gentleman, enjoyed music, but he was more interested in performers than in composers. As an old man he heard some songs by 'the last Mr. Pursal' at Pepys's house[4]; but he does not say what they were or what he thought of them, and of Purcell himself he has nothing to tell us.

The lack of personal testimony compels us to depend almost entirely on official records. Purcell passed all his life in the service of the king and the church. His name occurs frequently

[1] Brit. Mus., Harl. 7342, fo. 12.
[2] *Flying Post*, 23rd–26th November 1695.
[3] *Memoirs of Musick* (ed. Rimbault), p. 96.
[4] 30th May 1698. All quotations from Evelyn's *Diary* are from the latest edition by E. S. de Beer. Bray's edition read 'Dr. Purcel' in this passage. For the question of Purcell's supposed doctorate see my paper, 'Fact and Fiction about Purcell,' in the *Proceedings of the Musical Association*, 1935–6, p. 110.

in state papers, in the Lord Chamberlain's lists and accounts, and in the records of Westminster Abbey. The information provided by these sources makes it possible to give a tolerably complete and reasonably accurate account of his career; and this can be supplemented by extracts from the rate-books of St. Margaret's, Westminster, by references to his published works, and by particulars of the many theatrical entertainments for which he is known to have written music. It still remains difficult to get any clear idea of his personality or character. The man who could provide music for the ribald indecency of tavern catches —the texts are comfortably bowdlerized in the Purcell Society's edition—was clearly no anchorite; but enthusiasm for hearty drinking songs is not necessarily the mark of a confirmed debauchee. Portraits sometimes give a clue to character, but Purcell's are rather puzzling. The picture attributed to Kneller in the National Portrait Gallery shows us an idealized youth; we note the large nose, the humorous mouth, a touch of melancholy in the eyes and a hint of the double chin which is quite definite in the frontispiece to the *Sonatas of III Parts*. Here too we have the humorous, almost jolly mouth and the prominent Roman nose. But there seems to be also a note of comfortable complacency— or is that merely the effect of the flowing wig and the lace cravat? The engraving suggests a portly clubman in his prime rather than a rising young composer. Even in Closterman's dignified portrait, which seems to strike a mean between two extremes and may be the most faithful record of the three, the personality of the sitter remains elusive.[1]

Beyond these evidences of the past we have nothing to give us the man behind the music. Anecdotes of his private life—some scurrilous—have been preserved, but they are not contemporary and their authenticity is very doubtful. Imaginative biography, so popular at the present day, is a dangerous pastime, particularly if its subject is a great artist. Since history will not tell us more

[1] For an analysis of Purcell's character based on his handwriting see F. H. Walker, 'Purcell's Handwriting,' *Monthly Musical Record*, September 1942.

of Purcell, we must be content with a plain, unvarnished tale: the appointments he held, the commissions he undertook and the astonishing industry of a life of creative activity cut short in its prime.

Nothing certain is known of his antecedents. According to O'Hart's *Irish Pedigrees* [1] the family can be traced back to Sir Hugh Porcel, who came over from Normandy with William the Conqueror. There were branches of the family in several English counties in the Middle Ages, and an Irish branch was established in the twelfth century. The Oxfordshire Purcells, who were the lords of Newton-Purcell, lasted till the sixteenth century, and a cadet of this branch, Roger Purcell, was the founder of the Shropshire Purcells at the close of the twelfth century. Both the Irish Purcells and the Shropshire family were flourishing in the seventeenth century. [2] O'Hart goes on to say that from an off-shoot of the latter 'descended the famous musician, whose career is well known'; but he brings forward no evidence, and the assumption that Purcell's career is well known should perhaps put us on our guard against accepting the rest of his information.

It is true that the coat of arms printed on the title-page of Purcell's *Sonatas of III Parts* bears the three boars' heads which are common to the arms of both the Shropshire and the Kilkenny Purcells; and there is no reason for supposing that he was not related to one or other of these branches. But there were a large number of Purcells in London in the seventeenth century, as any one can see who takes the trouble to look through the parish registers which have been printed; and until a satisfactory genealogy that will relate them all together has been established it is unsafe to state definitely what has not yet been proved. The late Dr. Grattan Flood, whose industry in establishing the biographies of English musicians was only exceeded by his enthusiasm for his native island, claimed Purcell as an Irishman and declared that

[1] Vol. ii, p. 347 seq.
[2] For the latter see *The Visitation of Shropshire, 1623*, published by the Harleian Society, pp. 411–14.

he had succeeded in tracing his grandfather and great-grandfather.[1] But no evidence in support of his theory has been published, and it seems likely that here patriotic zeal has proved stronger than judgment.

Henry Purcell appears to have been born in the summer or autumn of 1659. The registration of his baptism has not been discovered and may never have been recorded. Parish registers are notoriously defective for the Commonwealth period. The date of his birth, however, is generally assumed to have been some time between June and November of this year on the evidence of the memorial tablet in Westminster Abbey, which records that he died on 21st November 1695 'anno aetatis suae 37mo.,' and of the words 'aetat. suae 24' on the title-page of his *Sonatas of III Parts*, published in 1683. He may have been born at Westminster, since his father lived there after the Restoration. Certainly it was at Westminster that his boyhood and indeed his whole life—apart from casual migrations with the court—was spent. How different was the London he knew from our own gargantuan metropolis can be seen at a glance by turning over one or two of the maps and prints of the period. A short walk from the abbey down Tothill Street brought the townsman to the open country, and north of Piccadilly all was pasture and heath. Not far from Palace Yard one could hire a boat and travel down the river—the quickest way to the City— passing on the north the houses and palaces of the great and on the south the empty wastes of Lambeth Marsh. Further east was the City itself and London's only bridge spanning the river to reach Southwark on the southern side. A narrow, picturesque, provincial town it would seem by modern standards; yet it was England's capital and the centre of her government.

The boy grew up in an ideal environment. His father, Thomas

[1] Bridge, *Twelve Good Musicians*, pp. 139–41; Grattan Flood, 'Irish Ancestry of Garland, Dowland, Campion, and Purcell,' *Music and Letters*, 1922, pp. 64–5.

Purcell,[1] was a professional musician who had a distinguished career in the royal service from the Restoration till his death in 1682. Of his life during the Commonwealth—a lean time for church musicians—we have no record. Pepys tells us how he met 'Mr. Lock and Pursell, Maisters of Musique,' at Westminster Hall in February 1660, when the question of Charles II's return was still in the balance. They went to the coffee-house together, where they had 'variety of brave Italian and Spanish songs, and a canon for eight voices, which Mr. Lock had lately made on these words: *Domine salvum fac regem,* an admirable thing.'[2] But whether this Mr. Purcell was Thomas or the elder Henry[3] is quite uncertain.

On the restoration of Charles II Thomas Purcell secured a place as a tenor in the reconstituted choir of the Chapel Royal at Whitehall, and as such sang at the king's coronation, wearing the special scarlet allowed for the occasion.[4] This was a great day for loyal Englishmen and all the more impressive as so many years had passed since the full trappings of royalty had last been seen. Pepys, who had been a boy of seven when the Civil War broke out, was so excited that he got up at four o'clock and waited till eleven in the north transept of the abbey to see the ceremony. The king's band of violins attended and looked very smart in their red vests. Of the music he heard little owing to

[1] Letter from Thomas Purcell to John Gostling, 8th February 1679 (printed by Cummings, p. 28): 'I have received the favor of yours of the 4th with the inclosed for my sonne Henry. . . . My sonne is composing wherin you will be chiefly concern'd.' For the significance of this letter and a discussion of the evidence for Purcell's parentage see Appendix E.

[2] 21st February 1660. 'Mr. Lock' is, of course, Matthew Locke, the composer. The phrase 'Maisters of Musique' means that they were professional musicians; cf. 16th August 1660, where there is a reference to 'Captain Cooke . . . and other Maisters of Musique.'

[3] They appear to have been of the same generation and were therefore probably brothers or cousins.

[4] *King's Musick,* p. 269; *Cheque Book,* p. 128.

the noise. Evelyn, who speaks of 'anthems & rare musique playing with *Lutes, Viols, Trumpets, Organs & Voices* &c.,' seems to have been more fortunate.[1]

The elder Henry Purcell was also a musician. He is probably to be identified with the 'Mr. Henry Persill' who took the part of Mustapha in Sir William D'Avenant's experimental opera *The Siege of Rhodes* when it was first produced in London in 1656.[2] Like his brother Thomas, he was successful in getting a place as a gentleman of the Chapel Royal and as a musician for the lute and voice. He was also appointed a senior singing-man (or lay-clerk) and master of the choristers at Westminster Abbey, where he took up his duties on 16th February 1661. He died on 11th August 1664 and was buried two days later in the east cloister of the abbey.[3]

Of Thomas's large family only two, Henry and Daniel, seem to have followed their father's profession. Francis became a groom of the Privy Chamber and in 1682 succeeded his father as groom of the robes.[4] Edward, who was born in 1655 or 1656 (as his epitaph shows), became a 'gentleman usher daily waiter assistant' in the royal household. His duties included assisting in the arrangements for the king's journeys from London to Windsor, Newmarket and elsewhere.[5] He remained in this post for ten years. Later he entered the army. As a lieutenant in Colonel Trelawny's infantry regiment he served with distinction in Ireland and Flanders, being eventually promoted to the rank of lieutenant-colonel. The

[1] Pepys and Evelyn, 23rd April 1661. Cf. *King's Musick*, p. 131; Baker's *Chronicle*, p. 817.

[2] The list of the cast is printed in the first edition of the libretto (1656). For *The Siege of Rhodes* see p. 106.

[3] *Cheque Book*, pp. 13 and 128; *King's Musick*, pp. 124 and 151; *Abbey Registers*, p. 161; Westminster Abbey Precentor's Book, fo. 3 and *passim*.

[4] See Appendix E.

[5] *Cal. Treas. Books*, 15th September 1673, 8th June 1681, 2nd December 1682, 18th April 1683; Chamberlayne, *Angliae Notitia*, 14th ed. (1682), pt. i, p. 166.

rest of his career is best told in the words of his epitaph in the tiny parish church of Wytham, a few miles north-west of Oxford:

HE assisted S^R GEORGE ROOK in taking GIBRALTAR, and the PRINCE of HESSE in the memorable defence of it. HE followed that PRINCE to BARCELONA, and was at the taking of MOUNTJOY, where that brave PRINCE was killed: and continued to signalize courage in the seige [*sic*] and taking of that city: in the year of our LORD 1705. HE enjoyed great services until the much lamented death of his late Mistress QUEEN ANN: when, decayed with age, and broken with misfortunes, he retired to the house of the Right Hon^{ll} the EARL of ABINGDON.

He died JUNE 20TH, 1717 AGED 61 YEARS.[1]

His body rests beneath the chancel of the church. Charles became a sailor and died at sea off the coast of Guinea. Of Matthew and Joseph we know little more than their names.[2]

Like several other musicians in the royal service Thomas Purcell was not content with a single post. The cost of living had gone up since pre-Commonwealth days,[3] and even though the salaries of the gentlemen of the chapel were raised in 1662 from £40 to £70 a year,[4] he probably found the sum insufficient for a married man with a family. The death of Henry Lawes in October 1662 created a vacancy in the private music for lutes, viols and voices, to which Thomas was appointed a few weeks later.[5] Lawes, celebrated song composer, 'the Priest of *Phoebus* Quire,' as Milton called him, was one of the few members of Charles I's Chapel Royal choir to re-enter the royal service at

[1] Epitaph at Wytham. At one time the stone was partially covered by choir-stalls, but these have now been removed.
[2] See Appendix E.
[3] The gentlemen of the Chapel Royal, in a petition dated September 1662, plead that diet, rents and apparel have increased in price since the reign of James I and that £40 then was better than £80 now (*Cal. S. P. Dom.*).
[4] *Cal. S. P. Dom.*, 14th October 1662, October 1663, etc.; *Cal. Treas. Books,* 9th November 1664; *Cheque Book,* p. 96.
[5] *Cheque Book,* p. 13; *King's Musick,* p. 151 (10th November 1662).

the Restoration. He was already an elderly man in 1660 and had had a serious illness in the winter of 1660–1.[1] His death severed yet another of the links that bound Restoration music to the old traditions. The emoluments of Thomas's new post were £32 2s. 6d. per annum, which included £16 2s. 6d. for his livery. And a very handsome livery it was: 'a camlet gown, garded with black velvet and furred,' a damask jacket and a velvet doublet.[2]

Young Henry Purcell must have shown signs of ability at an early age, if the three-part song, *Sweet tyranness, I now resign,* published in Playford's *Musical Companion* in 1667, is by him and not, as is commonly assumed, by his uncle.[3] At any rate his father thought him sufficiently promising to get him into the choir of the Chapel Royal. A popular tradition, for which there is no foundation, asserts that he was only six years old at the time. It seems an unusually early age; and indeed analogy would suggest that the tradition is false. Blow, Wise and Humfrey, who are cited by Hawkins as belonging to what he calls the 'first set of chapel children' after the Restoration, were respectively eleven, twelve and thirteen in 1660, and these ages, if they are not exceptional, would suggest that ancient and modern practice were much the same.[4] All that we know definitely about Purcell's history as a choirboy is that his voice broke in 1673.[5] Beyond that lies the territory of invention.

[1] Pepys, 30th December 1660.
[2] *King's Musick*, pp. 151–2; *Cal. S. P. Dom.*, 16th February 1663. 'Camlet' was a material made out of silk and wool. The name is due to the fact that it was originally made from camel's hair.
[3] The fact that it was reissued as a solo song, together with other songs by Purcell, in *New Ayres and Dialogues* (1678) suggests that the attribution to the elder Henry may be incorrect.
[4] Wise's age is only conjectural; but as his voice broke in 1664 (*King's Musick*, p. 168) he was almost certainly not more than twelve in 1660.
[5] *King's Musick*, p. 263.

CHAPTER II

AT THE CHAPEL ROYAL

THE children of the chapel were twelve in number.[1] They were under the direction of a master, who not only taught them to sing but was also responsible for seeing that they were housed and fed, that their clothes were washed regularly, and that they received a proper general education. The allowance for each boy's expenses in the past had been £15 4s. 2d. per annum, but the increase in the cost of living made it necessary to raise it to £30 in 1661.[2] As servants of His Majesty the choirboys had their official uniforms, or liveries, particulars of which are given in the Lord Chamberlain's records:

For each of them, one cloak of bastard scarlett cloth lyned with velvett, one suit and coat of the same cloth made up and trimmed with silver and silk lace after the manner of our footmen's liveries, and also to the said suit three shirts, three half shirts, three pairs of shoes, three pair of thigh stocking, whereof one pair of silk and two pair of worsted, two hats with bands, six bands and six pairs of cuffs, whereof two laced and four plain, three handkerchers, three pairs of gloves and two pieces and a half of rebon for trimming garters and shoestrings.

And at Easter, for their summer liveries, for each boy one cloak of bastard scarlett lined with sattin and one doublett of sattin with bastard scarlett trunk hose made and trimmed up as aforesaid, with three shirts, three half shirts, three pair of shoes, three pair of thigh stockings, whereof one pair of silk and two pairs of worsted, two hats with bands, etc.[3]

Their general education appears to have consisted principally

[1] *Cal. S. P. Dom.*, 12th September 1661; *King's Musick*, p. 136.
[2] *Cal. S. P. Dom.*, 14th October 1661.
[3] *King's Musick*, p. 136 (cf. p. 229).

of writing and Latin.[1] They also had lessons on the lute, violin
and organ.[2] The proficiency they acquired on the latter instrument is evident from the fact that several of them were given
important positions as cathedral organists at quite an early age.
As far as one can tell, the boys were properly looked after. Even
the older ones were apparently sent to bed at eight o'clock.[3]
When they were ill with smallpox or spotted fever or laid up,
as once happened, with a broken leg, special allowances were
made for doctors' fees and sick-room expenses, which included
the provision of a nurse.[4] In cold weather they had a fire in
their music room.[5]

The atmosphere of the choir school, small though it was, must
have been much like that of the modern preparatory boarding-
school, to which boys are sent from all over the country. It was
essential that the king's chapel should have the best voices obtain-
able, and for this purpose successive masters of the children
travelled all over England—to Newark, Lincoln, Rochester,
Peterborough, Worcester, Lichfield, Canterbury, Oxford, Cambridge, Gloucester and Hereford—in search of suitable boys.[6]
What the organists in these towns said when their best boys were
taken from them is not recorded. So usual was the practice that
a warrant for payments to the master of the children in 1673 is
specifically endorsed: 'In this warrant was nothing for fetching
children from several cathedrals, as is sometymes.' [7]

The first master of the children after the Restoration was Henry
Cooke—Captain Cooke, as he was always called, in compliment
to the rank he had held in the Royalist army during the Civil
War. He has not always been kindly treated by historians. It
is true that what we have of his music does not encourage a belief

[1] *King's Musick*, pp. 143, 157, etc.
[2] *King's Musick*, pp. 157, 170, 224, 231, etc.
[3] Pepys, 27th August 1664.
[4] *King's Musick*, pp. 177, 231, 260, 312, 327, 367.
[5] *King's Musick*, p. 167, etc.
[6] *King's Musick*, pp. 134, 224, 231, 290, 312, 338, 367.
[7] *King's Musick*, p. 254.

in his gifts as a composer [1]; but there is nothing to show that he
was in any sense an amateur or unfitted for his job. Indeed, all
the evidence points the other way. The value of a choir-trainer's
work is to be seen in his results. Cooke's results were remarkable
in themselves, but they appear even more remarkable when we
consider the difficulties he had to face. Every choirmaster knows
that one of the things he particularly dreads is the departure of
his older boys before the younger ones are sufficiently advanced
to take their place; he relies on the continuance of a tradition.
Cooke had no tradition to depend on; he was starting, so to speak,
from scratch. The Chapel Royal choir had naturally been dis-
banded during the Commonwealth; Cooke's task was to build
up a tradition with an entirely new set of boys. As time went on
he would be able to draw on the resources of the reconstituted
cathedral choirs in various parts of the kingdom; but at the outset
he had to depend largely on good fortune and his own instinct
for finding the right boys.

Of that early uphill struggle we know little. We can only
guess at the disappointments and exasperation that he had to
endure in the course of the first few months. The preparation
of the special music for the king's coronation in April 1661 must
have caused him grave anxiety. There is a hint of late sessions
in the entry in the Lord Chamberlain's records which speaks
of £2 16s. to Henry Cooke 'for torches and lights for practising
the musick against his Majesty's coronation.' [2] Matthew Locke
tells us incidentally, in the course of a vehement argument with
Thomas Salmon, that for over a year after the Chapel Royal was
reopened it was necessary to fill up the treble parts of the anthems
and services with cornetts and men singing falsetto, 'there being
not one Lad, for all that time, capable of Singing his Part readily.' [3]

[1] See, for example, the consecutive octaves between tune and bass
in the three-part song 'Long have I thought it was in vain,' printed in
Playford's *Musical Companion*, p. 201, and other consecutives in an
anthem quoted by J. C. Bridge in *Musical Antiquary*, ii, p. 70.

[2] *King's Musick*, p. 136.

[3] *The Present Practice of Music Vindicated* (1673), p. 19.

Locke was not a moderate writer, and one has half a suspicion that he is exaggerating here. It is difficult to believe that there was not a single boy able to sing properly. If Blow, Humfrey and Wise were among the first set of boys, it seems odd that they should have displayed so little sign of nascent musicianship. Pepys was an occasional visitor to the chapel, but there is no suggestion in his diary that the boys were as incapable as this. He does mention, it is true, that on one occasion the anthem was badly sung, which seems to have amused the king.[1] But accidents like this will happen in the best choirs. When he tells us how he went along one Saturday in February 1661 to hear the boys practise under Cooke, he says nothing to imply that the singing was inadequate; on the contrary it was 'rare Musique.'[2]

Nevertheless it is probable enough that the singing of the boys as a whole was not always reliable; and in the very early stages the music may have been sung by men only. It is perhaps significant that Pepys, speaking of a service in July 1660, says: 'Here I heard very good music, the first time that ever I remember to have heard the organs and singing-men in surplices in my life,' without any mention of the boys.[3] But when he refers to anthems 'sung by Captain Cooke,' there is no need to suppose that the music was entirely for solo voice or voices; he is presumably speaking of the 'verse' sections only.[4] The use of cornetts in the chapel, either as a makeshift or to strengthen the voices, is attested by Evelyn and can be paralleled from Westminster Abbey, where a cornett player was paid a regular salary from 1661 to 1667; and Roger North tells us that 'in the north, where good, or at least skillful voices were scarce and I am sure at Durham and Carlile if not at York, the Quires in time of memory have had wind musick to supply the want of voices and sound great.'[5]

[1] 14th October 1660.
[2] 23rd February 1661. The text reads 'Captain Cooke and his boy,' but the singular is unlikely.
[3] 8th July 1660.   [4] 12th August 1660; 18th May 1662.
[5] Evelyn, 21st December 1662; W.A.M. 33695, fo. 4ᵛ, etc.; *Musicall Gramarian*, p. 6.

The cornett, a wooden intrument with a small cup-shaped mouthpiece, now obsolete, was considered the best substitute for treble voices. 'What,' asks North in the same passage, 'can yeild a tone so like an eunuch's voice as a true cornet pipe?' Elsewhere he tells us that 'the Labour of the Lips is too great, and it is seldom well sounded,' [1] in which case the remedy must often have been worse than the disease. The king, one may suppose, had the best cornett players in his private wind music, who could easily be detailed for service in the royal chapel. Dr. William Child, the senior organist, was himself a cornett player—not by any means a unique example of versatility.[2] Evelyn, as a true conservative, enjoyed 'the antient grave and solemn wind musique' and regretted it when the use of cornetts in the chapel was abandoned.[3]

Cooke possessed one excellent qualification as a choir-trainer: he was a first-rate singer himself. Pepys was convinced that he had 'the best manner of singing in the world.' [4] Six years before the Restoration, when Evelyn heard him sing to his own accompaniment on the lute, he was already considered the best singer 'after the *Italian* manner' in England.[5] The quoted words are significant, as we shall see later. During the Commonwealth he had established a reputation as a teacher. As early as 1651 he is mentioned in Playford's *Musicall Banquet* as one of a number of 'excellent and able Masters' for the voice and viol.[6] He could also claim to have assisted at the birth of British opera. He had

[1] *Life of the Right Honourable Francis North* (1742), p. 135.

[2] *King's Musick,* p. 123.

[3] Loc. cit. Evelyn's experience of cornett-playing seems to have been happier than North's. He speaks of it as 'that instrument . . . in which the English were so skilfull.' But it should be remembered that he was not so keen or competent a critic as North, and it is clear from this passage that he was prejudiced.

[4] 27th July 1661.   [5] 28th October 1654.

[6] The only surviving copies of this work are in the Bodleian Library and the Huntington Library (San Marino, California). A facsimile of the relevant page is printed in Scholes, *The Puritans and Music,* facing p. 166.

appeared as Solyman in D'Avenant's *The Siege of Rhodes* in 1656 and had composed some of the songs for it. He was, in fact, a thoroughly experienced musician and an admirable choice for the post of master.

A tradition has grown up that Cooke was inordinately vain; one recent biographer of Purcell calls him 'the intolerably conceited Captain Cooke.' The tradition derives from a foolish remark of that old gossip, Anthony Wood, and from an incident recorded by Pepys. Wood, in his collection of manuscript notes on English musicians (now in the Bodleian Library), after confirming Evelyn's testimony to Cooke's reputation as a singer, suggests that he was eclipsed by Pelham Humfrey, 'and then as 'tis said the captaine died in discontent and with greif.'[1] This idiotic piece of tavern tittle-tattle is too absurd to be taken seriously. It is quite possible that when Humfrey 'came up,' as Wood quaintly puts it, Cooke had to look to his laurels. But it is ridiculous to suggest that he succumbed to a mortal attack of professional jealousy. Certainly he approved of Humfrey sufficiently to accept him as a son-in-law.[2]

Pepys's evidence is equally suspect. The occasion was a day in February 1667. He and Cooke were both guests at a dinner party given by Dr. Clerke, physician to the royal household. The party does not seem to have been a success. Pepys admits that he never wanted to go in the first place, and to make matters worse the dinner was 'an ill and little mean one, with foul cloth and dishes, and everything poor.' Talk ran on plays and operas, in the course of which 'Captain Cooke had the arrogance to say that he was fain to direct Sir W. Davenant in the breaking of his verses into such and such lengths, according as would be fit for music, and how he used to swear at Davenant and command him that way, when W. Davenant would be angry, and find fault with this or that note; but a vain coxcomb I perceive he is, though he

[1] Bodleian, Wood D 19 (4), fo. 37ᵛ.

[2] See the petition from Humfrey's widow, *Cal. Treas. Books*, v, ii, p. 1369, where she is described as 'relict of Pelham Humphrey and daughter to Henry Cooke, late Master of his Majesty's Chapel.'

sings and composes so well.' A little later Pepys complains of Cooke's 'bragging that he doth understand tones and sounds as well as any man in the world, and better than Sir W. Davenant or anybody else.' Cooke may have had rather an important air which annoyed Pepys, whose liver was probably restive as a result of the dinner. But it is a little unfair to give him a reputation for conceit on the strength of evidence which is plainly coloured by personal pique. After all, Cooke, as a professional musician, knew what he was talking about; and Pepys, though he had self-importance enough for half a dozen men, was only an amateur.[1]

Cooke's troubles were not confined to the initial hard work of getting an inexperienced choir into shape. Like most of Charles II's servants he had the greatest difficulty in getting any money out of the Treasury. In spite of the general retrenchment of household expenses which became necessary in 1663 the king had expressed his intention of continuing the augmented salaries that had lately been granted to the children and gentlemen of the chapel.[2] But, as members of the royal household came to learn to their cost, the issue of a royal warrant was no guarantee of payment; they might be lucky if they received their salaries and liveries some years in arrear. Cooke must have been at his wits' end to find the money to feed and clothe the boys. In 1666 he, Thomas Purcell and the other gentlemen of the chapel petitioned the king for payment, on behalf of themselves, the children of the chapel and the ex-choristers, pointing out that no money had been assigned to the Treasurer of the Chamber for that purpose. The king was suitably impressed; he informed the Lord Treasurer that he thought 'his honour concerned therein,' and expressed the wish

[1] 13th February 1667. In another passage (14th September 1662) Pepys says that he noticed Cooke overdoing his part in an anthem, 'which I never did before.' Apart from that he has nothing but praise for Cooke's singing, even though on the unfortunate occasion mentioned above he thought it inferior to the Italian music he had heard the day before.

[2] *Cal. S. P. Dom.*, 22nd December 1663.

that there should be 'full and punctual payment' of everything
due, when money was next assigned to the Treasurer of the
Chamber.[1] But the royal wish, however sincere, was not sufficient to ensure payment at a time when financial embarrassment
was acute. Two years later things were so bad that Cooke
refused to let the boys attend the chapel. He appeared before
the Lords of the Treasury, who declared that they were scan-
dalized at his action. Cooke retorted that the boys' clothes were
so worn out that they were obliged to keep indoors.[2]

Some time before, possibly in 1667, a scheme of retrenchment
had been drawn up, in which it was proposed that the children
of the chapel should have black gowns and plain suits like those
worn by the king's scholars at Westminster.[3] The proposed
economy does not appear to have been adopted. The choristers
were allowed to keep their scarlet cloth and silk lace, and they
could congratulate themselves that they were at least wearing the
correct livery, even if the cloth was in holes and the lace in tatters.
Cooke continued to bombard the authorities. He was still asking
for money for the boys' clothes in 1670. This time he drew up
a petition to the king, in which he stated that the children were
reduced to so bad a condition that they were unfit to attend His
Majesty or to walk the streets. Could he have an order for their
liveries? The charge was not great, and the king himself had
promised that the liveries should be continued. To Cooke's
personal application the Lords of the Treasury made sympathetic
reply. The king, they said, wished the clothes to be made as
before. Unfortunately the officers of the wardrobe had no money,
and Cooke was requested to raise a loan on the funds on which
the wardrobe had orders. Eventually it was ordered that the bills
should be paid out of the revenue from wine licences.[4]

[1] *Cal. S. P. Dom.*, 28th May 1666.
[2] *Cal. Treas. Books*, 24th January 1668.
[3] *Cal. Treas. Books*, VII, iii, App. V, p. 1650.
[4] *Cal. Treas. Books*, 7th December 1669, 5th July 1670 (cf. *Cal. S. P. Dom.*, 30th June 1670), 26th September 1671; *Cal. S. P. Dom.* June 1670.

Depressing though these sordid troubles were, there was compensation in the excellent material which Cooke had at his disposal. When all due allowance has been made for the skill and thoroughness of his training, it still remains true that boys like John Blow and Pelham Humfrey, to mention no others, must have been endowed with exceptional ability. While they were still choristers they began to compose anthems for the king's chapel. Tudway, who was himself a chorister, tells us that Charles II encouraged these budding composers 'by indulging their youthfull fancys,' and that at least once a month they produced something new. He goes further and claims that the secularization of church music to which he took such vigorous exception may be traced to these youthful efforts, all composed—so we are to believe —in the lively style which alone could please His Majesty.[1] What truth there is in this suggestion we shall have to consider later. Elsewhere Tudway gives a particular instance of the children's ability—the so-called *Club Anthem* by Humfrey, Blow and Turner, written, we are told, to celebrate a great victory by the Duke of York over the Dutch, the king's composers being unwilling to undertake the composition of an anthem at such short notice.[2] The genuineness of the anecdote has been suspected, since the naval victory to which Tudway refers took place off Lowestoft in June 1665, when Humfrey appears to have been abroad. But there is no reason for doubting the collaboration of the three boys.

Reliable evidence of the activities of some at least of the children of the chapel is afforded by an interesting collection of the words of anthems sung there (and generally in the cathedrals and collegiate churches of England and Ireland), which was issued by the Rev. James Clifford in 1663 and reached a second edition in the following year. It appears from the compiler's preface that many people in the early years after the Restoration were puzzled by the singing of anthems, which indeed must have been a

[1] Brit. Mus., Harl. 7338, fo. 3. I quote the passage in full on p. 199.

[2] Brit. Mus., Harl. 7339, fo. 239^v.

complete novelty to the younger generation. Clifford declares
that the purpose of his collection is

that the people may follow the Choire in their Devotions without any
loss or mistake, and be encouraged to learn to assist and consort in the
same melody. To which, I shall use this only motive, that since it
will be all and our sole employment in Heaven, it will be a wretchless [1]
and unexcusable neglect not to mind it here on earth

—a naïvely comforting justification of the practice of choral
music. Most of the anthems in this book are by Elizabethan or
Jacobean composers—a significant point—but one or two of the
older Restoration composers are also included, and in the second
part there are no fewer than twenty by Cooke himself (including
three sung at Charles II's coronation [2]) and fourteen by children
of the chapel: five by Pelham Humfrey, three by John Blow and
six by Robert Smith, who later wrote music for the theatre—'a
very excellent fellow,' in D'Urfey's opinion.[3] We have also the
independent witness of Pepys, who heard a five-part setting of
the fifty-first psalm by one of the choristers—'a pretty boy'—and
was told that there were four or five of them that could do as
much.[4]

The boys were not neglected when the time came for them to
leave the choir. After their voices had broken they were still
maintained by the Treasury, with an allowance of £30 a year
and clothing, presumably until they found employment.[5] Most
of them, we may imagine, kept up their music. Cooke was
annoyed that Tom Edwards, who had entered Pepys's service,
had 'no time to mind his singing nor Lute,' a complaint that Pepys
was quite prepared to answer, apparently to the satisfaction of the
captain, who 'desired me that I would baste his coate.'[6] Later
there is a delightful account of two ex-choristers paying a visit

---

[1] Old form of 'reckless.' [2] Baker's *Chronicle*, p. 817.
[3] *The Fool turn'd Critick* (1678).
[4] 22nd November 1663. It has been assumed, without sufficient
justification, that the 'pretty boy' was Humfrey.
[5] *King's Musick*, passim. [6] 10th April 1665.

to Pepys and joining with his boy in three-part songs. Their skill was extraordinary, but the sound of their broken voices, which they were unable to keep in tune, was very disagreeable.[1] We have no statistics of the various professions which the children of the chapel eventually adopted. Many of them, we know, were retained in the royal service and became gentlemen of the chapel or instrumentalists in the royal band. But there must have been several, like Tom Edwards, who preferred to take up other work and for whom an education in the Chapel Royal was a useful testimonial.[2]

Such was the society, small in numbers but rich in promise and full of activity, in which Henry Purcell passed three or four years of his boyhood. If we are to believe the tradition which assigns to him an *Address of the Children of the Chapel Royal to the King, and their Master, Captain Cooke, on his Majesties Birthday, A.D. 1670,*[3] he lost no time in following the example of his clever predecessors, Humfrey and Blow, and showing what he could do as a composer. Certainly he must have derived a valuable stimulus from Cooke's instruction. That was cut short when Cooke died in 1672, with hundreds of pounds still owing to him from the Treasury.[4] His successor was Pelham Humfrey, an ex-chorister and his son-in-law. Humfrey had travelled on the Continent after leaving the choir in 1664, his expenses having been paid out of the Secret Service funds. On his return he was

[1] 21st August 1667. The two boys, according to Pepys, were Blaeu and Loggings. I agree with Bridge (*Twelve Good Musicians*, p. 109) that the former is probably to be identified with Blow. Blow's voice had then been broken for more than two years and he was over eighteen; but every choirmaster has had boys who could make some sort of treble noise at this age, and Pepys's account emphasizes the unpleasantness of the tone.

[2] Pepys, 31st May, 7th and 17th August 1664, etc.

[3] According to Cummings (p. 20) a copy of this work, in the handwriting of Pelham Humfrey, was in the possession of Dr. Rimbault. But no one seems to know where it is now or, indeed, if it ever existed.

[4] *King's Musick*, p. 246.

taken into the royal service again as a lute-player and a gentleman of the Chapel Royal, and in the same year in which he succeeded Cooke as master of the children was also appointed composer for the violins jointly with Thomas Purcell.[1]

Much has been made of Humfrey's stay on the Continent. We have Pepys's word for it that he came back from France 'an absolute Monsieur,' full of conceit, very contemptuous of the king's musicians and proud of his intimate association with the king.[2] But what he learned abroad is another matter. It is often stated that Charles II sent him abroad expressly to study under Lulli, but we have no precise evidence for this or any certain knowledge that he ever met Lulli at all. Those who point eagerly to his residence in France as a significant detail in the growth of French influence on English music are apt to forget that Humfrey was sent to Italy as well. As a promising boy he was to be given the opportunity of absorbing all that the Continent had to offer. Italy, then as later, was the goal of the aspiring musician. The effect of his experiences on his music must be discussed in a later chapter. Pepys, it may be remarked in passing, had no great opinion of the compositions which 'the little fellow' brought out when he came back to England.[3] But what Pepys thought is not necessarily a safe guide. He is too often treated by writers on the seventeenth century as an infallible oracle.

If Humfrey brought Italian influences to bear on the boys under his instruction there was nothing new in that. Cooke, it will be remembered, had acquired a reputation as a singer 'after the Italian manner'—which implies residence in Italy or at least study with Italian masters—and encouraged his boys to sing Italian songs when they were not engaged in the chapel. Pepys heard him and two of the boys give some samples of Italian music at Lord Sandwich's house and thought it quite the best music he

[1] *King's Musick*, pp. 178, 185, 240; *Cheque Book*, pp. 14 and 213.
[2] 15th November 1667.
[3] 1st and 16th November 1667.

had ever heard.[1]   Of the important part played by Italian musicians at the court and in London generally at this time I shall speak later.

Humfrey did not long survive his father-in-law. He died in 1674 and was succeeded by another ex-chorister, John Blow, who was also organist of Westminster Abbey.[2]   Purcell's voice had broken in the previous year and he had left the choir with the usual grant of £30 a year for maintenance and the various articles of clothing ordinarily supplied to choristers on leaving.[3]   We do not know exactly what instruction he received from Blow, who was his senior by about ten years. No doubt, as with other boys of particular promise, it took the form of more specialized training in certain branches of music. Blow, if he had any discrimination, must have realized the boy's unusual gifts.[4]   In later years he could shine in the reflected glory of his pupil's accomplishments; when his friends prepared the epitaph for his monument in Westminster Abbey they did not omit to mention that he had been 'Master to the famous Mr. H. Purcell.'

[1] 21st December 1663. A few years later (16th February 1667) he was less impressed when he heard a performance by some Italian musicians.
[2] *Cheque Book*, pp. 15–16.
[3] *King's Musick*, pp. 263, 264, 275, 315.
[4] Cf. the memorial tribute to Purcell by Henry Hall, organist of Hereford, printed in *Orpheus Britannicus*:

> '*Apollo's* Harp at once our Souls did strike,
> We learnt together, but not learnt alike.
> Though equal care our Master might bestow,
> Yet only *Purcell* e'er shall equal *Blow*:
> For Thou, by Heaven for wondrous things design'd,
> Left'st thy Companion lagging far behind.'

CHAPTER III

APPRENTICESHIP AND RECOGNITION

THERE can never have been any doubt of the profession Purcell was to adopt. Family tradition, his father's influential position among the court musicians and his own precocious ability all pointed to a musical career. His first appointment, made in the same year that his voice broke, was modest. On 10th June 1673 a warrant was issued

> to admit Henry Purcell in the place of keeper, maker, mender, repayrer and tuner of the regalls, organs, virginalls, flutes and recorders and all other kind of wind instruments whatsoever, in ordinary, without fee, to his Majesty, and assistant to John Hingston, and upon the death or other avoydance of the latter, to come in ordinary with fee.[1]

The appointment, it will be noticed, was unpaid. In other words Purcell, who was barely fourteen, was to be apprenticed to Hingston to learn by practical experience the elements of a very important side of the musical profession.

In the seventeenth century there was nothing humiliating or undignified in being employed as a repairer and tuner of instruments. The present-day distinction between the workman and the performer is a product of modern specialization. When the organ at Westminster Abbey, for example, was restored in the first year of Charles II's reign, Christopher Gibbons, the organist, was paid twenty shillings for his share in the work of tuning it.[2] Bernard Smith, one of the most famous of organ-builders, not only built an organ in St. Margaret's, Westminster, but was also organist of the church for thirty-two years—from 1676 till his

[1] *King's Musick*, p. 255.

[2] W.A.M. 33695, fo. 4ᵛ. For further details about the Westminster organ see pp. 35 and 79.

death in 1708.[1] John Hingston, to whom Purcell was now apprenticed, was a distinguished organist, viol-player and composer, and had enjoyed a reputation as a teacher during the Commonwealth. Practical musicianship at that time was comprehensive and versatility was considered normal. Hingston's supervision of the king's instruments was not confined to the royal chapel. He also had the care of instruments in the queen's private chapel, the banqueting hall at Whitehall, Hampton Court Palace and Windsor Castle.[2] Though he did not do all the work himself, he was responsible for seeing that it was properly carried out, and all payments for such work were made through him.

The absence of any payment for Purcell's post as assistant cannot have caused any serious embarrassment in his family. Thomas Purcell was as well off as any royal servant at that time could expect to be. By 1674, in addition to being a gentleman of the chapel, musician for the lute, viol and voice, and composer for the violins in association with Pelham Humfrey, he had also become groom of the robes and a musician-in-ordinary in succession to Dr. John Wilson.[3] Together these posts brought in a substantial sum, even though it might be necessary to wait several years before receiving payment. Everything goes to show that Thomas was a respected and influential musician. In 1674 he had the duty of making an agreement with Bernard Smith for setting up an organ in the king's private chapel at Windsor, and for several years he was charged with the distribution of the annual payment of £400 to the musicians who were in attendance in the Chapel Royal.[4] When they were summoned to attend the king at Windsor in 1674, he drew up the list of their names and signed it himself; the document, dated 15th May, is still to be

[1] *Westminster Records,* p. 63; St. Margaret's Vestry Books, 2416, pp. 21, 23, 38; 2418, p. 13.

[2] *King's Musick,* pp. 144, 146, 156, 200, 214, 298, etc.

[3] *King's Musick,* pp. 240, 252, 268; *Cal. Treas. Books,* 6th December 1671, 2nd October 1676; numerous other references.

[4] *Cal. Treas. Books,* 17th October 1673, 17th December 1674, etc.; *Cal. S. P. Dom.,* 1st September 1673.

seen in the library of the Royal Society of Musicians.[1] In 1672,
when Captain Cooke, marshal of the Corporation of Music, a
society for safeguarding professional interests, resigned on account
of illness, Thomas Purcell was appointed in his place.[2] Nor
was his own advancement his only cause for satisfaction. Two
of his sons were already in the royal service: Edward, the eldest,
had just been appointed gentleman usher daily waiter assistant,
and Henry was with Hingston, with the prospect of succeeding
eventually to a salaried post. And before long Daniel followed in
his brother's footsteps and became a child of the Chapel Royal.[3]

Of Henry's early experiences as an organ-tuner we know
nothing. It is quite possible that he accompanied Hingston on
his journeys to the king's country residences and so acquired a
practical knowledge of different types of instruments. His progress in the art must have been rapid, for in little more than a year
after his appointment as assistant he was entrusted with the tuning
of the organ at Westminster Abbey, receiving the usual sum of
£2 for the year's work.[4] He may have owed this contract, which
was renewed in the three following years, to Blow, who had been
appointed organist of the abbey as early as 1668 [5]; but it is unlikely
that favouritism alone secured him such responsible work at the
age of fifteen. We must assume that he had already acquired a
thorough proficiency under Hingston's instruction. In the second
year of his association with the abbey, 1675–6, he was paid £5
'for pricking out'—i.e. copying—'two bookes of organ parts.' [6]

---

[1] It is printed in Cummings, p. 15. [2] Brit. Mus., Harl. 1911, fo. 10.
[3] He is mentioned among the children of the chapel who attended
the king at Windsor from 14th August to 26th September 1678 (*King's
Musick,* p. 339). As he is unlikely to have been more than fifteen at
the time, the date of his birth would be 1663 at the earliest.
[4] W.A.M. 33709, fo. 5; similar entries in 33710, 33712 and 33713.
The abbey accounts are from Michaelmas to Michaelmas. The first
payment is in Michaelmas 1675, and therefore covers the year September
1674 to September 1675.
[5] W.A.M. 33702, fo. 2; Precentor's Book, fo. 104.
[6] W.A.M. 33710, fo. 5ᵛ.

It is generally stated that Purcell was appointed official copyist to the abbey at this time. This is incorrect. There was no permanent copyist. All the treasurer's accounts tell us is that from time to time—by no means every year—payments were made to certain individuals for copying music and binding services and anthems. Thus in the next year, 1676–7, William Tucker, one of the minor canons and a gentleman of the Chapel Royal, was paid £20 'for coppying out some musick bookes for the use of the church'[1]; in the year 1678–9 Stephen Bing, one of the lay-clerks, received thirty-eight shillings 'for writeing 29 sheetes and 23 staves,'[2] and so on. The error of referring to Purcell as official copyist would be of small importance if biographers had not enlarged on the theme by stressing the responsibility and importance of the imaginary office. Emphasis is laid on the havoc wrought in cathedral music libraries during the Commonwealth. The ravages, it is said, had to be repaired by copying from the few printed copies that survived. Attention is drawn to the influence which the copying of the anthems of the great Elizabethan masters must have had on an impressionable youth.

All this is very impressive, but it does not strictly accord with the facts. Quite apart from anything else, it does not seem to have occurred to anyone as rather odd that sixteen years after the Restoration it should still have been necessary to continue copying Elizabethan anthems. The necessity is largely a figment of the imagination. In the very first year of Charles II's reign the abbey authorities bought from John Playford, the publisher, a set of Barnard's printed collection of services and anthems, in addition to borrowing another set for four or five Sundays.[3] Purcell's task in 1675–6 consisted simply in writing out organ parts, presumably of new anthems by Restoration composers. The influence of Elizabethan and Jacobean composers on Purcell's style is not in

[1] W.A.M. 33712, fo. 5ᵛ.
[2] W.A.M. 33714, fo. 6. Cummings confused him with the Rev. Stephen Bing, minor canon of St. Paul's.
[3] W.A.M. 33695, fo. 5.

dispute; but it need not be attributed to entirely imaginary activities. As a choirboy in the Chapel Royal he had had abundant opportunities of becoming acquainted with the works of pre-Restoration composers. As I have already pointed out, the greater part of Clifford's *Divine Services and Anthems* consists of the words of anthems by Elizabethan and Jacobean musicians. Later Purcell himself confessed his interest in his predecessors by transcribing works by Gibbons, Byrd, Tallis and other old masters into his own manuscript book.[1] If we want to have some idea of what music was copied at the abbey we may compare the list of anthems and services transcribed into the books of the Chapel Royal between 1670 and 1676.[2] Out of sixty-five anthems in this list only four are by pre-Restoration composers. The remainder are either by men like Child who had survived the Civil War or younger musicians like Blow who had grown up after the Restoration; there are eleven by Wise, eleven by Tucker, nine by Child, nine by Blow and six by Humfrey.

In the summer of 1677 death came to Matthew Locke, that stormy petrel of Restoration music, fit to be ranked, says Roger North, 'with Cleomenes King of Sparta, who was styled *ultimus heroum*.'[3] Purcell succeeded him as composer for the king's violins.[4] Precocity indeed! The boy was only eighteen, but he was given a post that had been held by one of the most distinguished musicians of the time and involved no small responsibility. He had as colleague his father, who had been a composer for the violins since 1672. Here again we may suspect the working of influence, and no doubt ambitious malcontents complained of favouritism when they saw a youngster promoted over their heads. The appointment was in one way peculiarly appropriate. Locke seems to have been an intimate friend of the Purcell family. We have already seen him in the company of one of the elder Purcells, and Cummings prints a letter from him to Henry which suggests a close friendship.[5] To that friendship Purcell himself testified

[1] Fitzwilliam 88, dated 1681–2.
[2] *King's Musick*, pp. 305–7.
[3] *Memoirs*, p. 96.   [4] *King's Musick*, p. 322.   [5] *Purcell*, p. 27.

by writing an elegy 'on the Death of his Worthy Friend, Mr. Matthew Locke,' which was published two years later in the second volume of Playford's *Choice Ayres, Songs and Dialogues*. The unnamed poet sang the praises of one

> whose skilful harmony
> Had charms for all the ills that we endure

—words which posterity can readily apply to Purcell's own greater genius.

The king's band of twenty-four violins—including, of course, every branch of the violin family—had been instituted soon after the Restoration in imitation of the *Vingt-quatre violons du Roi* at the French court. We first hear of them at Charles II's coronation on 23rd April 1661, when they attended in scarlet livery and took part in the anthems.[1] This was not, as has sometimes been supposed, the first appearance of violins in the royal service. They had played at the funeral of Queen Elizabeth in 1603 and again at the funeral of James I in 1625; and as early as 1621 there was an official composer for the violins. Ten years later there is a detailed list of fourteen musicians for the violins, giving their particular instruments—treble, contratenor, tenor, low tenor and bass.[2] The new band, however, was clearly more elaborate and ambitious, and its organization may be traced directly to Charles's residence in France, where he must have become acquainted with Louis XIV's players.

The twenty-four violins did not replace the older organizations —the music for lutes, viols and voices and the wind music— though they undoubtedly occupied first place in the king's favour. Their duties were principally to play at court functions wherever the king was in residence. According to Anthony Wood, Charles liked to have them playing before him at meal-times, 'as being more airie and brisk than viols.'[3] They did not at first take part in the services in the Chapel Royal. Wind instruments

[1] *King's Musick*, p. 131; Baker's *Chronicle*, p. 817.
[2] *King's Musick*, pp. 45, 53, 57, 76.
[3] *Life and Times*, vol. i, p. 212.

and viols were still being used there in August 1662.[1] But four
months later there was introduced, in Evelyn's words, 'a Consort
of 24 Violins betweene every pause, after the *French* fantastical light
way, better suiting a Tavern or Play-house than a Church.' He
adds that 'this was the first time of change.'[2] Curiously enough
Pepys writes of the innovation of instrumental symphonies on
14th September of the same year, saying simply that it was 'the
first day of having vialls and other instruments to play a symphony
between every verse of the anthem,' though not the first time that
symphonies were used, since he mentions them a week earlier.
Later, on Christmas Day, four days after Evelyn's experience, he
speaks of 'a good anthem . . . with vialls.' If 'vialls' is to be
taken literally the change from the old to the new system would
appear to have been gradual.

The innovation was certainly a shock to conservative opinion.
We can see that from Evelyn's account. There was no particular
objection to the instruments, which were familiar enough, though
old-fashioned musicians like Thomas Mace were bitterly opposed
to them; it was the use of purely instrumental music in divine
service to which Evelyn, and no doubt others of the same temper,
took exception, especially when the music played was modelled
on the French practice and hence, in their view, frivolous. We
shall have to consider later the part played by the king in encou-
raging this innovation and the influence his patronage had on
the style of church composition. From Evelyn's account it
appears that originally the whole band played in the chapel; but
we know that later on a system was introduced by which only a
few of the players served at a time. A list has been preserved of

[1] *King's Musick,* p. 147: 'Order that Robert Strong and Edward
Strong are to attend with their double curtolls in his Majesty's Chappell
Royall at Whitehall, and Thomas Bates and William Gregory with
their violls, every Sunday and Holy day, and all the rest to wayte in
their turnes.' 'Curtall,' or 'curtoll,' was the old name for the bassoon.
Cf. also *King's Musick,* p. 128 (9th March 1661): warrant for payment
of £30 'for two double sackbutts for service in his Majesty's Chappell.'
[2] 21st December 1662.

the musicians to wait in the chapel during the months of October, November and December 1671, according to which five are to be on duty each month, 'soe that each person attend every third month, or they will answere the contrary.'[1] In the following spring the number had been increased to six each month.[2] The penalty for failure to attend at services or practices was suspension,[3] but even this threat was not sufficient to ensure regularity. In July 1672 the king had to complain that the violins were neglecting their duty in the Chapel Royal, and it was once more emphasized that any one who failed to attend, either to practise or to wait in the chapel, after receiving notice from Thomas Purcell or Pelham Humfrey (the two composers at that time), would be suspended.[4]

In its early years the band had included some famous players, foremost among them the Swedish virtuoso Thomas Baltzar, who was appointed at the end of 1661 at a salary of £110 a year.[5] Contemporary evidence is unanimous in praise of his brilliant execution. Evelyn had heard him play in 1656 and was astounded:

His variety upon a few notes & plaine ground with that wonderfull dexterity, as was admirable, & though a very young man, yet so perfect & skillfull as there was nothing so crosse & perplext, which being by our Artists, brought to him, which he did not at first sight, with ravish-ing sweetenesse, & improvements, play off, to the astonishment of our best Masters: In Summ, he plaid on that single Instrument a full Consort, so as the rest, flung-downe their Instruments, as acknowledging a victory: As to my owne particular, I stand to this houre amaz'd that

---

[1] *King's Musick*, p. 237.

[2] *King's Musick*, p. 243. All the players mentioned in these lists are members of the king's band of violins.

[3] *King's Musick*, p. 244 (15th May 1672).

[4] *King's Musick*, p. 245.

[5] *King's Musick*, p. 140. He was born at Lübeck but is more than once described as 'the Swede.' Pulver (*Biographical Dictionary*, p. 24) thinks he was not a member of the band but a private musician. There is in any case no evidence for the statement in *Grove* that he was leader of the band. Cf. *King's Musick*, p. 207.

God should give so greate perfection to so young a person: There were at that time as excellent in that profession as any were thought in Europ: *Paule Wheeler*, Mr. *Mell* and others, 'til this prodigie appeared.

Anthony Wood was no less impressed when he heard Baltzar at Oxford two years later, particularly by his use of the high positions, which seem to have been unknown in England at that time.[2] He adds, however, that Davis Mell (who also became a member of Charles II's band) 'playd sweeter'; and corroborative testimony is forthcoming from Roger North, who admired Baltzar's mastery and commented on his use of double-stopping, but was compelled to admit that 'his playing, compared with our latter violins, was like his country rough and harsh.'[3] He died in 1663 and was buried in Westminster Abbey.[4]

Davis Mell seems to have been the most considerable of the English violinists in the original band. He had been one of the royal violinists as early as 1625, when he is mentioned among the players at James I's funeral,[5] and must have been considerably older than Baltzar, since Evelyn particularly remarked on the latter's youth in 1656. During the Commonwealth he was active as a teacher. He was also one of five musicians who in 1657 petitioned the Council's Committee for the Advancement of Music to permit the formation of a professional corporation or college of musicians. The petitioners, who included John Hingston, are described as 'Gent. of his Highness Musique.' Mell was, in fact, one of the small and privileged band who were attached to Cromwell's 'court' during the Protectorate, and as such he attended the Protector's funeral in 1658. On the restoration of Charles II he once more became one of the king's violinists

[1] 4th March 1656. Evelyn, like Wood, refers to him as 'the Lubicer,' from his birthplace.

[2] *Life and Times*, vol. i, p. 257.

[3] *Musicall Gramarian*, p. 30; cf. *Memoirs*, p. 100.

[4] *Abbey Registers*, p. 159 (27th July 1663): 'Mr. Thomas Balsart, one of the Violins in the King's service.'

[5] *King's Musick*, p. 57.

and was director of the 'four-and-twenty fiddlers' jointly with George Hudson. He died in 1662.[1]

Among the other original members of the band were Humphrey Madge, already a player of repute in 1653 and a friend of Pepys, whom he offended on one occasion by playing the fool on the violin when half drunk[2]; George Hudson, who, like Mell, had served under Charles I and Cromwell and had been a teacher during the Commonwealth[3]; and John Banister, who soon became a very important person. It is interesting to notice that, though the formation of the band must in the first place have been suggested by the similar body at the French court, there were no French players in it. Charles II certainly had a few French musicians on his establishment, but they did not belong to the twenty-four violins; and generally we find more references to Italian than to French musicians in the state papers.

In 1662 arrangements were made for twelve of the violins to form a special band 'for better performance of service' under the direction of Banister, who had previously been sent on a special mission to France with a view to studying French methods. The position of responsibility seems to have turned his head. 'After his returne,' says Wood, 'he became more admired, but then for some saucy words spoken to his maj.—(viz. when he called for the Italian violins he made answer that he had better have the English) he was turn'd out of his place.'[4] The story may be nothing more than another of Wood's gossipy and far from trustworthy anecdotes. But whether Banister used saucy words to the king or not, it is certain that he lost his post, the direction of the violins being transferred to the Frenchman Louis Grabu, who

[1] Playford's *Musicall Banquet* (1651); Scholes, *The Puritans and Music*, pp. 282–3 (where the petition is quoted in full); Burton, *Parliamentary Diary*, vol. ii, p. 521; *King's Musick*, pp. 114, 133, 147.

[2] Hookes, *Amanda* (1653); Pepys, 10th March 1660.   [3] See note 1.

[4] *King's Musick*, p. 159; *Cal. S. P. Dom.*, 2nd December 1661, 3rd May 1662; Bodleian, Wood D 19 (4), fo. 14. Note that Wood says 'Italian violins,' not 'French' as in Hawkins (p. 702) and many subsequent writers.

succeeded Nicholas Lanier as master of the king's music in November 1666. Only a month after Grabu's appointment as master an order was issued that Banister and the twenty-four violins were to 'obey the directions of Louis Grabu . . . both for their tyme of meeting to practise, and also for the tyme of playing in consort.'[1] Banister was furious at this interference with what he regarded as his prerogative, and tried to stop the passing of the king's privy seal confirming Grabu's superintendence of the violins, on the ground that there were arrears due to him from the Exchequer. Unfortunately he had been guilty of gross misconduct in the administration of the money assigned to the players under his direction, who complained of his fraudulent treatment and tyrannical caprice. The result was that the seal was passed and Banister was in disgrace, though he continued for a few years at least as a member of the band.[2] Of his subsequent activities outside the court circle we shall hear later. He died in 1679.[3] By 1677—the year of Purcell's new appointment—Grabu too had fallen into disgrace and bandy-legged Nicholas Staggins reigned in his stead as master of the king's music.[4]

One of Purcell's duties as composer for the violins must have been to write airs and dances for performance at court; the ephemeral character of such music and the limited circle to which it was introduced would be sufficient to explain why none of it has survived. The only string music by him that we possess—apart from incidental theatre music, symphonies in anthems and odes and one or two odd pieces—is the collection of fantasias in several parts, some of which at least belong to the year 1680.[5]

[1] *King's Musick*, pp. 190, 191, 193; *Cal. S. P. Dom.*, 12th November 1666.

[2] Pepys, 20th February 1667; *Cal. S. P. Dom.*, 29th March, 4th August 1667.

[3] *King's Musick*, p. 336.

[4] *King's Musick*, pp. 317–18; Thomas Brown, *Works*, 9th ed. (1760), vol. ii, p. 246.

[5] The four-part fantasias bear dates in June and August 1680 in the original manuscript (Brit. Mus., Add. 30, 930).

Whether they were scored for viols or violins—and tradition would suggest the former as the more probable—they cannot have been written for use at court. If there was one kind of music the king particularly detested it was the 'fancy,' as Sir Joseph Williamson, Under-secretary of State, learned to his cost. Charles's enthusiasm for music did not go beyond an appreciation of what was readily intelligible, with a straightforward rhythm to which he could beat time—as he did even in the Chapel Royal. Like the modern amateur who says: 'I know what I like,' he would listen to no argument but the evidence of his own ears.[1] We can imagine what he would have said to Purcell's fantasias, which are clearly chamber music intended for private performance by a few friends. We have, in fact, no positive evidence of Purcell's activity as a court composer until the year 1680. The only secular compositions that can be certainly assigned to the period 1677–9 are the songs which were published in *New Ayres and Dialogues* (1678) and *Choice Ayres,* book ii (1679).

[1] North, *Memoirs*, p. 103, *Musicall Gramarian*, p. 27; Pepys, 22nd November 1663.

CHAPTER IV

ABBEY, COURT AND STAGE

THE significance of Purcell's court appointment should not be overlooked. It did not guarantee a reputation; he had yet to make his name as a composer. But he now had constant opportunities for perfecting himself in his art, and the duty of composing for a permanent orchestra must have done for him what residence at Eisenstadt did for Haydn at a more mature age. Towards the end of 1679 came a new appointment, which must have had a similar influence on his church music: he succeeded Blow as organist of Westminster Abbey.[1] Among the many amiable legends that have gathered round Purcell's career is the story that Blow, struck by his pupil's brilliance, resigned the organist's post in his favour. It may be said at once that there is not the slightest evidence for this story, nor is it worth while to consider other possible explanations of the change.

There is nothing surprising in Purcell's being appointed at such an early age. Parallels are not wanting among earlier and contemporary musicians. Blow was under twenty when he succeeded Albert Bryan as organist at the end of 1668, if the generally accepted date of his birth is correct. Michael Wise must have been about the same age when he was appointed organist of Salisbury Cathedral in the same year, and Thomas Tudway was still in his early twenties when he became organist of King's College, Cambridge, in 1670.[2] It is unfortunate that the precentor's book for the period including Purcell's connection

[1] W.A.M. 33715, fo. 2. These are the treasurer's accounts from Michaelmas 1679 to Michaelmas 1680.

[2] The dates are from West, *Cathedral Organists*. The ages are conjectured from the dates when they were children of the Chapel Royal.

with the abbey is lost, so that we are without the actual declaration
that he made on taking office. But we have the oath taken by
Blow in 1668, and as the two must have been similar it is worth
reproducing:

I John Blow being to be admitted into the place of Mr. Albertus
Bryne late organist of the collegiate church of Westminster, doe promise
due obedience, diligent attendance and conformity to the laudable
customes of the sayd church; and if I shall be hereafter preferrd to any
other place which may prove prejudiciall to my attendance in the sayd
church; I will be content to relinquish all my right, title and interest
unto the same, unto which I doe willingly subscribe, serving the first
yeare upon approbation only, beginning December . 3 . 1668.

JOHN BLOW.[1]

Similar oaths were taken by the lay-clerks on appointment
Purcell's salary as organist was £10 a year, which was exactly
what each lay-clerk received, and he was also paid £8 a year
for the rent of a house.[2]

Having tuned the organ for four years in succession—from
1674 to 1678—he cannot have been a stranger to it; and it is
quite possible that he had had lessons on it from Blow. The
instrument was at that time on the north side of the choir.[3] It
had suffered badly in the Civil War, when troops were quartered
in the abbey, who 'brake downe the Organ, and pawned the
Pipes at severall Ale-houses for pots of Ale.'[4] When the damage
was repaired is not certain; but at any rate the organ was in use
again by the autumn of 1660, when the novelty of it attracted
curious crowds.[5] The musical establishment of the abbey was
similar to that of the Chapel Royal, except that there were far
fewer men. During the time that Purcell was organist it consisted normally of four petty canons (choirmen in holy orders),

[1] W.A.M., Precentor's Book, fo. 104.
[2] W.A.M. 33715, fo. 2 and 5.
[3] A plan of the abbey at James II's coronation in 1685 is in Sandford,
between pp. 80 and 81.
[4] Ryves, *Mercurius Rusticus* (1646), p. 215.
[5] Pepys, 4th November and 30th December 1660.

twelve lay-clerks or singing-men, one of whom was master of the choristers, an organist and ten boys.[1] All these were under the authority of the dean and chapter, to whom they were bound to show due respect and reverence. A chapter minute of 1686 orders that

the Quiremen as they passe in the Quire to doe their Offices shall according to the Old Custome come into the Middle of the Quire and there make due Reverence towards the Deanes and Prebendaries Stalls after they have first done it towards the Alter.[2]

In the same year instructions were given that all the officers of the church, including the choirmen, were to receive Holy Communion at least three times a year according to the rubric, i.e. at Easter, Whitsun and Christmas.[3]

The abbey records tell us nothing of the private lives of the musicians who served there. In such a mixed assembly there must have been many curious personal idiosyncrasies. If we want a sidelight on personalities we must call in the aid of the irrepressible Thomas Brown, who, be it noted, was a sincere admirer of Purcell's gifts. Not the least amusing section of his *Letters from the Dead to the Living* is Blow's imaginary answer to Purcell's equally imaginary letter from the shades. The following extract shows how a keen-eyed satirist could react to the pompous routine of cathedral life:

I have no novelties to entertain you with relating to either the *Abbey* or *St. Paul's*, for both the choirs continue just as wicked as they were when you left them; some of them daily come reeking hot out of the bawdy-house into the church, and others stagger out of a tavern to afternoon prayers, and hick-up over a little of the *Litany*, and so back again. Old *Claret-face* beats time still upon his cushion stoutly, and sits growling under his purple canopy, a hearty old-fashion'd bass, that deafens all about him. Beau *Bushy-wig* preserves his voice to a miracle, charms all the ladies over against him with his handsome face, and all over

[1] W.A.M. 33715–33728, *passim*.
[2] W.A. Chapter Minutes, 1683–1714, fo. 12.
[3] Ibid. fo. 13.

head with his singing. Parson *Punch* makes a very good shift still, and lyrics over his part in an anthem very handsomely.[1]

In 1680, the year after his appointment at the abbey, Purcell was active as a composer for the court, the chamber and the stage. In the summer he set down in his private manuscript book that astonishing record of his own virtuosity and his attachment to the old style, the fantasias for strings, written—so the dates suggest—in a fever-heat of enthusiasm and inspiration. In September, as composer in ordinary to the king, he had the duty of composing 'a Song to welcome home His Majesty from Windsor,' entitled *Welcome, vicegerent,* in which he was required to lavish his talent on such insipid and fulsome lines as

> Your influous approach our pensive hope recalls,
> While joyful sounds redouble from the walls,
> As when Apollo with his sacred lyre
> Did in the Theban stones a harmony inspire,

and

> His absence was Autumn, his presence is Spring
> That ever new life and new pleasure does bring,
> Then all that have voices, let 'em cheerfully sing,
> And those that have none may say: 'God save the King.'

In the same year he composed the incidental music and songs for Nathaniel Lee's tragedy, *Theodosius, or the Force of Love,* which was performed at the Duke's Theatre in Dorset Garden. This is explicitly stated by John Downes to have been the first music Purcell ever composed for the theatre.[2] The piece seems to have been popular. Thirty-one years later it was still a favourite with the ladies, and at the end of the eighteenth century the songs and

---

[1] Thomas Brown, *Works,* 9th ed. (1760), vol. ii, p. 248.

[2] *Roscius Anglicanus* (ed. Summers), p. 38. Downes was associated with the Duke's Theatre from 1662 to 1706, originally holding the post of prompter. In the chronology of Purcell's dramatic music I follow Barclay Squire's reconstruction in the *Sammelbände der Internationalen Musikgesellschaft,* v, pp. 489–564.

processional music (the latter apparently now lost) continued to be performed.[1]

There were at this time two principal theatres in London. The first of these was in Catherine Street, where Drury Lane Theatre now stands. The previous Theatre Royal had been burnt down in 1672; the new one, designed by Wren, was opened two years later. Here plays were performed by the king's company, under the direction of Thomas Killigrew. The other company, the Duke of York's, had since 1671 occupied a theatre in Dorset Garden, in the management of which a prominent part was played by the enterprising Thomas Betterton. In 1682 the rival companies joined forces and continued to use the two theatres, Dorset Garden—the larger of the two—being preferred for spectacular productions.[2] In view of Purcell's own contribution it is hardly necessary to point out that instrumental music played an important part in the Restoration theatre. At first the orchestra was placed above the stage in what was known as the music-room, and this practice seems to have been retained for some time at the Dorset Garden theatre.[3] However, when the first Theatre Royal (the predecessor of the 1674 building) was opened in the year 1663, Killigrew introduced the innovation of placing the orchestra in front of and partly below the stage —as it is in the modern theatre—a procedure that failed to satisfy Pepys, who found it impossible to hear the basses and not very easy to hear even the first violins. The players—at least for ceremonial performances—were members of the twenty-four violins of the king's band, twelve of whom served at the Theatre Royal and twelve at Dorset Garden. On special occasions, such as the performance of Shadwell's operatic version of *The Tempest* at Dorset Garden in 1674, the two sections were amalgamated. Clothes were as important as the dinner jacket to which the modern orchestral player is condemned, and rich stuffs were

[1] *Spectator* No. 92 (15th June 1711); Burney, vol. iii, p. 479 *bis*.
[2] Squire, op. cit., pp. 492–3; Nicoll, *Restoration Drama,* App. A.
[3] Pepys, 7th November 1667: 'Forced to sit in the side Balcone over against the Musique-room at the Dukes-House.'

ordered to adorn the musicians. Even though the first step had been taken towards a sunken orchestra, the authorities did not anticipate Wagner's contention that the players should be heard but not seen.[1]

Purcell continued his association with the theatre in 1681, writing one of his most beautiful and expressive songs, *Retir'd from any mortal's sight,* for Nahum Tate's adaptation of *Richard II*[2] —announced for political reasons as *The Sicilian Usurper* and taken off after two performances—and in December contributing a setting of *Blow, Boreas, blow* to D'Urfey's comedy, *Sir Barnaby Whigg, or No Wit like a Woman's.* The latter is not one of his more inspired productions, but it achieved some popularity and was reprinted in *Orpheus Britannicus* after his death. It was still in great favour when Burney was a young man, but, adds the doctor, it 'seems now more superannuated than any of his popular songs'—a pertinent judgment.[3] In the summer Purcell again had the opportunity of welcoming home his royal master with music. *Swifter, Isis, swifter flow* is an appeal to the river to restore its royal burden speedily to the capital. It must therefore have been written to celebrate Charles's return from Windsor at the end of August.[4]

Purcell probably married some time during 1681, since his first child was born in the summer of the following year. Nothing is known of his wife beyond the fact that her Christian name was

[1] Nicoll, op. cit., pp. 61–2; Pepys, 8th May 1663; *King's Musick,* pp. 175, 176 (cf. pp. 211, 263, 266); Shadwell's *The Tempest,* Act I: 'The Front of the Stage is open'd, and the Band of 24 Violins, with the Harpsicals and Theorbo's which accompany the Voices, are plac'd between the Pit and the Stage.'

[2] It is not certain that Purcell's setting was written for this production, but the fact that it was published in *Choice Ayres* ,book iv, in 1683, is suggestive.

[3] Burney, vol. iii, p. 494.

[4] Luttrell, 27th August 1681. Vaughan Williams (Purcell Society's edition, vol. xv, p. iv) thinks it was written on the occasion of the return from Newmarket in October.

Frances [1]; but since one of her children was christened Mary
Peters it has been assumed that Peters was her maiden name. [2]
Nor do we know anything of the domestic life of the young couple.
Tradition, preserved by the industrious Hawkins, relates that
Purcell was a man of intemperate habits and given to late hours,
that his wife, indignant at these excesses, refused to admit him
after midnight, and he consequently caught a cold which brought
on his death. Gossip of this kind is generally invented about persons
of distinction; it has nothing to do with sober history. Mrs. Purcell's
affectionate references to her late husband in her dedicatory preface
to *Orpheus Britannicus*—a posthumous collection of his secular songs
—are far more likely to give a true picture of their relationship.   It
was possibly on his marriage that Purcell moved to a house in
Great St. Ann's Lane, Westminster (now St. Ann's Street). [3]

1682 continues the tale of royal service.   In the spring Purcell
was among the musicians who attended the king at Windsor [4]
and at the end of May he was obliged to waste his energy on yet
another of those pompous and sycophantic welcome songs that were
the price of patronage.   This time it was the Duke of York whose
return to the capital had to be celebrated in song.   The occasion was
the conclusion of his three years' service as High Commissioner of
Scotland.   'What,' asks the fortunately anonymous bard,

> What shall be done in behalf of the man
> In whose honour the King is delighted,
> Whose conduct abroad
> Has his enemies awed

---

[1] *Abbey Registers,* p. 74.   The registers of All Hallows the Less record
the baptism of Henry, son of Henry and Frances Pursell, on 9th July
1681.   If, as is quite likely, the father is the composer, the marriage will
have to be put back to 1680 and John Baptista (see p. 45) will be the
second son.

[2] The J. B. Peters who witnessed Purcell's will in 1695 was probably
her brother.

[3] He paid rates for this house in 1682 (Bridge, 'Purcell's Birthplace
and Residences,' *Musical Times,* 1895, p. 733).

[4] *Cal. Treas. Books,* 17th May 1682.

> And every proud rebel affrighted,
> With whose absence his Prince
> Will no longer dispense
> But home to the joys of his Court has invited?

Tedious and inept tribute was paid to the hero of the hour:

> York, the obedient, grateful, just,
> Punctual, courageous, mindful of his trust.

And the bells rang and bonfires were lit in London town, and the public—as the public will—took part in joyful demonstrations,[1] though the majority of them would probably have been just as happy if the noble duke had remained in Scotland.

On 14th July Purcell succeeded Edward Lowe as one of the three organists of the Chapel Royal, where his father had given faithful service in the choir for over twenty years and where he himself had learned the traditions of English church music as a boy.[2] A minute in the *Cheque Book,* dated 19th December 1663, describes the duties of the post:

> Of the three Organistes two shall ever attend, one at the organ, the other in his surplice in the quire, to beare a parte in the Psalmodie and service. At solemne times they shall all three attend. The auncientest organist shall serve and play the service on the eve and daye of the solemne feastes, viz: Christmas, Easter, St. George, and Whitsontide. The second organist shall serve the second day, and the third the third day. Other dayes they shall waite according to their monthes.[3]

The organists were therefore members of the choir with extra-ordinary duties to perform. From the list of the gentlemen of the chapel printed in Sandford's account of James II's coronation in 1685 it appears that Purcell was a bass. Some confusion has arisen as a result of a passage in the *Gentleman's Journal* for November 1692, which tells us that at a performance of Purcell's *Ode on St. Cecilia's Day* in that year the second stanza—a counter-tenor solo—'was sung with incredible Graces by Mr. *Purcell* himself.' But there is nothing unusual or remarkable in the fact that a man who was once a bass should cultivate a counter-tenor. We have

---

[1] Luttrell, 27th May 1682.　[2] *Cheque Book,* p. 17.　[3] *Cheque Book,* p. 83.

an example of the reverse process in Thomas Blagrave, also a gentleman of the Chapel Royal, who sang counter-tenor in 1674 at Windsor and bass at the coronation in 1685.[1] Indeed it was not unknown for a singer to cultivate both at once. Mr. Pordage, whom Evelyn heard in 1685, had 'an excellent voice both Treble & base.'[2]

The gentlemen of the Chapel Royal numbered thirty-two, of whom eight were clerks in holy orders, three were organists, one was master of the children and one clerk of the cheque.[3] The salary at the Restoration was £40 a year, but the singers soon found that this was not sufficient. The cost of living had gone up a hundred per cent, and they were obliged to ask for an increase, so that they should not have to depend on other churches for their daily bread. They even went so far as to suggest that confiscated property might be used to supply their needs. Among their grievances was the fact that they had to attend every day and also that they had no allowance for expenses when the court moved to Windsor, Hampton Court or wherever it might be. Their petition was so far successful that the salary was raised to £70 in 1662, an increase proportionate to that already assigned to the children of the chapel, and this augmentation was continued when general expenses were cut down in the following year. As we have seen already, this did not guarantee prompt payment. In 1666 Captain Cooke, Thomas Purcell and other gentlemen had to petition for money due to them and the children of the chapel. Ten years or so later came another petition, claiming payment of £877 7s. for attendance at Windsor in 1674 and stating frankly that the want of the money had brought the gentlemen to serious embarrassment. The Treasury minute appended to this petition is typical of bureaucracy in all ages; it says: 'Resolution hereon: let something be done.'[4] In addition to the regular salary there

[1] Sandford, p. 71; *King's Musick*, p. 269.
[2] Evelyn, 27th January 1685.   [3] *Cheque Book*, p. 128.
[4] *Cal. S. P. Dom.*, 22nd June, September (p. 476), 14th October 1662, 24th September, 1st November, 22nd December 1663, 28th May 1666; *Cal. Treas. Books,* 9th November 1664, v, ii, p. 1374; *Cheque Book,* pp. 95-7.

were one or two bonuses given annually, among them New Year presents from the Treasurer, the Dean of the Chapel and the Lord Almoner, and a lump sum of £20 divided among the gentlemen in lieu of three deer which it had formerly been the king's custom to present once a year.[1]

The regulations governing the conduct of the gentlemen of the chapel were strict. They were required to live in or near the City of London and they were not allowed to be members of any other choir.[2] They were to come into chapel in an orderly manner, 'decently habited in their gownes and surplices (not in cloakes and bootes and spurrs),' and be regular and punctual in their attendance. It was only on Sundays and holy days and their eves that they were all obliged to attend. On weekdays there was a system by which a certain number were in attendance for a month at a time. When in attendance they had to be present at daily matins and evensong, at ten in the morning and four in the afternoon, as well as at the Sunday services at nine and four. Gentlemen who were prevented by illness from being present were obliged to provide substitutes. To be late was a serious offence. If a man appeared after the first *Gloria Patri*—i.e. at the end of the first set of responses—he was fined sixpence; if he came after the first lesson he was reckoned absent and had to pay the usual fine of one shilling for weekdays and two shillings for Sundays and holy days.[3] When the court removed to Windsor a select number of the gentlemen of the chapel were required to attend.[4] Nor was their service confined to the sacred offices. When Shadwell's version

---

[1] *Cheque Book*, pp. 121 and 125; *Cal. S. P. Dom.*, 18th July 1663, 12th July 1665, 2nd August 1667, etc.

[2] This rule does not seem to have been invariably insisted on; e.g. at James II's coronation in 1685 seven of the gentlemen of the chapel were also choirmen of Westminster Abbey and had to be replaced in the abbey choir by substitutes (Sandford, p. 70). Purcell himself was simultaneously organist of Westminster and of the Chapel Royal.

[3] *Cheque Book*, pp. 81–3 (order of the chapter held by the Bishop of Winchester, Dean of the Chapel, 19th December 1663).

[4] *King's Musick*, pp. 235, 269, 294, 339, etc.

of *The Tempest* was given at the Duke's Theatre in May 1674, while the king was out of London, members of the choir took part in the production and were allowed to stay in London during the week, going down to Windsor merely for the week-end.[1]

Purcell knew intimately several of his new colleagues. They included his former master, John Blow—now a doctor of music by the grace of the Dean of Canterbury [2]—who was master of the children; Stephen Crespion, the precentor of Westminster Abbey [3]; John Abell, celebrated counter-tenor, who had recently returned from Italy [4]; William Child, the veteran senior organist, still vigorous at the age of seventy-six; Thomas Blagrave, clerk of the cheque, versatile instrumentalist, friend of Pepys and 'a gentile and honest man' [5]; Edward Braddock, master of the choristers at the abbey and Blow's father-in-law [6]; Michael Wise, ex-chorister of the chapel, organist of Salisbury and a turbulent spirit [7]; William Turner, also an ex-chorister and a distinguished composer; and, far from least, the Reverend John Gostling, 'that stupendious Base,' whose virtuosity is sufficiently commemorated in those fantastically difficult solos—with a compass of two octaves and more—that Purcell introduced into his anthems and

[1] *King's Musick,* p. 271.

[2] This is said to have been the first Lambeth degree in music. It was given by the Dean of Canterbury as the archbishopric was temporarily vacant (Grove).

[3] W.A.M. 33706, fo. 6, etc.; *Cheque Book,* p. 15.

[4] *Cheque Book,* p. 17; Sandford, p. 70; Evelyn, 27th January 1682. Evelyn calls him 'the famous Trebble,' which shows how remarkable Abell's compass must have been and also how little Evelyn knew about voices.

[5] *Cheque Book,* p. 13; *King's Musick,* pp. 122, 124, etc.; Pepys, 21st June, 9th December 1660, 7th March 1662, etc.; Bodleian, Wood D 19 (4), fo. 23ᵛ.

[6] *Cheque Book,* p. 12; W.A.M. 33703, fo. 2.

[7] *King's Musick,* p. 167; West, *Cathedral Organists,* p. 101; Bodleian, Wood D 19 (4), fo. 136ᵛ. On St. Bartholomew's Day, 1687, 'he was knock'd on the head & kil'd downright by the Night-Watch at Salisbury for giving stubborne & refractory language to them' (Wood).

odes.[1] With these and others the young organist must have found himself in congenial company.

On the last day of July Thomas Purcell died. The full tale of his official posts has already been told. The amount that he actually received in cash was less impressive. Five years after his death there was still owing to his widow the sum of £220 12s. 6d. For all his assiduity he can hardly have died a wealthy man. By his will, made on 4th June 1681, he left his wife his house in Pall Mall, together with the furniture and other appointments and money owing to him from the Treasury, and £5 to each of his children, to be paid out of the arrears of his salary. On 2nd August he was laid to rest in the cloisters of Westminster Abbey.[2]

A week later the same building was the scene of a more joyful ceremony, when Henry Purcell's firstborn son was christened John Baptista.[3] The name has an Italian ring, and the suggestion has been made that it implies an indirect compliment to some foreign musician—perhaps Lulli, Draghi, or Vitali. A much more likely clue is afforded by the J. B. Peters who witnessed Purcell's will in 1695. This would appear to be John Baptist Peters, who was so proud of his name that he gave it to two of his own children. If we accept the reasonable supposition, mentioned above, that Mrs. Purcell's maiden name was Peters, the probability is that John Baptist was her brother and that she named her own son after him. It is perhaps significant that John Baptist Peters christened two members of his large family Frances and Henry.[4] If John Baptista Purcell had lived he might have given the world precise information about his name; but, like so many children in that insanitary age, he did not survive the perils of babyhood. He died when he was little more than two months

---

[1] *Cheque Book* p. 16; Evelyn, 28th January 1685. See Appendix E.

[2] *Cheque Book*, p. 17; *King's Musick*, p. 381 (18th February 1687); P. C. C. 138 Cottle, 8th November 1682; *Abbey Registers*, p. 205.

[3] *Abbey Registers*, p. 72. But see p. 40, n. 1.

[4] Registers of St. Mary le Bow (published by the Harleian Society).

old and was buried, like his grandfather, in the cloisters of the abbey.[1]

During this anxious time Purcell had been at work on another welcome ode for the king, which was performed four days after the burial of his infant son. Charles and the duke had been for their annual visit to Newmarket, and arrived back in London on 21st October. Again an anonymous poet pays fulsome homage to the returning monarch:

> The summer's absence unconcerned we bear
> Since you, great Sir, more charming fair appear,
> Scattering the mists of faction with our fear.
>
> Shine thus for many years, and let the sight
> Your friends encourage and your foes affright,
> Like Joshua's sun, with undiminished light.

How little the empty records of history communicate! There is nothing to tell us what Charles thought of this crawling syco-phancy or—more important—what Purcell's own attitude was to such a string of platitudes. Perhaps, pure musician that he was, he was indifferent to the quality of the words he set. It may have been all one to him whether it was Dryden or some miserable hack. Like Schubert he had the power of transfiguring the second-rate. During this year he had also written a number of anthems and signed the fly-leaf of his manuscript with the pious prayer: 'God bless Mr. Henry Purcell.'[2] Some at least of these anthems seem to have been composed for Westminster Abbey, as well as a service, probably the service in B flat of which Blow made a copy in 1683.[3]

---

[1] *Abbey Registers*, p. 206 (17th October 1682).

[2] Fitzwilliam MS. 88. The beginning of the manuscript is dated 13th September 1681 and the end 10th September 1682.

[3] W.A.M. 33717, fo. 5ᵛ (accounts ending Michaelmas 1682): 'Paid for writing Mr. Purcell's Service & Anthems, 30s.'; Fitzwilliam MS. 117.

CHAPTER V

ROYAL MUSIC

In June 1683 Purcell ventured into print on his own account for the first time with a work which, as far as we know, marks a new departure—the *Sonatas of III Parts* for two violins and bass with organ or harpsichord. The set of twelve sonatas was published in separate parts at a subscription price of ten shillings, the price after publication being raised to fifteen shillings. Subscribers were invited to come personally to the composer's house in St. Ann's Lane to fetch their copies,[1] which could also be purchased by the general public from Playford & Carr at the Temple. The young composer had evidently decided that his first published work should be issued with fitting ceremony. On the title-page he is proudly described as 'Composer in Ordinary to his most Sacred Majesty, and Organist of his Chappell Royall,' and the first violin part is enriched with an engraved portrait, which we are assured is the 'vera effigies Henrici Purcell, aetat. suae 24.' The work is dedicated to the king, by whose royal favour the composer declares he has been emboldened to lay his compositions at His Majesty's 'sacred feet.' The preface, addressed to the 'ingenuous [2] reader,' deserves quotation in full:

Instead of an elaborate harangue on the beauty and the charms of Musick (which after all the learned Encomions that words can contrive commends it self best by the performances of a skilful hand, and an angelical voice:) I shall say but a very few things by way of Preface, concerning the following Book, and its Author: for its Author, he has

---

[1] *London Gazette,* 24th–28th May and 7th–11th June 1683.

[2] 'Ingenuous,' like the synonymous and more familiar 'gentle,' is a complimentary term. For a note on this preface see p. 230, n. 1.

faithfully endeavour'd a just imitation of the most fam'd Italian Masters;
principally, to bring the seriousness and gravity of that sort of Musick
into vogue, and reputation among our Country-men, whose humor,
'tis time now, should begin to loath the levity, and balladry of our
neighbours: The attempt he confesses to be bold, and daring, there
being Pens and Artists of more eminent abilities, much better qualify'd
for the imployment than his, or himself, which he well hopes these his
weak endeavours, will in due time provoke, and enflame to a more
accurate undertaking. He is not asham'd to own his unskilfulness in
the Italian Language; but that's the unhappiness of his Education,
which cannot justly be accounted his fault, however he thinks he may
warrantably affirm, that he is not mistaken in the power of the Italian
Notes, or elegancy of their Compositions, which he would recommend
to the English Artists. There has been neither care, nor industry
wanting, as well in contriving, as revising the whole Work; which had
been abroad in the world much sooner, but that he has now thought
fit to cause the whole Thorough Bass to be Engraven, which was a
thing quite besides his first Resolutions. It remains only that the English
Practitioner be enform'd, that he will find a few terms of Art perhaps
unusual to him, the chief of which are these following: *Adagio* and
Grave, which import nothing but a very slow movement: *Presto Largo,*
Poco Largo, or *Largo* by it self, a middle movement: *Allegro,* and *Vivace,*
a very brisk, swift, or fast movement: *Piano,* soft. The Author has no
more to add, but his hearty wishes, that his Book may fall into no other
hands but theirs who carry Musical Souls about them; for he is willing
to flatter himself into a belief, that with such his labours will seem
neither unpleasant, nor unprofitable.

However flattered the king may have been by the dedication of
these sonatas, he had little time to spare for music just then. By
the end of June he was busy unravelling the complexities of the
Rye House Plot, which had been designed to overthrow the
monarchy by murder and set up a republic or a dukedom under
the puppet Monmouth. The whole country was profoundly
moved by the news, and addresses of congratulation on Charles's
escape continued to pour into Whitehall. When Purcell had
to compose another welcome ode for the king a few months later,
it was not surprising that the text made specific references to the
ineffectual seeds of revolution. Towards the end of July Prince

George of Denmark arrived in London, having come to marry Princess Anne, daughter of the Duke of York by his first wife and a patron of Purcell's art.[1] As though to emphasize the grimness of royal power in the midst of nuptial celebrations, several of the Rye House conspirators were executed at Tyburn the day after his arrival, and the following day the noble Lord Russell fell a victim to the executioner's 'butcherly strokes.'[2]

A week later, on 28th July, the royal wedding took place at Whitehall. Purcell celebrated the occasion with an ode, *From hardy climes and dangerous toils of war*—a reference to the prince's mother country and the recent warfare in which he had been engaged. He was indeed said to be a man of valour, though 'somewhat heavy,' and had actually rescued his brother, the King of Denmark, in a battle against the Swedes, 'when both those Kings were engaged very smartly.'[3] From the husband's origins the poet turned to the expected results of the union, foretelling that

> as ev'ry king that reigns
> Thro' Europe shares the blood that fills your veins,
> So shall the race from your great loins to come
> Prove future Kings and Queens of Christendom.

Vain prophecy! Of all Anne's numerous progeny none survived to wield the sceptre; when she died, worn out with cares and sickness, a German prince succeeded to the British throne. After the wedding Charles, not sorry to escape from the turmoil of government, repaired to Windsor and from there to Winchester.[4] On 9th September a solemn thanksgiving was celebrated for his delivery from violence [5]; and when at the end of the month he returned to London he was welcomed with an ode which seized

---

[1] Dedication of *A Choice Collection of Lessons* (1696).
[2] Evelyn, 19th–21st July 1683.
[3] Evelyn, 25th and 28th July 1683.
[4] Luttrell, 1st and 30th August 1683.
[5] Evelyn, 9th September 1683.

eagerly on the opportunity for topical reference.[1] The author of
Fly, bold rebellion, the fifth of Purcell's welcome songs, was able
to extend the customary compliments by rejoicing, no doubt
sincerely, that

> The plot is displayed and the traitors, some flown
> And some to Avernus by Justice thrown down.

And the composer duly provided his bass soloist with a resonant
bottom D on the final monosyllable.

In November Purcell wrote the first of his odes for St. Cecilia's
day, a setting of words by Christopher Fishburn, beginning:

> Welcome to all the pleasures that delight
> Of every sense the grateful appetite.

The ode was published in the following year with a dedication to
the gentlemen of the Musical Society, who organized the celebrations. From the title-page it appears that St. Cecilia's day was
'annually honour'd by a public *Feast*'; but nothing is known of
the celebrations before this year, and the fact that Blow's ode for
the following year is described as 'A Second Musical Entertainment' suggests that Purcell was the first to compose an elaborate
work for the occasion. From 1684 the meetings were held at
Stationers' Hall. It was for this celebration that Dryden in 1687
wrote his ode, *From harmony, from heavenly harmony,* originally set
to music by Draghi with one or two low C's for Gostling and

---

[1] The king returned on 25th September (Luttrell). The date of the
ode is uncertain. Vaughan Williams (Purcell Society's edition, vol.
xv, p. vi) suggests three alternative dates: the end of June, the end of
September and the end of October. The first of these is impossible,
since the conspirators were not executed till July. Arundell (*Henry
Purcell,* p. 97) points out that October is unlikely as the court was in
mourning for the King of Portugal, the queen's brother. I cannot,
however, agree with him that 9th September, 'as being the appointed
day for rejoicing, is more probable than' 25th September, since 9th
September was a Sunday and—more important still—the king was still
at Winchester.

subsequently by Handel.[1] Writing of the 1691 celebrations, the *Gentleman's Journal* describes the feast as

one of the genteelest in the world; there are no formalities nor gatherings, like as at others, and the appearance there is always very splendid. Whilst the company is at table, the hautboys and trumpets play successively.

To the year 1683 belongs a setting of a Latin hymn to St. Cecilia, *Laudate Ceciliam,* also intended for the celebration on 22nd November; but where it was performed cannot be certainly determined. Another ode for St. Cecilia's day, *Raise, raise the voice,* is said on the evidence of two late manuscripts to date from this year, but their authority is of doubtful value.[2]

In December John Hingston died and Purcell succeeded him as keeper of the king's wind instruments. His duties embraced not only the supervision of regals, virginals and organs, but also the care of flutes and recorders. The salary was £60 a year plus expenses.[3] The post was no sinecure. Hingston had been kept very busy repairing, setting up, moving and tuning the king's organs at Whitehall, St. James's, Hampton Court and Windsor. The detailed accounts in the Lord Chamberlain's records tell of a lively activity.[4] The new appointment must have brought Purcell into even closer touch with Bernard Smith, whom he was able to serve in an extraordinary competition that took place in the following year. In the autumn of 1682 Smith had been invited to set up an organ in the Temple Church. Subsequently a similar invitation was issued to another distinguished organ-builder, Renatus Harris. It was then decided, in February 1683, that both builders should erect their organs in one of the Benchers' halls, so that the better of the two could be chosen for the church, and in May a committee was appointed to adjudicate.

[1] Husk, *An Account of the Musical Celebrations on St. Cecilia's Day,* pp. 10 seq.

[2] Arkwright, Purcell Society's edition, vol. x, p. v.

[3] *King's Musick,* pp. 361 and 364.

[4] *King's Musick,* pp. 298–300, 334–5, 361–2, etc.

It is clear from what followed that the whole confusion was due to the rivalry between the Benchers of the Inner Temple and those of the Middle Temple. At the end of May 1684 Harris submitted a petition to the former in which he announced that his organ was ready and asked to be allowed to set it up in the church, for which the necessary permission was given. The public competition must have begun some time after this. According to Tudway, Smith engaged Blow and Purcell to demonstrate the excellence of his organ, while Harris invoked the aid of Draghi, also an eminent organist, and 'they thus continued vying with one another near a twelvemonth.'[1] By June 1685 the Benchers of the Middle Temple decided that 'the tedious competi-cion' had gone on quite long enough. They recorded their preference for Smith's organ, 'both for sweetnes and fulnes of Sound (besides the extraordinary Stopps, quarter Notes, and other Rarityes therein) . . . and that the same is more ornamentall and substantiall.' Harris's they felt to be 'discernably too low and too weake.' It was not to be expected that the rival Benchers would concur in this decision. They retaliated by advocating the appointment of impartial judges, adding significantly 'and such as are the best Judges of Musick,' to be nominated by both houses.

The controversy continued and the Benchers of the Inner Temple were still pressing for impartial judges in February 1686. Tudway says that the final decision was made by Sir George Jeffreys, whose reputation rests on a rather less recondite administra-tion of justice. Whatever truth there may be in this, it is certain that the actual purchase of Smith's organ was not completed till June 1688. So ended a memorable contest. Tradition has it that partisan zeal waxed violent among the supporters of the two builders. Burney tells us that he had it from 'old Roseingrave'

[1] Tudway's account is contained in a letter to his son, which is unknown apart from the quotations from it in Hawkins (p. 691). Tudway actually says that Harris employed Lulli, which is manifestly impossible. Hawkins made the almost certain suggestion that it was Draghi, whose Christian name was also Baptist.

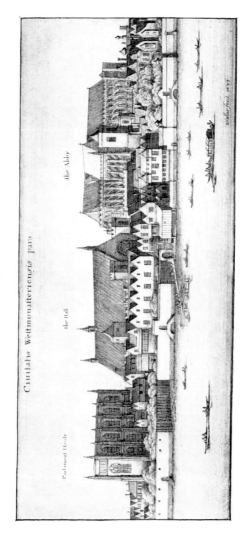

Parliament House   the Hall   the Abby

Civitatis Westmonasteriensis pars

WESTMINSTER FROM THE RIVER THAMES

W. Sherwin, sculp.

THE CORONATI

JAMES II, 1685

PURCELL IN HIS TWENTY-FOURTH YEAR

London: 8th of Feb: 78

S[r]

I have rec[eiv]d y[e] favor of yours of G: 4[th] w[th] y[e] Inclosed, for my Sonne Clency. I am sorry wee are like to be w[th]out you soe long as your[s] menc[i]ons: but is very likely you may have a Summons to appeare among[st] Sooner then you Imagin: for my Sonne is Composing; wherin you will be cheifly Conc[erned] However your oratory and eye, where you are most be Consi[d]- -derd and your Conueniencie, euer Complyde w[th]all: in y[e] meane time assure your self I shall be Carefull of your Con- -cern[s] heir by minding and Refreshing our masters memo- -ry of his Gratious promis when there is occasion. my wife Retu[r]n[s] -ns thanks for y[r] Compliment w[th] her service. and pray y[e] Giue both our Respects and humble service, to D[r] Belk and his La- -dy and beleeue euer that I am

&[c]

D[r] perce is in towne but
if I vue not seen him since
I haue performd G[r]
Compliments to D[r] Blow
with Turner &c:

your affectionatt and humble Seruant
Purcell

I flauti and humble &c amy are preparing for you

LETTER FROM THOMAS PURCELL TO JOHN GOSTLING

FINAL PAGE OF THE CORONATION ANTHEM,
'MY HEART IS INDITING'

Henry Purcell

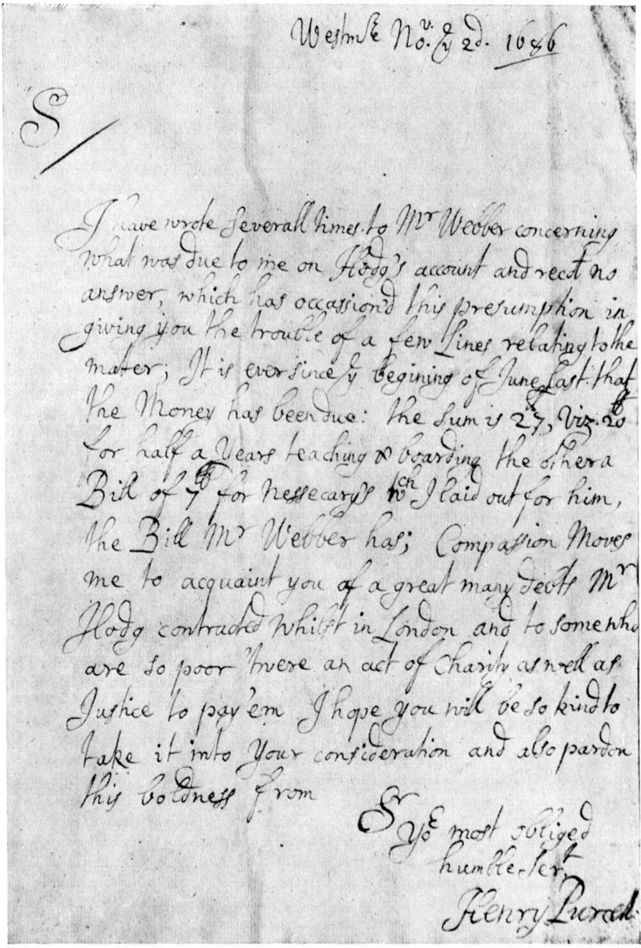

Westm^r No.^r y^e 2^d. 1696

S^r/

I have wrote severall times to Mr Webber concerning
what was due to me on Hogg's account and rec^d no
answer, which has occasion'd this presumption in
giving you the trouble of a few lines relating to the
mater; It is ever since ye begining of June last that
the Money has been due: the Sum is 27, Viz: 20
for half a years teaching & boarding the other a
Bill of 7 for nesseary^s wch I laid out for him,
the Bill Mr Webber has; Compassion Moves
me to acquaint you of a great many debts M^r
Hodg contracted whilst in London and to some who
are so poor 'twere an act of Charity as well as
Justice to pay 'em I hope you will be so kind to
take it into Your consideration and also pardon
this boldness from

                        S^r y^r most obliged
                          humble ser^t
                          Henry Purcell

LETTER FROM PURCELL TO THE DEAN OF EXETER

he poured into one poignant moment the full vehemence of passionate protest. For him too the end was near and inescapable.

On 21st November he made his will:

> In the Name of God Amen I Henery Purcell of the Citty of Westm^r. Gentl. being dangerously Ille as to the Constitution of my Body But in good and perfect Mind and Memory (thanks bee to God) Doe by these presents publish & Declare this to bee my last Will & Testam^t. And I doe hereby Give & bequeath unto my Loveing Wife Frances Purcell All my Estate both real & personall of what Nature & kind soever, to her & to her Assignes for Ever And I doe hereby Constitute & Appoint my said Loveing Wife My sole E[x]ecutrix of this my last Will & Testam^t. revokeing all Former Will or Wills Witness my Hand and seale this Tewent[i]eth First Day of Novemb^r. Annoq. Dni. 1695 And in the seaventh yeare of the Raigne of King William the Third &c.
>
> H. PURCELL.[1]
>
> Sign'd seal^d. published &
> Declar'd by the sd. Henry Purcell
> in the presence of
> W^m. Eeles: John Capelin
>   J. B. Peters.

On the same day he died.[2] It was the eve of St. Cecilia's day. The dean and chapter of Westminster decided unanimously that he should be buried in the abbey, without any charge being laid upon his widow. At her suggestion the last resting-place was chosen in the north aisle, at the foot of the organ which he had played for over fifteen years. The funeral solemnity was splendid. The whole chapter attended in vestments and the joint choirs of the abbey and the Chapel Royal were present. The music was by Purcell himself—the anthem and the dirges which he had

[1] P.C.C. 243 Irby, 7th December 1695. The above transcript is a faithful copy of the original will, which contains the autograph signatures. The careless spelling and the fact that the writing deteriorates towards the end suggest that the document was drawn up in great haste. Purcell's signature is so smudged and blurred as to be barely recognizable. J. B. Peters was probably Purcell's brother-in-law (see p. 45).

[2] *Cheque Book*, p. 21; *H.M.C., Bath MSS.*, vol. iii, p. 67; *Post Boy* 21st–23rd November 1695.

written for the queen's funeral eight months before.[1] On a pillar
adjoining the tomb was erected at Lady Howard's expense a
marble tablet recording that the composer had 'gone to that
blessed place where only his harmony can be exceeded.' 'He is
much lamented,' wrote the *Post Boy*, 'being a very great Master of
Musick.' The simple tribute is more eloquent than all the verses
that were dedicated to his memory. We need do no more than
echo it and find our justification in his work.

[1] *Flying Post*, 23rd–26th November 1695; *Post Boy*, 26–28th
November 1695; Luttrell, 26th November 1695; *Abbey Registers*, p. 238.

CHAPTER VIII

ASPECTS OF THE PERIOD

IT would be tempting at this point to sketch in detail the society in which Purcell lived and worked. To the modern observer it appears a curious mixture of barbarity and refinement. On the one hand we have the development of intellectual culture that was the inheritance of the Renaissance, the love of beauty and splendour in literature, music and architecture, the inquisitive interest in philosophical speculation and scientific experiment that laid the foundations of modern knowledge, and an elegance in dress and deportment that verged on foppishness but none the less gave colour and dignity to London life; on the other a system of sanitation that was 'oriental in its simple grandeur,'[1] a coarseness in the enjoyment of animal pleasures that almost belies the super-ficial refinement, the most primitive methods of dealing with the problems of death and disease, and a callousness towards the sanctity of human life that has all the air of a savage survival.

We are accustomed to look at Restoration England through romantic spectacles. It is well sometimes to try to get a more truthful picture. Evelyn—one of the most gentle and cultured humanists of his day—after seeing the reeking quarters of the regicides brought in baskets from the gallows was content to exclaim: 'O miraculous providence of God!'; and Pepys, though he was afterwards affected by the sight of the severed limbs hanging up at Aldersgate, could happily go off to eat oysters after having seen Major-General Harrison hanged, drawn and quartered at Charing Cross, with the single observation that the victim looked 'as cheerfully as any man could do in that condition.'[2] Nor was this all. Pepys's cold-blooded accounts

[1] Bryant, *The England of Charles II*, p. 16.
[2] Evelyn, 17th October 1660; Pepys, 13th and 20th October 1660.

87

of brutality to his own servants strike us oddly from a man who had had a university education and was acquainted with the highest in the land. Of the deplorable condition of public health at the time his diary gives us an illuminating record. Comparatively little attention was paid to personal cleanliness, and infant mortality was shockingly high. All this background of filth and horror lay behind the gorgeous façade of Restoration architecture and the brave show that survives in the work of the portrait-painters and poets of the day.

For these details of the world in which Purcell moved—details by no means irrelevant if we would see him as he actually lived—the reader must go to the pages of the diarists and those modern historians who have skilfully re-created the atmosphere of a past age. Here we must confine ourselves to the part played by music in the social whirlpool of London life. The changes effected by the king's return had their repercussions in the musical world. A foreign invasion began that has gone on ever since. Not that either foreign music or musicians were unknown in England before the Restoration. Edward VI, Mary and Elizabeth had all maintained a company of Italian musicians, including both string- and wind-players. James I seems to have favoured Frenchmen, no doubt through the influence of his consort, Anne of Denmark; at the funeral of Prince Henry in 1612 there were four French and five Dutch musicians in attendance. Some of the Italian musicians, however, remained in the royal service and were present at the king's funeral in 1625. Charles I's queen naturally brought over a number of musicians from her native France, and the court establishment included a French harpist. The Commonwealth interrupted the tradition of foreign attendance on the ruler—Cromwell preferred Englishmen—but it did not exclude the independent virtuoso. Thomas Baltzar, the violinist, was already charming the ears of English amateurs in 1656.[1]

The same thing happened with foreign music. It was the importation of the Italian madrigal under the Tudors that helped

[1] *King's Musick*, pp. 8, 10, 11, 12, 13, etc., 50, 52, 57, 59, 70, etc.; Scholes, *The Puritans and Music*, p. 148. For Baltzar, see p. 29.

to create the indigenous English product. French dance measures also became popular and continued so throughout the Commonwealth; it was during the suspension of the monarchy that Playford published his *Court Ayres, or Pavins, Almaines, Corants and Sarabands* (1655). So popular were Italian songs at this time that Henry Lawes, in the preface to his *Ayres and Dialogues* (1653), protested against the English habit of depreciating native musicians, claiming that 'our own Nation hath had and yet hath as able Musitians as any in *Europe*'; and he satirized the prevailing fashion by setting to music a list of Italian song-titles, presenting the result as 'a rare *Italian song*.' The influx of foreigners that followed Charles II's restoration was not a new phenomenon; it was rather an intensification of a process that had begun over a century before.

Several of these foreign musicians were in the king's service. As we have seen already, this did not necessarily ensure a livelihood. John Hingston, the organist and composer, to whom Purcell was apprenticed as an organ-tuner, told Pepys on one occasion that many of the king's musicians were on the point of starvation, their salaries being five years in arrears.[1] But employment at court would at any rate give a man standing and bring him to the notice of the aristocracy. The king's residence in Paris during his exile naturally led to particular interest in French music. As early as 1660 there were French musicians at court, for whom the king showed his preference in the bluntest fashion. In 1663 we have the names of a special band of these players, six in number, and from 1666 to 1674 a Frenchman, Louis Grabu, was actually master of the king's music. When masques were performed the Frenchmen's experience of ballet must have been invaluable.[2]

Enlightened opinion, however, was in favour of Italian musicians. Sir Bernard Gascoigne wrote from Italy, saying that he had found a eunuch in Florence with an excellent voice, as well

[1] Pepys, 19th December 1666.
[2] Pepys, 20th November 1660; *King's Musick*, pp. 162, 193, 280, 290, 318, 332; *Cal. S.P. Dom.*, 23rd July 1663.

as a girl of sixteen, well trained, 'who sings in reasonable perfection.' He gave it as his opinion that the king would be well
advised to send for them and dismiss 'those Frenchmen that are
not worth a fiddlestick.'[1] Before long Italian musicians were
added to the already overburdened establishment at a cost of
£1,700 a year, largely through the agency of Thomas Killigrew,
the theatrical impresario, who visited a number of European
courts to find the best material. A list of 1666 mentions a con-
tralto, a tenor, a bass, 'the poet, the woman, the eunuch,' and the
two Albricis, Vincenzo and Bartolomeo, the former of whom had
been a pupil of Carissimi. The Albricis were officially styled
the king's composers. Privileged visitors to court had the opportunity of hearing these 'rare *Italian* voices' in the king's private
chamber, or it might be from a barge in the Thames beneath
the queen's drawing-room. So important was the Italian music
that an official master was appointed, Giovanni Sebenico, who
also had the duty of attending in the queen's chapel.[2]

Some of these musicians seem to have suffered, as Roman
Catholics, from the agitation that followed the so-called 'Popish
Plot' of 1678. On 18th November 1679, the day after an effigy
of the Pope was carried past the queen's windows and burned at
Temple Bar, a petition was referred to the Treasury from four of
the Italians—including Bartolomeo Albrici and Giovanni Baptista
Draghi, who had by this time succeeded Sebenico as master—in
which they explained that they had left the service of foreign
princes at the king's request, that they were now forced to go
away through prosecution and that their salaries were four years

[1] *Cal. S.P. Dom.*, 7th June 1664.
[2] *Cal. S.P. Dom.*, 25th March 1665, 1st and 31st March 1666,
(June) 1666 (p. 484), 29th April 1668, 25th May 1671, April 1673
(p. 194); *King's Musick*, pp. 203, 222, 256; Evelyn, 24th January 1667;
Pepys, 12th February 1667, 28th September 1668. The 'Seignor
Joanni' mentioned in the last entry as an outstanding singer is clearly
Sebenico, not Draghi as has been suggested. Draghi was always
known as Signor Baptista, and besides did not pretend to be a singer
(see 12th February 1667).

in arrear.[1] Apparently, however, the scare was a false alarm.
Francesco Galli, one of the petitioners, was still in London
exhibiting his talents on the harpsichord in 1682 and Draghi
retained his position as organist to the queen.[2] With the accession
of a Roman Catholic king in 1685 the position of the Italians
became even more secure. Both Albrici and Draghi found
employment in James II's 'Popish chapel,' Albrici as a 'Gregorian'
and Draghi as organist.[3]

A further contribution to the cosmopolitan character of London
musical life was made by Charles II's queen, Catherine of Braganza. She brought with her a number of Portuguese musicians,
whom she insisted on retaining even when the other members of
her suite were sent back to Portugal. She had no love, it seems,
for the English and French musicians. On the other hand there
was little admiration among the English courtiers for the Portuguese. The Venetian resident informed his government that they
disgusted everybody with their discordant concerts, and both
Pepys and Evelyn were very disappointed in their performance.[4]
As time went on Italians were drafted into the service of the
queen's chapel at St. James's, which may account for the improve-
ment noticed by Pepys in 1666. In the following year, and
frequently afterwards, he speaks definitely of Italian music there,
though there were still some Portuguese musicians on the staff
as late as 1684.[5] It is impossible to tell the nationality of 'Mr.
Ferdinando,' who was in charge of the choristers in the chapel

---

[1] *Cal. S.P. Dom.,* 18th November 1679; Shadwell, preface to *Psyche,*
(1675).

[2] Evelyn, 27th January 1682; Chamberlayne, *Angliae Notitia,* 14th ed.
(1682), pt. i, p. 223. Evelyn, as usual when mentioning Italian
musicians, says simply 'Signor *Francesco,*' but the identification seems
probable enough.

[3] *Cal. Treas. Books,* 5th July 1687, 20th March 1688.

[4] *Cal. S.P. Venice and Northern Italy,* 21st July and 8th September
1662; Evelyn, 9th June 1662; Pepys, 21st September 1662.

[5] Pepys, 1st and 15th April 1666, 7th April 1667, etc.; Chamberlayne,
Angliae Notitia, 15th ed. (1684), pt. i, p. 221.

during 1664 and 1665. He may possibly, as the editor of *King's Musick* suggests, have been the same as Ferdinand de Florence, one of the king's French musicians, who was appointed in 1663 and threatened with dismissal—perhaps actually dismissed—in 1665.[1]

In addition to these establishments there was another, maintained by the queen-mother, Henrietta Maria, at Somerset House. Here the music was directed by a Frenchman, Anthony Robert, who spent forty years in her service.[2] When she died in 1669 the palace passed into the possession of Queen Catherine, who took up her residence there in 1671.[3] It must have been during the years 1671-7 that Matthew Locke, who is said to have become a Roman Catholic, served her as organist, in association first with Sebenico and then with Draghi. After Charles's death the queen continued to reside there; and even when the accession of William III made Roman Catholicism an unpopular religion, she was permitted to retain the use of her chapel, with Draghi as organist and master of the music.[4]

Royal patronage gave the foreigners a distinction that society was not slow to appreciate. Those who were fortunate enough to retain their positions settled down comfortably to take their place in English musical life. Draghi became so acclimatized that he was commonly spoken of as Mr. Baptist. Their success encouraged others to follow their example. There was 'a great flocking hither of forrein masters' from Germany, France and Italy.[5] Nicola Matteis, the celebrated Italian violinist, came over

[1] *King's Musick*, pp. 162, 167, 169, 178; *Cal. S.P. Dom.*, 23rd July 1663, February 1665 (p. 227), 1670 (p. 637).

[2] *King's Musick*, p. 321. [3] *Cal. S.P. Dom.*, 1st June 1671.

[4] Bodleian, Wood D 19 (4), fo. 86ᵛ; North, *Memoirs*, p. 95, *Musicall Gramarian*, p. 30; Chamberlayne, *Angliae Notitia*, 14th and foll. ed. (1682, etc.); Brit. Mus., Add. MSS. 15897, fo. 35; Elegy on Locke's death by Purcell. It is curious that Locke is described as an organist as early as 1664 (*King's Musick*, p. 169) but without any specification of the post. The dates of his alleged conversion and appointment to the queen are unknown.

[5] North, *Memoirs*, p. 106.

some time before 1674 and before very long had all London at
his feet. Evelyn thought him the most wonderful player he had
ever heard. At first his superior manner told against him; when
invited to play at court 'he behaved himself fastously,' insisting
on absolute silence during the performance, which was not in
the least what the courtiers were used to. But the enthusiasm of
one or two amateurs, including the Under-secretary of State, won
him the support of the fashionable world. His friends explained
to him that the English must be humoured; and their advice was
so successful that he began coining money and added to his
income by publishing his own works. An attempt to capture
Paris in the same way was less fortunate; he found 'that pistolls
did not walk so fast as ginnys.'[1]

Pietro Reggio, who had been in the service of Queen Christina
of Sweden, also came to explore the English gold-mine.[2] He
made a reputation as a singer and so far embraced English
culture as to set several of Cowley's poems to music. He also
wrote some of the music for Shadwell's version of *The Tempest,*
and the poet returned the compliment by writing some introductory verses for a volume of Reggio's songs published in 1680.
Shadwell was generous with his eulogy:

> Thou canst alone preserve my perishing Fame,
> By joyning Mine with Thy Immortal Name.
> Heroes and Conquerours by Poets live;
> Poets, from Men like Thee, must Life receive:
> Like Thee! where such a Genius shall we find,
> So Quick, so Strong, so Subtile, so Refin'd,
> 'Mongst all the Bold Attempters of thy Kind?

This is sickening enough, but Louis Maidwell, who honoured
the same publication with a set of Latin hexameters, went further
and dragged in the stalest classical commonplaces to adorn the tale:

> Aeterno dignus per saecula vivis honore,
> Dum Parthus Tigrim bibet, aut Germania Rhenum.

---

[1] Evelyn, 19th November, 2nd December 1674, 20th November
1679; North, *Memoirs,* pp. 122–8, *Musicall Gramarian,* pp. 34–7.
[2] Evelyn, 23rd September 1680, 25th July 1684.

To complete the chorus of praise Thomas Flatman threw in a comparison with Arion, singing on his dolphin to the admiring denizens of the waters. None of these three worthies could have guessed that the young organist of Westminster would be honoured in after years when the object of their admiration had long been consigned to the dusty folios of the historians and lexicographers. A combative tone in Reggio's preface and a note of championship in the poetic tributes suggest that not all London was willing to accept him as a genius. One catches a glimpse of rival camps— pro-Reggio and anti-Reggio.

The reputation won by these visitors brought them pupils. When Evelyn wanted his daughter Mary to learn music he sent her as a matter of course to Reggio for singing and to Bartolomeo Albrici for the harpsichord, with such success that she was accounted, if we may trust a proud father, their best pupil.[1] Matteis was in great demand as a teacher for the violin and helped by his example to stimulate the taste for Italian music. Those Englishmen who could afford it were not content to learn from foreigners at home; they went abroad and imbibed their culture from the fountain head, whether in France or in Italy.[2] Those who achieved proficiency in their studies came back to England to reap their reward. Even before the Restoration Captain Cooke had a reputation as a singer after the Italian manner; and in 1654 an English singer, Thomas Stafford, had come to Paris from Rome with Carlo Caproli to sing the part of Prometheus in the latter's opera, *Le nozze di Peleo e di Teti*.[3] We have already seen how Pelham Humfrey, Cooke's pupil and Purcell's master, was sent to France and Italy at the king's expense. Later Mrs. Knight, a famous singer, paid a visit to Italy and returned to sing 'incomparably.' John Abell, the counter-tenor, did the same, and Mr. Pordage, a priest, enchanted a select audience on his return

[1] Evelyn, 7th February 1682, 14th March 1685.
[2] Pepys, 18th June 1666; North, *Musicall Gramarian*, p. 37, *Memoirs*, p. 124–5.
[3] Prunières, *L'Opéra italien en France avant Lulli*, pp. 168–70. For Cooke, *v. supra*, p. 13.

from Rome by singing in the style of the Venetian recitative.[1]
More significant still, Nicholas Staggins, who succeeded Grabu
as master of the king's music in 1674, was given leave of absence
in 1676 to spend a whole year in Italy 'and other foreign parts.' [2]

A further impetus to the cultivation of Italian music was given
by the stage. The development of opera during this period will
be discussed in the next chapter. Here it will be sufficient to
mention the influence that Italian drama, both spoken and musical,
had on the Restoration theatre. In Aphra Behn's *The Feign'd
Curtizans* (1679) there is actually an Italian song, beginning

> Crudo amore, crudo amore,
> Il mio core non fa per te,

a circumstance that argues either a high degree of intelligence in
the audience or, more probably, the powerful domination of an
alien fashion.[3] Wits could afford to make merry over Society's
devotion to Italian music. In Southerne's *The Wives' Excuse, or
Cuckolds make Themselves* (1691)—a title sufficiently indicative of
contemporary taste—there is some sharp satire on fashionable
concerts. In the first act, after an Italian song has been sung,
Mr. Friendall invites opinions on the music. Mr. Wellvile confesses his admiration for the vocal part, not having understood
a word of it; to which Mr. Friendall ingenuously replies:

Nor I, faith, *Wellvile,* but the words were *Italian,* they sung well, and
that's enough for the pleasure of the ear.

Later, when there is a call for an English song, Mr. Wellvile
concurs, exclaiming:

Any Song, which won't oblige a man to tell you he has seen an
Opera at *Venice* to understand.

There must, in fact, have been a good deal of snobbery in the
prevailing taste.

[1] Evelyn, 2nd December 1674, 27th January 1682, 27th January 1685.
[2] *King's Musick,* p. 284; *Cal. S.P. Dom.,* 26th February 1676.
[3] Nicoll, op. cit., p. 249.

Purcell

Yet it would be a mistake to suppose that this interest in foreign products was all assumed. Thomas Killigrew, the theatrical impresario, had been to Rome over and over again to hear the music there, though he could neither sing nor play a note, and Philip Howard, brother of the Duke of Norfolk, was genuinely enthusiastic about the music at St. Peter's, as indeed one might expect from a Roman Catholic priest.[1] Pepys himself, for all his desire to be in the fashion, was no empty admirer and realized that a knowledge of Italian was essential in order to appreciate their vocal music.[2] Lord Guilford, himself an amateur composer, was keenly interested in Italian songs and transcribed a large number as a recreation when affairs of state lay heavy on him.[3] Publishers also moved with the times. Playford's *Musical Companion* (1667) contains several Italian songs, and in 1679 Godbid and Playford issued together a *Scelta di canzonette italiane de più autori,* a collection of songs and cantatas by Luigi Rossi, Carissimi, Cesti, Stradella and other composers.[4] Pepys had heard music by Carissimi as early as 1664.[5] The numerous contemporary manuscripts preserved in the music school at the Bodleian Library tell a similar tale. Cazzati, Draghi, Carissimi, Merula, Bassani, Ziani and many other composers are represented in this collection.

The vogue of Italian music was also responsible for introducing to English audiences the *castrato,* who was to dominate the opera of the early eighteenth century. The establishment of Italian musicians at court and the requirements of the queen's chapel gave permanent employment to these phenomena, who were also heard at the theatre. The Frenchman, Italian trained, who sang in the revival of Fletcher's *The Faithful Shepherdess* in 1668 attracted great attention. The most spectacular of the *castrati* was Giovanni

[1] Pepys, 23rd January, 12th February 1667.
[2] Pepys, 12th and 16th February, 7th April 1667, 22nd March 1668.
[3] North, *Life of the Right Honourable Francis North* (1742), p. 296; cf. *Autobiography,* p. 85.
[4] A copy of this extremely rare work is in the British Museum, catalogued under Pignani.
[5] Pepys, 22nd July 1664.

Francesco Grossi, commonly known as Siface, who came over to England on the strength of a European reputation and sang at James II's Roman Catholic chapel at Whitehall. After much solicitation he also gave a private concert at Pepys's house before a select company. This was a great favour, 'the Signor,' says Evelyn, who was present, 'much disdaining to shew his talent to any but princes.' The reign of the opera star, with all his caprice and childish arrogance, had begun.[1] For obvious reasons the *castrato* remained a foreign importation. English singers contented them-selves with cultivating the counter-tenor and winning approbation without insulting nature.

Beside this Italian invasion interest in French music was in-considerable. It had flared up in the early years of Charles II's reign but could not withstand for long the assaults of a greater rival. North traces the decline of French music in London and the rise of Italian to the influence of Nicola Matteis [2]—a view that probably makes too definite and clear-cut a division between the two fashions but at any rate indicates the reasons that contributed to the change. The French music that was popular at the begin-ning of the Restoration period was principally instrumental and associated with dances. When Charles II established his band of twenty-four violins at court, it was only natural that their repertory should be modelled largely on the practice of the French court, and Lulli's instrumental style was imitated by English composers in dances and stately 'entries.'[3] The craze passed, as such fashions will, but it left its mark on the court masques, which naturally took their cue from the French *ballet de cour,* and through them on the English opera, such as it was; and it had also a further influence on church music through the introduction of instrumental symphonies. The dances in Purcell's theatrical

[1] Pepys, 7th April 1667, 12th and 14th October 1668; Evelyn, 30th January and 19th April 1687. The 'Eunuch' in D'Avenant's *The Siege of Rhodes,* pt. ii (Pepys, 2nd July 1661), was not a *castrato*; he was merely one of the characters in the piece.

[2] North, *Memoirs*, pp. 121–2.

[3] Ibid., pp. 102–3.

works and the overtures to his anthems and odes are a permanent record of the impression made by the French style.

With all this activity on the part of professional musicians, both English and foreign, private music-making continued to flourish. When Charles II came back to his throne the old traditions were still so strong that Pepys could be ashamed of an acquaintance for his inadequate performance on the viol.[1] It would be rash, however, to generalize too far from Pepys's individual case. He was an enthusiast, and even he did not profess to be an expert. Sight-reading was not a thing to be taken for granted; if successfully accomplished it was worth recording in the diary.[2] Similarly Evelyn, some years later, mentions a conversation with Lord Guilford, in which the latter told him that he had been brought up to music from a child, 'so as to sing his part at first sight'—which, if it had been a normal part of a gentleman's education, would hardly have been worth recalling.[3] It is clear, too, that there were people then, as now, who were ready to praise an amateur performance without any standards to guide them.[4] Evelyn's own observations on music are generally neither acute nor particularly well-informed. He can write, for instance, of a private performance given before Charles II:

I also heard Mrs. Packer (daughter to my old friend) sing before his Majestie & the Duke privately, That stupendious Base *Gosling*, accompanying her, but hers was so lowd, as tooke away much of the sweetenesse: certainly never woman had a stronger, or better voice could she possibly have govern'd it: She would do rarely in a large Church among the Nunns [5]

— which is entertaining gossip but not very enlightening criticism.

Where there was enthusiasm music was practised as vigorously as string quartets are in every town in England to-day. One has

---

[1] Pepys, 26th April 1660.   [2] Pepys, 16th January 1660.
[3] Evelyn, 8th February 1684.   [4] Pepys, 6th June 1661.
[5] 28th January 1685.

only to turn over the pages of Pepys's diary to find constant references to impromptu music-making. When the business of the day was over—which was comparatively early in Restoration times—it was the natural thing for so ardent a music-lover to meet his friends for part-singing or fiddling. This activity was not confined to the aristocracy and the middle classes. When Pepys called on Lady Wright a few months before the king's return, her butler invited him into the buttery and not only gave him a glass of sack but also played a piece on his lute; and Lord Sandwich's German footman was an excellent performer on the theorbo.[1] When Pepys himself engaged servants he preferred those who were musical and liked to have them taking part with him in his favourite recreation. He was delighted to find that Tom Edwards, the ex-chorister of the Chapel Royal, could read anything at sight, and was glad that Mary Mercer, his wife's maid, proved to be a competent performer on the harpsichord and the viol. He also taught her to sing, whether, as he says, from a love of music or for the opportunity it afforded for a little light relief from matrimony is not quite clear; there was probably some truth in Mrs. Pepys's acid observation that he had never taken any pains to teach his own wife.[2]

Amateurs also ventured on composition. Pepys's own excursions in the art under the direction of John Berkenshaw are well known. Lord Sandwich, Master of Trinity House, and Silas Taylor, once a captain in Cromwell's army, both composed anthems, the Duke of York remarking rather unkindly that Taylor 'was a better store-keeper than anthem-maker, and that was bad enough, too.'[3] It was inevitable, however, that private music-making should suffer from the advent of the foreign virtuosos. The exquisite performances heard in the fashionable *salons* of the wealthy put to shame the well-meant efforts of

[1] Pepys, 25th January 1660, 7th December 1661.

[2] Pepys, 4th and 9th September 1664, 30th July 1666, etc.

[3] Pepys, 14th January, 24th February 1662, etc.; 14th December 1663, 29th June 1668.

home-grown amateurs, and even enthusiastic music-lovers found it irksome to have their private meetings judged by experts.[1]

One result of the new professionalism was to encourage the practice of listening to music. Hitherto the privilege of hearing good music had been largely confined to court and aristocratic circles; now it was thrown open to a wider public. The music-meetings at the Post Office, to which Pepys refers in 1664, were probably private occasions [2]; but public concerts seem to have begun about the same time. At first they were primitive and simple in character, beginning at a house near St. Paul's Cathedral, where there were organ recitals 'and some shopkeepers and foremen came weekly to sing in consort, and to hear and enjoy ale and tobacco.' Most of the music at these meetings was taken from Playford's book of catches, the third edition of which was published in 1667 with the title *Catch that Catch Can, or the Musical Companion.* Here no charge was made except for the drinks. A more ambitious venture was undertaken by John Banister, whom we have met already as one of the king's violinists and a bitter rival of Louis Grabu. In 1672 he opened a concert room in White-friars, 'rounded with seats and small tables, alehous fashion. One shilling was the price, and call for what you pleased.' These concerts continued, in various buildings, until 1678.

More distinguished was the 'Gentlemen's Meeting,' which began with the private practice of music in the French instrumental style. When the performers' fame spread abroad, they repaired to a tavern in Fleet Street, the owner of which continued to give concerts with professional players after the society came to an end, and 'the good half crownes came in fairely.' Inspired by the success of this undertaking the professionals had a concert hall prepared in Villiers Street, York Buildings, which soon became the principal musical centre in the town. Here prima-donnas, virtuosos from Italy and plain Englishmen appeared before

[1] Pepys, 22nd and 29th July, 12th August 1664. The 'Seignor Pedro' mentioned in these passages may be one of the queen's Portuguese musicians; he has also been identified, conjecturally, with Reggio.

[2] Pepys, 10th August, 5th October 1664.

the public; here too concerts were given in honour of distinguished persons, such as the Princess of Denmark or Prince Louis of Baden. North disapproved of the concerts because they were badly organized, no attention being paid to the construction of the programme:

> Now a consort, then a lutinist, then a violino solo, then flutes, then a song, and so peice after peice, the time sliding away, while the masters blundered & swore in shifting places, and one might perceiv that they performed ill out of spight to one and other.

But if the concerts were as badly managed as this it is strange that they lasted well into the eighteenth century. There is more probability in North's other suggestion that their decline was due to unsuccessful competition with the theatre.[1]

No chapter on Restoration music would be complete without a mention of the concerts given by Thomas Britton, the 'small-coal man,' in a room over his shop in Clerkenwell. Beginning in 1678, if we may trust Hawkins, he soon attracted a large and influential circle of music-lovers. His concerts, in spite of the modest surroundings in which they were held, did much to disseminate a knowledge of the latest masterpieces from the Continent. The Bodleian Music School possesses a copy in Britton's handwriting of Corelli's Opus 1, which we are told was 'used at his Assembly for many years.' A man of wide interests and culture, he was loved and respected by all who knew him. He witnessed the rise of Purcell's genius and its sudden extinction, and lived to welcome Handel to his meetings.[2]

---

[1] North, *Memoirs*, pp. 107–15, *Musicall Gramarian*, pp. 30–3, *Autobiography*, p. 72. North's inimitable account is well worth reading for its own sake. A number of relevant advertisements from the *London Gazette* are quoted by Hawkins, p. 763.

[2] Hawkins, pp. 762, 788–92; Bodleian, Mus. Sch. c. 75.

CHAPTER IX

MUSIC AND DRAMA

PURCELL was a prolific composer. The collected edition of his
works already runs to twenty-six volumes (1942), and there are
more to come. It is true that a certain proportion of the area
covered by the printed notes is taken up by modern editors'
realizations of the figured bass or reductions for pianoforte of the
full score. But even so the composer's industry remains remarkable when we consider that practically all his surviving work
was produced in the space of fifteen years, between 1680 and 1695.
It is important to remember, too, that nearly all his instrumental movements are fully scored in four or sometimes five parts
and that the details of the part-writing are worked out with
scrupulous care. Purcell may have been busy, but he was
clearly not slapdash; and he had a sufficient regard for some at
least of his work to think it worth while to make fair copies. The
magnificent autograph volume in the Royal Library (now housed
on permanent loan in the British Museum) is an abiding testimony
to his patience and thoroughness.

This large output covered many fields—the court, the theatre,
the church and the chamber. To all he contributed music that
claimed and has won survival, however ephemeral the occasions
for which it was composed. It might be thought odd at the
present day that a cathedral organist should provide music for
theatrical entertainments, many of which were in questionable
taste. But the seventeenth century did not recognize any water-
tight compartments for the musician's art; the whole world was
his to conquer. 'Men of our profession,' says Dr. Blow in Tom
Brown's imaginary correspondence, 'hang between the church and
the playhouse, as *Mahomet's* tomb does between the two load-

stones, and must equally incline to both, because by both we are equally supported.'[1] It was Brown, too, who wrote in a poem dedicated to Purcell's memory:

> And surely none but you, with equal ease,
> Cou'd add to *David,* and make *D'Urfy* please,[2]

suggesting not that it was unusual to do both but that Purcell did both consummately well.

Not that he was merely a cathedral organist. Far more important than his post at the abbey were the services he rendered at court, as organist of the Chapel Royal and as a member of the king's private music. And the theatre was bound up with the court. Its audience was drawn not from the citizens of London, who looked askance at its licence and immorality, but from the aristocracy and the king's immediate circle. It is true that most of Purcell's dramatic music dates from the reign of William III, when the king was too busy with wars to devote much time to the pleasures of the capital; but the old associations between the court and the theatre remained, and the queen, for all her piety and devotion, frequently graced the theatre with her presence.[3]

It is unlikely, therefore, that Purcell's music for the theatre was known to a wide circle. It would not, for instance, have travelled outside London as his church music did. But that it had a public is evident from the fact that much of it was published, either in Purcell's lifetime or shortly after his death. When *Dioclesian* made his reputation in 1690 the success was sufficient to justify him in issuing the full score; and his fame so far survived him that *Orpheus Britannicus,* which contains a large number of songs from the plays, ran into three editions. The only church music that was published until eighteenth-century editors

---

[1] *Works,* 9th ed., vol. ii, p. 248.

[2] Printed in *Harmonia Sacra,* pt. ii (1693) and in Brown's *Works* 9th ed., vol. iv, p. 99.

[3] Nicoll, *Restoration Drama,* pp. 5–19, 352, 356–7.

undertook its collection was the festal *Te Deum* and *Jubilate*; and that was written for a special occasion, and regularly performed in subsequent years. The dramatic music does not represent the whole Purcell, but it forms a very large and highly characteristic part of his output and makes a convenient starting-point for a general survey of his work.

The history of dramatic music in England is curious.[1] This country has generally been slow to follow continental developments, whether as a result of her peculiar geographical position or because a native caution makes our composers reluctant to assimilate foreign styles and habits until they have been carefully examined. When opera first came to birth in Florence at the end of the sixteenth century in the form of an attempted re-creation of Greek drama, England remained content with the old practice of using music merely as an incidental addition to the structure of a play. The idea of a play set to music throughout, with the natural inflections of speech and the emotions of dramatic narrative interpreted by a single vocal line, was still something foreign and remote. Solo song, of course, was recognized and accepted. The madrigalists appreciated the possibilities of a voice-part accompanied by strings, and at the turn of the century the lute-song came to England from the Continent and emphasized still more the idea of a subordinate accompaniment to the voice. But the complete application of these principles to the drama had yet to be made, and when it was made—as it turned out—they were soon abandoned.

Though English musicians were shy of imitating Italian opera, they did not hesitate to make use of the new recitative, which they introduced into the court masques, a hybrid form of entertainment which generally included dialogue, singing and dancing. As early as 1617 Nicholas Lanier, later master of the king's music and a connoisseur of painting, had set the whole of Ben Jonson's *Lovers made Men* 'after the Italian manner, *stylo recitativo*.' Some years after this he was sent to Italy to buy pictures for the king's

[1] The standard work on this subject is Dent, *Foundations of English Opera*.

collection and must have used the opportunity to become further
acquainted with the declamatory style. He was, says Roger
North, 'a nice observer of the Itallian musick . . . and more
especially of that, which was most valuable amongst them, I
mean the vocall.'[1]

The masques, which were very fashionable under the first
two Stuart kings, were less material for the musician than for the
scenic artist. The provision of sumptuous stage settings and
elaborate machinery was regarded as essential to a successful production, and the fact that the performances took place at court
made expense a negligible consideration. The Civil War put
an end to these royal *divertissements* but did not kill the masque,
which was carried on by less exalted performers. When the
Commonwealth was established the Government laid a ban on
stage plays but had no objection to entertainments in which
music played a part. The most important of the masques
produced during this period was Shirley's *Cupid and Death,* with
music by Matthew Locke and Christopher Gibbons, which was
performed privately in honour of the Portuguese ambassador in
1653. Others were written specially for school performance.[2]

Meanwhile Italian opera, which in its own country had developed from a court entertainment into a public spectacle, had been
brought to Paris, largely through the efforts of Cardinal Mazarin,
the first performance taking place in 1645. It is significant that the
young Prince Charles, living in exile in Paris with his mother,
attended several operatic performances and concerts at this time.[3]
Another exile was also living in Paris at this time, Sir William
D'Avenant, who had produced several court masques during the
reign of Charles I. In addition to the Italian operas another
type of entertainment was given by French actors and musicians.
This consisted of heroic tragedies with spectacular scenic effects
and a certain amount of music, both vocal and instrumental.
The principle on which they were constructed is outlined by

[1] *Musicall Gramarian,* p. 19.
[2] Dent, op. cit., p. 81; Scholes, *The Puritans and Music,* p. 194.
[3] Prunières, op. cit., pp. 95 and 101.

Corneille, whose *Andromède,* with music by Dassoucy, was performed in 1650. He explains that each act has

a flying machine with a consort of music, which I have employed only
to satisfy the ears of the spectators, while their eyes are engaged in
watching the machine sink or rise again or concentrating on something
that prevents them from paying attention to what the actors might be
saying. . . . But I have taken good care that nothing should be sung
that was essential to the understanding of the play, because as a general
rule words that are sung are imperfectly heard by the audience, owing
to the confusion resulting from a number of voices singing together;
and they would consequently have created great obscurity in the body
of the work if it had been their function to convey any important
information to the listener.[1]

England still remained ignorant of opera. Only those who
could afford to travel were acquainted with the possibilities of the
new form. Evelyn had his eyes opened when he visited the opera
at Venice in 1645,

which are Comedies & other plays represented in Recitative Music by
the most excellent Musitians vocal & Instrumental, together with variety
of Seeanes painted & contrived with no lesse art of Perspective, and
Machines, for flying in the aire, & other wonderfull motions. So taken
together it is doubtlesse one of the most magnificent & expensfull
diversions the Wit of Men can invent.[2]

The whole performance held them 'by the Eyes and Eares til two
in the Morning.' It was not until 1656 that opera was introduced
into England and then in a curious hole-and-corner fashion in
order to escape the Commonwealth ban on public theatres. *The
Siege of Rhodes,* written by D'Avenant with music by Henry
Lawes, Captain Cooke, Matthew Locke, Charles Coleman and
George Hudson, was given before a small audience at Rutland
House, Aldersgate, in the City.[3] The circumstances are well

[1] Preface to *Andromède.* [2] Evelyn, June 1645.
[3] Wood, *Athenae Oxonienses* (ed. Bliss), vol. iii, p. 805. The libretto
was published in the same year.

described by Dryden in his preface to *The Conquest of Granada* (published 1672):

> For Heroick Plays, . . . the first light we had of them on the *English Theatre* was from the late Sir *William D'Avenant*: It being forbidden him in the Rebellious times to act Tragedies and Comedies, because they contain'd some matter of Scandal to those good people, who could more easily dispossess their lawful Sovereign than endure a wanton jeast; he was forc'd to turn his thoughts another way: and to introduce the examples of moral vertue, writ in verse, and perform'd in *Recitative Musique*. The Original of this musick and of the scenes which adorn'd his work, he had from the *Italian Opera's*; but he heighten'd his Characters (as I may probably imagine) from the example of *Corneille* and some *French Poets*. In this Condition did this part of Poetry remain at his Majesties return. When growing bolder, as being now own'd by a publick Authority, he review'd his *Siege of Rhodes,* and caus'd it to be acted as a just *Drama*.

It will be noticed from this account that Dryden derives the *Siege of Rhodes* jointly from Italian opera and Corneille, and also that he regards it as the parent, as indeed it was, of the heroic drama of the Restoration period. Indeed, the last sentence seems to imply that when the work was revived in 1661 after the king's return it appeared in a revised version as a play with music rather than as an opera.

The new form was still a tentative experiment. When Evelyn went to see a performance of D'Avenant's opera in 1659 he thought it 'much inferior to the Italian composure & magnificence.'[1] The two nouns are significant. Scenery, no less than music, was considered indispensable in opera. We have just seen how Evelyn in Venice was impressed both by the recitative and by the scenic effects. So now he particularly described D'Avenant's work as 'a new *Opera* after the *Italian* way in *Recitative Music & Sceanes*.' The English public, too, seems to have been slow to accept the new style. D'Avenant himself, in *The Playhouse to be Let* (1663), puts into the mouth of one of his characters (an actor) the conventional objection to recitative, that

[1] 5th May 1659.

it is unnatural; to which the musician replies with a reasoned definition of its function:

> Recitative Musick is not compos'd
> Of matter so familiar, as may serve
> For every low occasion of discourse.
> In Tragedy, the language of the Stage
> Is rais'd above the common dialect;
> Our passions rising with the height of Verse;
> And Vocal Musick adds new wings to all
> The flights of Poetry.

There was no immediate attempt to follow up D'Avenant's lead; indeed D'Avenant himself, though he had produced two other so-called operas at the end of the Commonwealth period, failed to develop his innovation. We hear of projects to perform Italian operas in 1660, 1664 and again in 1667, but there is no record that anything ever came of them.[1] The public taste was for a different kind of entertainment. When next a complete opera was performed in London it was a French importation. There had been opposition in Paris to the Italian opera almost from the first, and before long French composers began to produce operas of their own. When the French composers had success-fully driven Cavalli out of Paris in 1662 they proceeded to disagree among themselves. Lulli, an ambitious Italian who had begun his career as a dancer and had already written music for several *comédies-ballets*, purchased in 1672 the monopoly of pro-ducing operas which Louis XIV had previously granted to the poet Perrin and the musician Cambert in 1669. Cambert came over to London—a sensible thing to do, since the king, as we have seen, took an interest in French musicians. He brought with him Perrin's opera *Ariane, ou le Mariage de Bacchus,* which was set to music by Grabu and performed at the Theatre Royal in the spring of 1674 by the 'Royal Academy of Music,' an institution

[1] *Cal. S.P. Dom.*, 22nd October 1660; Pepys, 2nd August 1664, 12th February 1667.

obviously copied from its French original.[1] This seems to have been the work that Evelyn saw on 5th January; he describes it as an '*Italian Opera* in musique, the first that had ben in *England* of this kind'—by which he evidently intended some distinction from D'Avenant's productions which he had seen in 1659 and 1662. [2]

It was eleven years before Grabu again set an opera. At the end of 1674 he lost his place as master of the king's music and was succeeded by Nicholas Staggins. After making application for arrears of salary he was allowed to return to France in 1679, together with his wife and three children. However, he was back again by 1685, having probably been brought over by Betterton, who had been negotiating with him in Paris in 1683, and collaborated with Dryden in an English opera on the French model—*Albion and Albanius*.[3] In the preface to this work, the fortunes of which have already been related, Dryden explained his theory of opera. The plot should be of a specific kind:

> The suppos'd Persons of this musical Drama [i.e. of opera in general], are generally supernatural, as Gods and Goddesses, and Heroes, which at least are descended from them, and are in due time, to be adopted into their Number

—an out-of-date opinion, since Italian opera had long ceased to confine itself to the supernatural and had turned eagerly to purely historical themes. Accepting his postulate Dryden goes on to point out that the recitative takes the place of the 'lofty, figurative, and majestical' language that would normally be employed in a spoken play on such a subject. He distinguishes carefully the arias, or, as he calls them, '*The Songish Part*,' where the object is 'to please the Hearing, rather than to gratify the understanding,' pointing out, however, that English is inferior to Italian, since it is weak in female rhymes.

[1] Documents relative to the French opera performances are quoted by Nicoll, op. cit., pp. 355–6.

[2] Evelyn, 5th May 1659, 9th January 1662, 5th January 1674.

[3] *King's Musick*, pp. 279, 284, 317, 319; *Cal. S.P. Dom.*, 31st March 1679; Lawrence, *The Elizabethan Playhouse*, 1st series, p.149; *H.M.C.*, Report 7, pt. 1, p. 290.

This is an interesting observation, since it indicates a specific desire to model English opera on the Italian, for which, indeed, Dryden expresses the greatest admiration; it does not seem to have occurred to him that an English librettist should make a virtue of the weaknesses of his language. When Dryden prides himself on his knowledge of Italian and French, he fails to realize that the author of an opera can dispense with foreign tongues so long as he knows his own thoroughly and has an intelligent understanding of music. It is difficult to say which is the odder—Dryden using his knowledge of French and Italian to compile an English libretto, or Grabu setting that libretto with an imperfect knowledge of the language. The fallacy of Dryden's point of view is that it assumes that English music will necessarily be modelled on the continental styles.

Albion and Albanius was a failure. For that, as we have seen, the political circumstances of the time were partly responsible; but it is at least probable, as Professor Dent has suggested, that the ineptness of the music, which aroused the contemptuous indignation of a contemporary versifier, was also responsible for its collapse. Only one other attempt was made to give a complete opera in London, and once again this was a foreign importation. Mr. W. J. Lawrence has recently shown, by a most ingenious and convincing argument, that Lulli's *Cadmus et Hermione,* first performed in Paris in 1673, was given in London by a French company in February 1686. 'The musicke,' wrote Peregrine Bertie to the Countess of Rutland, 'was indeed very fine, but all the dresses the most wretched I ever saw,' which suggests that public taste in spectacles had become exacting and severe. A month later Tom Jevon, in the prologue to his farce, *The Devil of a Wife,* poked clumsy fun at the French opera, burlesquing the air, 'Ah! Cadmus, pourquoy m'aimez-vous?' as 'A Cadmeus Pur qua, Mene Vou.'[1]

The performance of *Cadmus* is important, not only as an

[1] Lawrence, 'The French Opera in London,' *The Times Literary Supplement,* 28th March 1936; Nicoll, op. cit., p. 350; *H.M.C., Rutland MSS.,* vol. ii, pp. 102–4.

example of French influence on the theatre in James II's reign, but more particularly because it preceded all Purcell's important works for the stage. It is probable that he saw this performance or at any rate knew the music, if it was he who appropriated the instrumental 'Entrée de l'Envie' in the prologue and used it for the dance that follows *Arise, ye subterranean winds* in *The Tempest*. That he was already acquainted with Lulli's instrumental style before this is evident from his welcome songs; but the presumption that he came into direct contact with one of Lulli's most significant works in 1686 gives us much more definite evidence to work on.

Albion and Albanius had no successor. The taste of the theatre-going public did not incline to pure and undiluted opera. Their point of view seems to have been similar to that of Saint-Evremond, who, while admitting that music had its place in the theatre, had no good word to say for a work that was sung throughout, however striking the production. As he observed in a sentence that defies adequate translation: 'Une sottise chargée de Musique, de Danses, de Machines, de Décorations, est une sottise magnifique, mais toûjours sottise.'[1] The failure of opera to take root in this country may have been due to the lack of public response in the first place or to a natural antipathy on the part of English composers. An acute foreign critic has remarked:

Music is not the natural means of expression for the Englishman to the same extent as it is for the Italian. He regards it as something higher than a mere vehicle of the emotions and passions; and this explains why in England music remained in a subordinate position to drama.[2]

There may be much truth in this. Certainly operatic triumphs have been won in this country not by English composers but by foreigners; the popularity of Handel in the eighteenth century is paralleled by the vogue of Wagner in our own.

Restoration England turned from opera as it was understood abroad and preferred to cultivate a hybrid form—dramatic spectacles in which music played a large and important part. Some

---

[1] 'Lettre sur les Opera,' *Works*, 5th ed. (1739), vol. iii, p. 284.
[2] Alfred Einstein, *A Short History of Music* (English trans.), p. 81.

of these were adaptations of existing plays, whether by Elizabethan
authors or by contemporary dramatists; others were specially
written for operatic performance. To the first class belong
Purcell's settings for *Dioclesian* and *The Fairy Queen*, to the latter
his *King Arthur*. One of the most popular of these adaptations
was Shadwell's version of *The Tempest*, which first appeared in
1674 and was frequently revived. Among the composers who
contributed music to it before Purcell took it over at the end of
his career were Banister, Humfrey, Reggio, Draghi and Locke.[1]
The first of the original semi-operas was *Psyche*, written by
Shadwell in imitation of the Molière-Lulli *comédie-ballet* with the
same title, the music to the English version being provided by
Locke and Draghi. This was performed in February 1675.[2] A
further stimulus to the cultivation of the hybrid form may have
been received from the performance at court of a French *comédie-
ballet*, *Rare en Tout*, by Mme La Roche-Guilhen with music by
James Paisible, one of Charles II's musicians, on 29th May 1677
(the king's birthday).[3]

The combination of music and dialogue provided by the
semi-operas remained popular throughout Purcell's lifetime, but
their vogue did not last; 'for some that would come to the play
hated the musick, and others that were very desirous of the musick,
would not bear the interruption that so much rehearsall gave.'[4]
North concludes that 'it is best to have either by it self entire,' and
Addison, writing on the essential difference between English and

[1] Nicoll, op. cit., p. 205; Dent, op. cit., p. 138; Squire, 'The Music
of Shadwell's "Tempest,"' *Musical Quarterly*, 1921, pp. 565–78; *King's
Musick*, p. 271.

[2] Nicoll, op. cit., p. 348. Downes, *Roscius Anglicanus* (ed. Summers),
p. 35, says February 1673, but this is probably a mistake, as the Lord
Chamberlain's warrant quoted by Nicoll distinctly says 'Feb. 27 1674
[i.e. 1675]: Psyche first Acting.' Both the text and the music were
published in 1675.

[3] Lawrence, *The Elizabethan Playhouse*, 1st series, p. 147; *King's
Musick*, p. 318.

[4] North, *Memoirs*, p. 117. 'Rehearsal' is a term used for speeches.

Italian opera, is of the same opinion. He approves Italian recitative, 'the Transition from an Air to Recitative Musick being more natural, than the passing from a Song to plain and ordinary Speaking, which was the common Method in *Purcell's* Operas.' He only objects to Italian recitative—that is to say, *recitativo secco* —when it is fitted with English words.[1]

With the restoration of Charles II the masque, which had been relegated to school and private performances during the Commonwealth, once more became a court entertainment. Here the passion for lavish display and elaborate dancing could most naturally be gratified. Of the performance of one of these masques—John Crowne's *Calisto,* given at Whitehall in the winter of 1674-5—the most comprehensive details have been preserved. Preparations went on for months beforehand, and large sums of money were spent not only on dresses, curtains and properties, but also on the music, which had been composed by Nicholas Staggins. The noble performers included the Duke of Monmouth and the two daughters of the Duke of York. Dancers, singers and instrumentalists of every kind were engaged, and the bill for the music came to over £220. The blaze of jewellery was dazzling. The music has not survived, which is a pity, as it would have been interesting to study its form and style. Crowne was good enough to say that 'Mr. Staggins has not only delighted us with his excellent composition, but with the hopes of seeing in a very short time a master of music in England equal to any France or Italy have produced.' The hope was fulfilled, but the master was not Staggins.[2]

Less spectacular but more significant was the masque, *Venus and Adonis,* with music by John Blow, which is thought to have been performed some time between 1680 and 1687.[3] The style of this shows an acquaintance not only with Lulli's instrumental

[1] *Spectator,* No. 29 (3rd April 1711).

[2] Nicoll, op. cit., pp. 357-60; *King's Musick,* pp. 280, 285, 286-7, 290, 471-6; Evelyn, 15th and 22nd December 1674.

[3] The work has been published by G. E. P. Arkwright in the *Old English Edition,* No. xxv, and by Anthony Lewis (Lyre Bird Press).

writing but also with the pathetic, expressive declamation of the Italians. There is no dialogue, and the work is rather a miniature opera than a masque, though it contains a fair proportion of instrumental movements for dancing. To the student of Purcell it is of particular interest as the direct forerunner of *Dido and Æneas*.[1] The influence of the masque can be seen in the spectacular operatic productions of the period—in Grabu's *Albion and Albanius,* for example, and in much of Purcell's work for the theatre, notably *Dioclesian* and *The Fairy Queen.*

[1] Earlier than this Locke had set a masque of Orpheus and Eurydice in Settle's *The Empress of Morocco* (1673); see North, *Musicall Gramarian,* p. 33, and Julian Herbage, 'Matthew Locke's Dramatic Music,' *Monthly Musical Record,* January 1937.

CHAPTER X

'DIDO' AND 'DIOCLESIAN'

'DIDO AND ÆNEAS' was Purcell's only opera, in the strict sense of the word. Like the Commonwealth masques it was composed not for the professional stage but for school performance. Grabu's *Albion and Albanius* was the last attempt to give the public a form of entertainment for which it was not yet ready. The peculiar circumstances under which *Dido* was produced isolate it not only from Purcell's other works but from the rest of the dramatic music of the period. Though the conditions of its performance link it up with the tradition of the masques, it is, like *Venus and Adonis*, a genuine opera, in that vocal music is predominant and dancing takes only a subordinate place. But it does not subscribe to the contemporary belief that an opera should be spectacular, since the resources of a boarding-school were inevitably more limited than those of Dorset Garden. And since a school production is generally a modest and unambitious undertaking, it is unusually short, taking little more than an hour to perform. In a word, it is a chamber opera for amateurs.

The origin of the libretto is to be found in Tate's *Brutus of Alba*, which had been given at Dorset Garden ten years before. Here we find under other names not only the prototypes of Dido, Æneas and Belinda, but also the witches who were so popular with Restoration audiences. *Dido* is not, however, an adaptation of *Brutus of Alba*; the verbal coincidences are so few as to be negligible. Tate, no less than Purcell, appreciated the conditions under which the performance was to be given and wrote his new libretto with those conditions in mind. As a poet he deserves all the unkind things that have been said about him, but whatever the literary quality of *Dido*—and it is on the whole very poor—there is no doubt that the text is thoroughly suitable for musical setting. There is little of Dryden's anxious preoccupation with feminine endings or literary graces. The style is plain and straightforward, with only one or two deviations into theatrical pomposity, and the words are such as any musician would welcome. One has only to think of occasional lines—'Peace and I are strangers grown,' 'Fear no danger to ensue,' 'Great minds against themselves conspire,' and so on—to see what opportunities lay ready to Purcell's hand. And how magnificently he seized those opportunities!

The story in its essentials is Vergil's. Æneas, fleeing from ruined Troy and bound for Latium, is driven by storm into Carthage, where the widowed Dido reigns as queen. Proximity leads to passion, felt and reciprocated; but the gods forbid their union. Æneas sails away to fulfil his destiny in Italy and Dido ends her sorrows with her own hand. To this simple story the poet has merely added the witches, as symbols of the malevolence of destiny, and modified the tragic ending by making Dido the victim of a broken heart.[1] The work begins with a short overture of the type established by Lulli—a slow introduction followed by a quasi-fugal *allegro*. Thereafter we are plunged straight into the anguish of love. Belinda, Dido's sister—corresponding to Anna in Vergil—plays the part of the confidante, a type familiar in seventeenth-century Italian opera and well exemplified by Arnalta in Monteverdi's *Incoronazione di Poppea*. She counsels cheerfulness and the chorus echo her advice, but in vain. Dido's pangs are beyond remedy. She confesses them in an aria that at once illustrates Purcell's gifts both of musical invention and of dramatic characterization. The movement is constructed on a simple ground bass of four bars, above which the queen's sighs are heard:

---

[1] This seems to be implied by the final recitative. There is certainly nothing in the text to suggest suicide, unless we interpret literally the words 'Elissa bleeds to-night.'

The large notes represent the original text. The small notes are from Professor Dent's vocal score (Oxford University Press).

As the song proceeds the bass becomes more insistent. It has been the background to the voice. Now it invades the singer's consciousness and its opening phrase shapes itself to her words:

Notice how Purcell extends the second half of the sentence to

make an irregular period of five bars—a characteristic touch.
The climax comes when the heart is so charged that there is
nothing more to add, and the strings, which have hitherto been
silent, enter as the voice ceases and take up the tale. Æneas
appears and presses his suit, Belinda gives approval, and the chorus
sing of the triumphs of love, followed by a majestic 'Triumphing
Dance' which recalls the stately chaconne—also in C major—in
Lulli's *Cadmus et Hermione*.

Scene ii brings us to the Sorceress's cave. The chorus are now
witches, singing 'Ho ho ho' as energetically and in the same
tempo as the three magicians in Lulli's *comédie-ballet, Pastorale
comique*—or we may compare the shattering 'Tôt tôt tôt' of the
chorus of Chalybes, forging steel, in the same composer's *Isis*.
Here we cannot help being struck by the unreality of Restoration
conventions. Purcell's instrumental introduction is solemn and
and impressive but it does not suggest the horror of the supernatural, and the choruses are jolly rather than frightening. The
witches may sing, 'Harm's our delight and mischief all our
skill,' but they might just as well be a crowd of rustic merrymakers
for all the music does to help illusion. The one really striking
moment is the suggestion of distant hunting-horns on the strings
when the Sorceress refers to the joint expedition. At the end of
the scene Purcell adopts a device that had already been used by
Locke in *Psyche* and introduces an echo chorus.

Act II introduces the hunting-party. It includes the stately
aria in which an attendant woman recites the melancholy fate of
Actaeon, the voice pursuing its own richly varied course above
one of those steadily moving basses in which the seventeenth
century delighted. Once again the entry of the strings at the end
supplies the culminating passion. The storm follows. Belinda,
brisk and practical as ever, urges the company to return to the
city in a lively little song that exactly hits off her nurse-like anxiety.
The chorus dutifully repeat her advice. Æneas, confronted by
a spirit in the guise of Mercury, learns that he must leave Carthage
that very night. The scene ends with his anguished realization
of the sacrifice that obedience entails.

The atmosphere changes completely in Act III. We are on the quay-side with the rough, homely members of Æneas's crew, who have received their sailing orders and are already preparing departure. The stir and bustle are vividly expressed in the orchestral introduction:

It will help us to appreciate Purcell's relationship to his contemporaries and predecessors if we compare with this two other instrumental pieces, the first from Blow's *Venus and Adonis* and the second from the introductory symphony to Ziani's opera, *La schiava fortunata*[1]:

[1] Quoted by Heuss, 'Die venetianischen Opern-Sinfonien,' *S.I.M.G.*, iv, p. 471.

The climax of Purcell's symphony is one of those swinging, inevitable tunes of which he seemed to hold the peculiar secret. It is a perfect match for Tate's racy jingle:

> Come away, fellow sailors, come away,
>> Your anchors be weighing,
>> Time and tide will admit no delaying;
> Take a boozy short leave of your nymphs on the shore,
>> And silence their mourning
>> With vows of returning,
> But never intending to visit them more,
> No, never intending to visit them more,

with a Scotch snap for the jaunty repetition, 'No, never.' When next we hear the chorus, after solos by the Sorceress and her henchwomen, they are witches, singing 'Destruction's our delight' in square-cut, four-part harmony, with little bits of imitation for the wicked 'Ho hos.' The style of this is similar to Lulli's sturdy homophonic choruses or those of the Venetian composers. Its origin is to be found in the popular part-songs of Renaissance Italy, with their imitative 'fa la las,' which had been domesticated in England by Thomas Morley before the end of the sixteenth century.

The time has come for farewell, and farewell is bound to be not only sad but stormy. Stung by Dido's reproaches, Æneas for a moment threatens to disobey Jupiter's decree. But the queen is ready to meet her fate and will hear of no weakening. With her heart breaking she sends him imperiously away. There follows one of the most impressive moments in the opera, when the chorus, fulfilling the function of its Greek prototype, comments gravely on the strange contradiction of human passions:

> Great minds against themselves conspire,
> And shun the cure they most desire.

The words sound perfunctory, but Purcell has set them to a solemn, chorale-like measure that rises to the proper height of tragic dignity. It leads straight into the final lament. With none but the faithful Belinda by her side, the queen, deserted and already in the shadows, sings her own threnody:

> Thy hand, Belinda, darkness shades me,
>   On thy bosom let me rest;
> More I would, but death invades me,
>   Death is now a welcome guest.
> When I am laid in earth, may my wrongs create
>   No trouble in thy breast;
> Remember me, but ah! forget my fate.

It has been said that the words will not scan, but that is not strictly true. The fifth line is clumsy and lop-sided, but it can just be fitted into a metrical scheme. Even so the verse remains a bungling piece of work. All the more remarkable then is the way in which Purcell has treated it. Of the first four lines he makes a pathetic recitative, and reserves the last three for one of his noblest lyrical inspirations, in which technique and passion are miraculously fused in one. It is constructed upon a ground bass, one of the favourite devices of the age. 'The practice,' says Burney, 'was Gothic,'[1] and damns it by implication, though he admits that some composers were successful in adopting it. The judgment is unsound, since no musical device is necessarily bad in itself. Undoubtedly the ground bass was a mine that Purcell in particular was apt to overwork; but here he struck a vein of purest gold:

---

[1] Vol. iii, p. 494.

The commonest type of ground bass used by the Italians was the descending scale, either diatonic or chromatic. Purcell here uses the latter, adding a cadence to complete it. The challenge of such a bass to a composer's invention is obvious. It is not enough in so pathetic an aria to supply a graceful melodic line and fill up the interval with conventional figured harmony. The successful treatment of a ground bass of this type depends on the skilful use of suspensions and discords. Purcell seizes on this opportunity in the second bar of the voice part, where the B flat is a suspension or 'hang-over' from the previous bar. The result is what is technically known as an appoggiatura in the second bar, a device that has been for several hundred years a peculiar vehicle for emotional expression in music. How close Purcell's kinship is to the Italian composers can be seen by examining the following extract from a song in Cavalli's *Egisto* (1642)[1]:

[1] Prunières, op. cit., musical example No. 11.

Here too we have the descending chromatic scale and the appoggiaturas, both of which Bach later used with such striking effect in the 'Crucifixus' of his Mass in B minor.

In Purcell's song the accompaniment is not for continuo alone but for strings. Nothing is left to chance and every detail of the harmony is preserved intact. When the voice turns from a flowing melody to the monotoned appeal, 'Remember me,' the violins take over the appoggiaturas and continue them to the end. In the last nine bars the orchestra alone sets the seal on the lamentation:

Handel may have had this passage in mind when he wrote the chorus 'How long, O Lord, shall Israel groan?' in *Susanna*, which is also over a chromatically descending ground bass. Purcell himself used the bass again in the introduction to the duet, 'In vain the am'rous flute,' in the 1692 *Ode on St. Cecilia's Day*, but not as a ground. What has once been worked perfectly is best left alone.

Dido's lament has justly come to be regarded as one of the great things in music. Here Purcell rises within narrow limits to monumental grandeur. The brief aria has a Miltonic dignity; in that last repeated 'Remember me' it is almost as though the musician, tearing himself away from the artificiality of court and theatre, had written his own epitaph. It is succeeded by a little

chorus that rounds off the work with the same tragic finality as
the last chorus in the St. Matthew Passion. And having sung
it once the chorus must sing it again so that the drooping
cadences may linger in the memory.

Dido is a masterpiece, but not, as is sometimes claimed, a flawless
masterpiece. Purcell was thirty when he wrote it, but he had had
very little experience of the stage; and indeed the limited scope of
the work would try the gifts even of a musician who had spent
long years in contact with the theatre. The work is sometimes
praised because it moves swiftly; but that is not necessarily a virtue
in opera. Opera, like the spoken drama, can afford to linger
over moments, to extend and elaborate an emotional crisis until
the spectator is himself willy-nilly caught and enfolded in the
passions of the persons on the stage. It is impossible not to feel
in *Dido* that the episodes and individual movements sometimes
succeed each other too rapidly. We learn of Dido's passion in
two exquisitely expressive arias, but of Æneas's we hear no more
than a few bars of recitative. When the two lovers sing together
at the end it is merely to fling protests at each other, and the
treatment is conventional. Conventional too is the duet of the
two witches in the last act, where the ready-made sequences of
Italian opera take the place of real horror. Indeed, Purcell is at
his weakest in dealing with the witches. It is the human beings
in this opera that have inspired him to his greatest heights. It
has been said that Dido 'is more than half a schoolgirl herself,
with a court of schoolgirls round her,'[1] but that is not quite true.
There is nothing callow in Purcell's Dido. She is from first to
last a tragic heroine. Professor Dent has pointed out that German
critics describe the work as 'Shakespearian,'[2] and it is easy to
realize the justice of the epithet.

I have ventured on these criticisms of the structure of *Dido*, since
it has become almost an article of faith with some Purcellians to
accept the work as faultless. The truth is that no composer
could adequately treat such a tremendous subject in what is, in

[1] Colles, *Voice and Verse*, p. 85.   [2] Op. cit., p. 188.

effect, a one-act opera. What makes *Dido* immortal is that it triumphs over its weaknesses. It will always hold our admiration and affection for its penetrating revelation of the profoundest secrets of human passion. Standing midway between the English masque and the Italian cantata it was the prelude to an achievement that was never realized, either by Purcell or by his successors. When Italian opera came to London in the eighteenth century, recitative had become mainly a conventional thread for linking together a succession of arias. Purcell's recitative, which clearly owes something to Locke, is faithful to the older model; it is a brilliant application of the declamatory style to the peculiar accents of English verse. It has nothing of the ambling fluency of Lulli's recitative. It is direct and forceful and moves constantly within the limits of common time. The conventions of chromatic progression and falling intervals—perfect and diminished fifths, perfect and diminished fourths—are used, but with an appropriateness that justifies every one of them. Only the florid clichés that have to do duty for storm and stress seem forced and unnatural.

Purcell's other operas are entitled to the name only in the limited sense given it in the Restoration theatre. They are properly 'semi-operas,' an apposition, not a combination, of drama and music. *The Prophetess,* more usually known by its alternative title, *Dioclesian,* appeared the year after *Dido and Æneas.* The play is an adaptation by Betterton of Fletcher and Massinger. The prophetess who gives her name to the work is Delphia; she foretells that Diocles, a private soldier in the Roman army, will become emperor:

> *Imperator eris Romae cum Aprum grandem interfeceris.*
>
> Thou shalt be Emperor, O Diocles,
> When thou hast kill'd a mighty Boar.

The prophecy is fulfilled when Diocles slaughters Aper, murderer of the late emperor. He is hailed as emperor by the soldiers. Difficulties arise when he transfers his affections from Drusilla, Delphia's niece, to Aurelia, who had previously offered to marry the man who avenged the late emperor's death. The situation is further complicated by the fact that Maximinian, who is Diocles's nephew, also loves Aurelia. War with the Persians follows and Diocles is victorious, since Delphia, who had previously assisted the Persians, forgives his treatment of Drusilla and aids him. Magnanimous in victory, he restores the Persian king to his kingdom and hands over the empire to Maximinian. An attempt on the part of Maximinian to kill Diocles is frustrated by Delphia, who proceeds to entertain the company with a country masque. The magnificence of this entertainment may be gathered from the description in the stage directions:

While a symphony is playing, a machine descends, so large it fills all the space from the frontispiece of the stage to the further end of the house, and fixes itself by two ladders of clouds to the floor. In it are four several stages, representing the Palaces of two Gods and two Goddesses. The first is the Palace of *Flora*; the columns of red and white marble breaking through the clouds; the columns fluted and wreath'd about with all sorts of flowerage, the pedestals and flutings inrich'd with gold. The second is the Palace of the Goddess *Pomona*: the columns of blue marble, wound about with all kind of fruitage, and inrich'd with gold as the other. The third is the Palace of *Bacchus*: the columns of green marble, wreath'd and inrich'd with gold, with clusters of grapes hanging round them. The last is the Palace of the Sun; it is supported on either side by rows of *termes,* the lower part white marble, the upper part gold. The whole object is terminated with a glowing cloud, on which is a chair of state, all of gold, the Sun breaking through the cloud, and making a glory about it; as this descends, there rises from under the stage a pleasant prospect of a noble garden, consisting of fountains, and orange trees set in large vases; the middle walk leads to a Palace at a great distance. At the same time enter *Silvanus, Bacchus, Flora, Pomona, Gods of the Rivers, Fauns, Nymphs, Heroes, Heroines, Shepherds, Shepherdesses,* the *Graces,* and *Pleasures,* with the rest of their followers. The Dancers place themselves on every stage in the machine; the Singers range themselves about the stage.

It is important to notice that though music plays a large part in *Dioclesian,* the principal actors do not sing; and this is characteristic of all the semi-operas of the period. One of the reasons for this may be the lack of experienced opera-singers in London at the time. Grabu, in presenting his *Albion and Albanius* to James II, declares that

the only Displeasure which remains with me, is, that I neither was nor could possibly be furnish'd with variety of excellent Voices, to present it to Your Majesty in its full perfection

—which may seem ungrateful to a country that was hospitable enough to offer Grabu employment, but probably has some basis in fact. The apologetic remarks made by Matthew Locke in the preface to *Psyche* point to a similar conclusion. The greater part of the music of *Dioclesian* takes place in the masque presented at the end of Act V. The rest is concerned mainly with the two ceremonial occasions—the song of triumph after the slaying of Aper and the jubilation after the victory over the Persians. There are also several dances, such as the one that occurs when a dreadful monster disintegrates into a number of Furies, and the celebrated song, 'What shall I do to show how much I love her?' during which Maximinian, whose passion is thus being hymned, characteristically stands silent, gazing on Aurelia.

The overture is preceded by two instrumental pieces—the 'First Music' and 'Second Music'—a survival of the Elizabethan practice of having a concert before the play began. In this case the late-comer who thought he could safely miss the 'First Music' would have been the loser; the opening movement is a finely dignified introduction to the work. The same dignity is apparent in the first chorus, where the voices sing 'Praise the thund'ring Jove, Pallas and Venus share' in rolling, Handelian counterpoint. For the period the scoring is elaborate, including two flutes, two oboes, tenor oboe, two trumpets and strings.[1] The trumpets inevitably colour the tonality of the music. At that time only two keys were normal for these instruments—C and D—and as the trumpets are used frequently a good deal of the work is in these two keys. The instrumentation is elaborate. Many of the

[1] The flutes (i.e. recorders) were probably played by the same players as the oboes, as in the early eighteenth century, since the two instruments are hardly ever found together. The introductory symphony to 'Shepherd, shepherd, leave decoying' in *King Arthur* is an exception.

songs are with continuo only, but one or two have parts for obbligato instruments and all the choruses are fully scored with independent string parts.

In 'Sound, fame, thy brazen trumpet sound'—not in itself a very characteristic song—Purcell has introduced one of those florid obbligatos to which he was naturally tempted by the virtuosity of the Shore family. Technically the most interesting instrumental movement is the chaconne in Act III, where two flutes conduct a canon at the unison above a ground bass—a brilliant *tour de force* and an indication that theatre audiences were quite prepared to hear something more than mere frivolity. Important too are the instrumental introductions to some of the songs. In 'What shall I do to show how much I love her?' the tune is played over on two oboes before the voice begins.

Writers on Purcell have always confessed their particular admiration for the masque in *Dioclesian*. It is undoubtedly the finest part of the work, if only because it hangs together as a consistent whole. Purcell here takes the pastoral conventions of his time and gives them a new vigour and freshness. No one can resist the two jolly Bacchanals who announce the coming of the crew of revellers. Their breezy, open-air heartiness has an English tang. Equally characteristic is the charming duet between the shepherd and the shepherdess, the shepherd beginning:

and she replying in the suavest three-in-a-bar, the whole being rounded off by a little dance, in which the quickening individuality of Purcell's melodic invention is seen at its best.

The masque ends with an elaborate song of the triumph of love, a theme that Purcell had already treated in *Dido and Æneas*. The whole chorus is built on a ground bass, conventional in form but rich in possibilities:

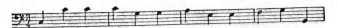

Burney pointed out that it had previously been used by Merula.[1] Subjects of this kind were the common property of all composers. The general structure of the movement, which is an elaborate chaconne, was probably suggested by the chaconne in Grabu's *Albion and Albanius*, a particularly depressing piece of work. Purcell here obtains variety not, as in Dido's lament, by changes of harmony achieved by suspensions, but by alternating the voices and instruments till the whole culminates in a splendid panoply of sound. The middle section is in the minor, with the fourth in the bass diminished, which results in some rather odd harmonic progressions. The splendour of the orchestration may be judged from this example, showing the return to the major:

It is not surprising that this music, so free from the insipid platitudes of the time, brought Purcell a reputation and forced the reluctant Dryden to conclude that there might possibly be an English composer worthy of his genius after all. To the fruits of that conclusion we may now turn.

CHAPTER XI

OTHER OPERAS

'KING ARTHUR' is unique among Purcell's semi-operas in that it was designed from the first as such; the others were adaptations. The reception given to *Albion and Albanius* had not encouraged Dryden to repeat the experiment of a *durchkomponiert* opera; but he made abundant provision for the introduction of songs, choruses and dances, and music plays a more important part than in *Dioclesian*.

The story of the play, which is a quaint mixture of historical legend and pure fantasy, is too complicated to be given at length. Briefly, it tells how Arthur, king of the Britons, and Oswald, Saxon king of Kent, are rivals for the hand of Emmeline, the blind daughter of the Duke of Cornwall. Already ten bloody battles have been fought and the Saxons have been driven back. It remains to launch the decisive conflict, the British leaders taking encouragement from the omen of St. George's Day. Oswald has the co-operation of a magician Osmond, who is further assisted by two familiar spirits, Grimbald and Philidel, one of the earth, the other of the air. Philidel, however, is sensitive and is persuaded by Merlin to transfer his services to the British side. When Grimbald tries to mislead Arthur and his troops, Philidel counteracts his malice by setting them on the right path.

Meanwhile Emmeline and her attendant Matilda are captured by Oswald and leave the stage crying: 'A rape, a rape!' More unpleasant experiences follow when Osmond presses his unwelcome attentions on her and, to impress her with love's power —her sight having by this time been restored—produces an impromptu display, in which a frozen country-side and people are warmed to life again by Cupid. Right begins to triumph

131

when Arthur, after successfully resisting the charms of two sirens, captures Grimbald, who had been masquerading as Emmeline, and so breaks the enchantments that are against him. In the last act the opposing armies come together and 'fight with Spunges in their Hands, dipt in blood.' Arthur meets Oswald in hand-to-hand combat and, disarming him, offers him his freedom. Emmeline is reunited to her royal lover, while Merlin announces that Arthur is the first of 'three Christian worthies' [1] and exercises his magic arts. The winds are banished and Britain's island rises from the sea,

> Fairest isle, all isles excelling,
> Seat of pleasures and of loves.

The whole company unites to sing the praises of St. George, and a general dance concludes the celebrations.

Unfortunately the music has not come down to us in a complete or wholly intelligible form. The score was not printed in Purcell's lifetime, and the manuscripts do not contain the whole of the music provided for in Dryden's text; nor is it always certain where the instrumental movements printed in *Ayres for the Theatre* should be introduced. The introductory music, too, is the subject of some confusion. The 'First Music' is the chaconne in F major from Purcell's welcome song for James II, *Sound the trumpet* (1687). The 'Second Music,' in D minor, also described as the overture, appears to be original. There is also another overture, or perhaps the overture proper, in D major, which has been transferred from the birthday ode for Queen Mary, *Arise my Muse* (1690). In spite of these problems there is quite enough material to enable us to appreciate Purcell's contribution to this patriotic spectacle, which sometimes verges perilously near pantomime, and to see how he reacted to the opportunities provided by the poet.

[1] Hence the full title, *King Arthur, or the British Worthy*. 'The Nine Worthies were equally divided among three religions; namely, three Pagans, Hector, Pompey and Alexander the Great; three Jews, Joshua, David and Judas Maccabaeus; and three Christians, Arthur, Charlemagne and Godfrey of Boulogne' (note by Sir Walter Scott).

The first act does not, on the whole, show Purcell at his best. The music for the Saxons' sacrificial rites has a contrapuntal stodginess that suggests the conventional oratorio rather than the heroic opera; nor are the Italian roulades of the alto solo, 'I call you all to Woden's hall,' entirely convincing. Only one passage deserves quotation, part of the setting of the not very inspiring lines (those feminine endings again!):

> Honour prizing
> Death despising,
> Fame acquiring
> By expiring,
> Die and reap the fruit of glory.

A brisker note is introduced by the characteristic, square-cut song of the Britons, 'Come if you dare, our trumpets sound,' which has an infectious swing.

It is the second act that first shows the riches of Purcell's talent. The rival choruses of Grimbald's and Philidel's spirits, 'Hither this way, this way bend,' are a delightful and ingenious inspiration; so too is Grimbald's persuasive song, 'Let not a moon-born elf mislead ye,' with its captivating cadence:

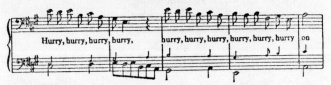

Fairies seem to have had a particular attraction for Purcell, though he was less happy with the grosser malevolence of hags and sorcerers. He was thoroughly at home too in pastoral scenes. Here, as in *Dioclesian*, he makes the most sophisticated conventions seem natural. 'How blest are shepherds,' sing the chorus, and Purcell's setting is so suave and graceful that we believe them without thinking twice about the discomforts of country life.

The third act is remarkable for the scene of the frozen wastes, from which the Cold Genius rises grimly like Erda in the *Ring*. Much has been written about the *tremolando* that Purcell has indicated for the strings, the soloist and later the chorus; but the effect was not new. Lulli had done the same thing in the fourth act of his *Isis* (1677), where the scene represents 'l'endroit le plus glacé de la Scythie'; and the use of *vibrato* was a commonplace in Italian opera. What distinguishes Purcell's music for this scene is not the method of performance but the extraordinary suggestiveness of the harmonic progressions, from the strange sliding semitones of the instrumental introduction to the discordant melancholy of the Cold Genius's concluding words:

Let me, let me,let me freeze a - gain,_____ Let me,

let me freeze_____ a - gain to death, let me, let me, let me

freeze_____ a - gain to death.

The rest of the act is conventional by comparison, though there is
much that is attractive in the counterpoint of voices and strings in
the duet for soprano and bass, 'Sound a parley, ye fair, and
surrender.'

In the fourth act the seductive song of the two sirens, 'Two
daughters of this aged stream are we,' in one of Purcell's favourite
keys—G minor—is followed by the imposing passacaglia in the

same key, 'How happy the lover,' set for oboes, strings, soprano, alto and bass solos and chorus over a descending ground bass. This is one of Purcell's finest achievements. The fifth act includes the baritone solo, 'Ye blustering brethren,' with its bustling *bravura* for the strings—a forerunner of 'Arise, ye subterranean winds'—and the curious juxtaposition of a pastoral trio in the Italian style, 'For folded flocks,' with an unmistakable English folksong, 'Your hay it is mow'd.' 'Fairest isle' has always been admired. It is a spacious tune, and the sentiment of the song is irreproachable. There is a patriotism that finds expression in banners and bugles and another less ostentatious— a patriotism of the spirit. Look beneath the conceits and conventions that form the crust of Dryden's text, and you will find the same emotion to which Rupert Brooke gave expression when he wrote that

the actual earth of England held for him a quality . . . which, if he'd ever been sentimental enough to use the word, he'd have called 'holiness.'[1]

Curiously enough, the actual text of the setting is the subject of dispute. Should the A in the third bar:

Fair - est isle, all isles_____ ex - cel - ling

be natural or flat? The editor of the revised edition published by the Purcell Society prints a flat, though there is substantial evidence, both manuscript and printed, for the natural—notably in *Ayres for the Theatre* and in *Orpheus Britannicus*. My own inclination is to follow these sources and accept the natural. It is quite true that 'the flattened seventh of the key was characteristic of the period and of Purcell,' but it was not a dominant, exclusive characteristic.

As a whole *King Arthur* is a singularly satisfying work. It needs, of course, a stage presentation. A concert performance

[1] Printed in the *Oxford Book of English Prose*, p. 1062.

without the dialogue is ridiculous and meaningless. There are one or two things in the music that are stiff and wooden, but the bulk of it is full of the most lively inspiration. It is more mature, both in technique and in imagination, than *Dioclesian,* and there is more variety in the invention. Purcell's interest in the more recondite aspects of his art has not prevented him from frankly indulging his peculiar gift of fresh and spontaneous tunefulness. The best movements in this opera, whether simple songs or elaborate contrapuntal structures, have that quality inseparable from fine craftsmanship—they appear inevitable.

Both in *Dioclesian* and in *King Arthur* masques are introduced as a concession to the prevailing taste; but they do not by any means exhaust the whole of the music to those operas. *The Fairy Queen,* on the other hand, is simply a succession of masques, which have so little connection with the play that no one who merely heard the music would have the remotest suspicion that the opera was an adaptation of Shakespeare's *Midsummer Night's Dream.* The passion for spectacle has led to the addition of a large number of characters not provided for in the original text—gods and goddesses, spirits, nymphs, shepherds, monkeys, Chinese dancers and the four seasons. Thus adapted, the play becomes a sort of revue, in which Shakespeare's scenes are merely episodes in a larger and more magnificent whole. The opera was so successful in 1692 that it was presented again in a revised version in the following year, with several new songs.[1] For over two hundred years the score was lost. It finally came to light in the library of the Royal Academy of Music in time to be used for the publication of the Purcell Society's edition in 1903. Though not wholly autograph, it was evidently the copy used at the first performance and it contains several numbers in Purcell's handwriting.

The Fairy Queen is the longest of Purcell's dramatic works. Though it lacks the unity of *Dioclesian* and *King Arthur,* consisting as it does mainly of a succession of songs and dances, the level of musical achievement is consistently higher than in either of these works. There are, it is true, one or two things that strike one as

[1] Purcell Society's edition, vol. xii, p. i.

bald and conventional, such as the trumpet fanfares in the overture, but for the most part the work is singularly fresh and inspired.
The subject, rich in fantasy, clearly appealed to Purcell's imagination, and he lavished on it all his ingenuity, wit and charm.
There is no lack of cunning devices. We find a double echo on
the model of the one in Locke's *Psyche* mentioned above, a double
canon at the octave and the fifteenth, elaborate coloratura, a fugal
canzona for strings and trumpets, ground basses and subtle
chromaticism. In the introductory symphony to the fourth act
Purcell has anticipated Bach's Christmas Oratorio by opening
with a timpani solo. Another interesting experiment in scoring
is the song, 'See, even Night herself is here,' where the accompaniment is entrusted to three upper strings, the cellos and basses
remaining silent. How thoroughly Purcell was influenced by
the Italian operatic fashion of his time is evident from the *da capo*
aria, 'Ye gentle spirits,' or the prelude to Act V, which sounds
like an anticipation of 'O ruddier than the cherry':

In the well-known song, 'Hark, the ech'ing air,' there is the
most generous use of coloratura, not only in the voice part but
also in the introductory ritornello for the trumpet, which we so
rarely hear on the instrument for which it was written. Beside
these florid excursions we may set some of those spreading tunes
in which Purcell delighted, made up not of the mere repetition
of phrase and sentence but covering a whole period. Such are
'If love's a sweet passion,' which Gay was glad to use later in *The*

Beggar's Opera, and 'Hark, how all things in one sound rejoice,' in which Purcell shows the happiest mastery of the Italian style. How simple, too, and yet how arresting is the end of the chorus sung over the sleeping Titania, where the very silence is eloquent! Once again we find Purcell yielding to the spell of the fairies in his settings of 'Trip it, trip it in a ring' and 'About him go,' which are full of the airy levity of a world that is more than human and instinct with the gracious fun that lies behind Shakespeare's own fantasy. Dr. Ernest Walker has well compared them to the incidental music written by Mendelssohn for *A Midsummer Night's Dream,* which has the same unquestioning innocence, the same gossamer frivolity.

In a different vein, but no less characteristic, is the dialogue between the shepherd Corydon and the shepherdess Mopsa, where it is difficult to say whether the background is supplied by the Italian *moresca* or the English country dance, so common is the pastoral idiom to the two countries. The two lovers are delightfully picked off in these homely, lilting strains:

with Mopsa returning the falsely modest reply of the maid who knows perfectly well what she wants. And when after the dance of haymakers the chorus sing:

> A thousand, thousand ways we'll find
> To entertain the hours,

we believe them as readily as we trust the praises of the shepherd's life in *King Arthur*, and are only too glad to hear repeated the strangely melancholy cadence of their song.

Delightful and ingenious as *The Fairy Queen* is, it is *The Indian Queen* and *The Tempest* that show the full flowering of Purcell's gifts as a composer for the stage. Both these works were written in the last year of his life and show him at the very height of his powers. The actual bulk of the music is less than in *King Arthur* and *The Fairy Queen*, but its significance is greater. The tentative fumbling and the easy acceptance of formulas that one cannot help noticing occasionally in the earlier works here give place to an assured mastery, a firm and experienced control. Purcell had hitherto been schooling himself in the latest developments of the Italian style, both vocal and instrumental, and the process of education is still apparent in *The Fairy Queen*. In *The Indian Queen* and *The Tempest* he seems at last to have mastered the style. No longer does he use technical devices for their own sake; he has made them his servants.

A simple test of the advance can be made by comparing the elaborate symphony in the fourth act of *The Fairy Queen* with a similar piece, described as a 'Trumpet Overture,' in *The Indian Queen*. In the latter work Purcell is no longer bound by the limitations of the trumpet's scale; he makes a virtue of necessity. It is obvious, of course, that the natural trumpet does not allow the composer any great freedom of harmonic development. Of the possible modulations the most obvious are those to the domi-nant of the key and to the relative minor. Purcell uses both in this overture, but mitigates their obviousness by the use of imitation:

The easy, confident swing of the tune is braced and strengthened by the vigorous treatment of the independent parts. The succeeding canzona shows a lively and convincing handling of a stock fugal form; the movement and development flow as naturally as in Handel's magnificent *Concerti grossi*. Purcell is sometimes spoken of as though he were pre-eminently a composer for the voice. This is not quite just. Masterly as his vocal music is, both in its treatment of the words and in its understanding of the singer's art, his instrumental music is no less significant. He had been brought up as a contrapuntist, and the counterpoint of his day was primarily instrumental. As in *The Fairy Queen* the symphony ends with an expressive *adagio*. The power and intensity of these nine bars is astonishing. The strings move forward with relentless determination. Towards the end the whole colour changes. The basses sink to a grinding B flat, which in its turn forces the upper strings into the minor, and the conflict is only resolved by the major third in the last bar. Few things in music suggest more vividly the implacable urge of destiny.

The story of *The Indian Queen*, which is adapted from a tragedy by Sir Robert Howard and Dryden, is once more concerned with the warfare of rival peoples. Montezuma, a young Peruvian general, captures Acacis, the Mexican prince, in battle. The

Inca invites him to choose his reward, but is little pleased when
Montezuma asks for the hand of his daughter Orazia. The pre-
sumptuous youth is forced to flee and in revenge throws in his lot
with the Mexicans. Here, too, he meets with difficulties, since,
having captured the Inca and Orazia, he wishes to keep them for
himself—a proposal that is unpopular with his new allies. Further
complications are introduced by the fact that Zempoalla, the queen
of the Mexicans, falls in love with Montezuma. She consults
the magician Ismeron, but without any appeasement to her
passion. The last act resolves all the complications. The
intended sacrifice of the Inca, Orazia and Montezuma at 'a bloody
Altar' is arrested by the action of Acacis, who, himself in love
with Orazia, commits suicide. Meanwhile it has been discovered
that Montezuma is actually the lawful king of the Mexicans and
has been proclaimed by the people. Zempoalla also commits
suicide, and the Inca consents to the union of Montezuma with
his daughter. This is the merest sketch of a plot which runs the
full gamut of the emotions proper to Restoration tragedy, but it is
a sufficient guide to the foundations on which Purcell's music
is built.

Here, as in *The Fairy Queen,* there is no attempt at local colour.
For all the music tells us, the action might be taking place in
St. James's Park. But that was thoroughly consonant with the
spirit of the age and with the traditions of the drama itself. It was
the business of the scene-painter and the dress-designer to provide
atmosphere; the poet and the musician contented themselves with
rising to the emotional heights suggested by the theme. In con-
sidering Purcell's music, we may pass over his setting of the
prologue, which is the least interesting part of the work. The
principal music of the play begins in Act II with a symphony [1] in
four movements, the second a canzona, in which there is some
play with triplets, and the third a slow *adagio* with a lingering
melancholy. The symphony leads straight into a short masque

[1] This is identical, except in key, with the introductory symphony of
the Queen Mary birthday ode, *Come ye sons of art* (1694), which is in
D, a tone higher.

performed before Queen Zempoalla. Fame and the chorus sing her praises to one of those simple and easy-stepping melodies which Purcell based on the scale of the natural trumpet, here heard in unison with the sopranos. Envy follows with a solo in which a characteristic Italian formula, used over and over again by Corelli and Handel, is exploited. An interesting detail of the score is the dramatic entry of the alto and tenor on the word 'hiss,' which has a naïve look on paper but would be thoroughly effective on the stage:

In the third act occurs the scene with Ismeron, the magician, whose incantation, 'Ye twice ten hundred deities,' has become one of Purcell's most celebrated bass songs. The solo that follows for the God of Dreams has an ingenious obbligato for solo oboe, and the duet for the two aerial spirits shows Purcell treating his favourite device of a ground bass with the most fluent mastery. Finally we have the immortal melody, 'I attempt from love's sickness to fly,' a perfectly polished gem and an outstanding example of Purcell's incomparable gift of melody. Almost equally beautiful, however, is the song, 'They tell us that you mighty powers above,' which comes in the fourth act, with its steady increment of passion in the third line:

No wonder the music of *The Indian Queen* was so popular that a pirated edition appeared almost at once, with an ingenuous address from the publishers to the composer, in which they neatly justified their action. It should be added that music for a masque of Hymen was written by Daniel Purcell and published in the spring of 1696 [1]; but whether this was used in the original production in 1695 or added for a revival after Purcell's death—which seems more probable—is uncertain.

The Tempest, one of those Shakespearian adaptations that were all the rage under the later Stuarts, is Purcell's most mature work for the theatre. It exhibits even more than *The Indian Queen* the complete absorption of the Italian style—even to the use of the *da capo* aria—and an unfaltering technical facility. It is delightful to see Purcell in the overture, [2] confident of his skill, gaily inverting the subject of the fugal allegro:

Of the songs the most famous is 'Arise, ye subterranean winds' —a magnificent piece of dramatic writing. How far Purcell outdistanced his contemporaries in his appreciation of dramatic propriety may be seen by comparing a few bars of the voice part with the opening of the setting written by Pietro Reggio for an earlier performance in 1674 (*see page 146*).

[1] Squire, op. cit, p. 530.
[2] Conjecturally assigned to this work by E. J. Dent.

The structure of Purcell's air is also interesting, since it is an excellent example of the Italian practice, frequently borrowed by Bach, of interpolating an instrumental symphony after the first vocal phrase, which is then repeated and developed.

The dance that immediately follows this song is taken from Lulli's *Cadmus et Hermione,* where it accompanies the entry of

Envy in the prologue. This is the only known instance in which
Purcell has borrowed music from another composer, and it would
be interesting to know the reason for the appropriation. *Cadmus
et Hermione* had been performed in London in 1686, and it is
likely enough that Purcell knew the music. But that is not
sufficient to explain why a man of such fertile invention should
have recourse to the work of others. As there is no autograph
of *The Tempest* we cannot be absolutely certain that Purcell
was responsible. But it is just possible that he had once copied
the music to this dance and finding it among his papers decided
to use it without bothering about its source. It is curious that
whereas the air of the dance in *The Tempest,* which is for violins
and continuo only, is practically identical with that in *Cadmus
et Hermione,* the bass has been radically altered. Evidently
Purcell, even if he knew the piece was Lulli's, was not so impressed by the Frenchman's reputation as to accept his harmony
(or his assistants' harmony) as well as the tune.

'Arise, ye subterranean winds' is only one of a number of
splendid arias, such as the lusty 'Æolus, you must appear,' with
its very Corellian instrumental symphony:

or the charming soprano solo, 'Halcyon days,' a *da capo* aria, in
which the suggestion of the first word draws a picture of sweet
placidity from the solo oboe; or another bass solo, also a *da capo*

147

aria, 'See, see the heavens smile,' where the bounding gaiety of
nature is happily interpreted by the violins:

It is a pity that these fine songs, which would be as effective on
the concert platform as in the theatre, are so little known. In
the introductory recitative to 'Come down, come down, my
blusterers,' Purcell even adopted the conventional cadence that
was to dominate *recitativo secco* for a century or more.

The Tempest is a treasury of good things. Again, in Ariel's
song, 'Dry those eyes,' Purcell takes the dusty formula of the ground
bass and makes it a living creature. This song is a remarkable
example of sustained invention, with the instruments subtly introduced at intervals to avert the threatened monotony of repetition.
Charming, too, are the settings of 'Come unto these yellow sands'
—Shakespeare seen through Restoration eyes—and 'Full fathom
five.' The latter offers chances for picturesque treatment,
which Purcell naturally seizes. The mysterious bell tolls in
the first bar of the continuo, and in the succeeding chorus
that curious shifting between flat and sharp seventh which
so often stamps his cadences is used to represent the sea-nymphs'
knell:

The dominant impression left by *The Tempest* is first admiration and joy and then a stab of regret that this abounding maturity and mastery was so soon after brought to nothing. If Purcell had lived twenty years longer he might himself have led the invasion of Italian opera and by adapting the style to the peculiar exigencies of the English tongue have given us a national opera able to withstand all the assaults of the alien. But of what use is it to wish that history had been otherwise?

CHAPTER XII

INCIDENTAL MUSIC AND SONGS

PURCELL'S activity as a composer for the stage was not confined to his 'operas.' He also wrote incidental music for over forty plays, the greater part of which has been preserved in song collections, in the volumes of *Ayres for the Theatre* published after his death, and in manuscript. I have already spoken of the important part played by music in the Restoration theatre. How far it was listened to is another matter. A visitor from France noticed that people gladly went to the theatre early to hear the music before the play began[1]; but the general evidence of conditions in the Restoration theatre seems to show that the decorum expected of an audience is a product of more recent date. Conversation, cat-calls and even free fights were quite likely to disturb the most important productions, in spite of Killigrew's conviction that he had inaugurated a new reign of law and order; and if the players had these difficulties to face, the musicians must more than once have suffered as well.[2] But there is no hint of this in Purcell's music, never a suggestion that it was written carelessly or contemptuously.

The great bulk of Purcell's dramatic music belongs to the years 1690–5 and so represents the period of his maturity. But even the earlier work has its distinction. In *Theodosius* (1680), his first work for the stage, the dignified solemnity of the sacrifice scene—the precursor of several others—and the spontaneous lyricism of songs like 'Hail to the myrtle shade' and 'Ah! cruel, bloody fate' already set a standard in advance of the work of his predecessors. Locke's *Psyche,* for all its gaiety and grace, is clumsy by comparison, and Humfrey's songs in *The Tempest* are insipid.

[1] Sorbière, *Relation d'un voyage en Angleterre* (1664), p. 167; cf. Magalotti, *Travels of Cosmo III* (1821), p. 191 (probably copied from Sorbière).

[2] Nicoll, *Restoration Drama,* pp. 15–19; Pepys, 12th February 1667.

The end of 'The gate to bliss does open stand' is characteristic. There is a touch of stiffness in the verbal accentuation, but how easily and naturally the melody moves to its climax and then falls to rest! Again, the song 'Retired from any mortal's sight,' contributed to *King Richard II* in the following year, is a remarkably subtle and expressive setting. Before long Italian influences, openly acknowledged in the *Sonatas of III Parts,* began to have their effect. We can see them in *Circe* (? 1690[1])—if this is to be attributed, as seems likely, to Purcell—where a single song contains an example of the florid concerted style and of the use of chromaticism to underline an individual word:

[1] Squire suggested 1685, but on the evidence of style I am inclined to put the music to *Circe* several years later.

We can also catch a glimpse of the relationship between Purcell's stage music and his anthems. The ground bass of the song, 'The air with music gently wound,' is first cousin to that of the opening section of the anthem, *In Thee, O Lord, do I put my trust.*

The mass of music that Purcell crowded into the last five years of his life is full of parallels to the 'operas.' What a rich store of instrumental music lies here industrious editors already know, and there is still more to be discovered. These pages abound in jigs, bourrées, minuets, slow airs and hornpipes, all finished off in Purcell's inimitable manner. The audiences were fortunate who could hear between the acts such clean, robust, uncompromising music as this rondeau from *Abdelazer* (1695):

The overtures, too, reflect the same influences that we have seen at work in the 'operas.' Most remarkable are those short *adagio* movements which sometimes follow the second movement, as in the symphony to the third act of *The Indian Queen*. Here solemnity was not confined to tragedy. Indeed the style of the instrumental movements rarely gives any indication of the character of the play. One would hardly gather from the previous example that *Abdelazer* was a tragic piece any more than the *adagio* in the overture to *The Gordian Knot Untied* (1691) leads one to expect a comedy. The finest *adagio* is that in the overture to *Bonduca* (1695), where we may suppose Purcell to have been stirred by the suggestion of the tragic theme:

This is a fitting companion to the *adagio* in *The Indian Queen*.

There are also several examples of that brisk trochaic rhythm which is often found in the second movement of the French overture and was several times employed by Handel. In the introduction to *Sir Anthony Love* (1691) the orchestra seems almost to have become infected with St. Vitus's dance, so insistent is the hopping measure. Counterpoint there is in plenty, as well as pure homophony. Nor did Purcell always trouble to follow slavishly the text-book rules. At the end of a jig in *The Old Bachelor* (1693) he only avoids a whole succession of consecutive fifths by the skin of his teeth.

Delightful as the instrumental movements are, it is the songs that have endeared Purcell most to posterity. One has only to mention 'Nymphs and shepherds,' 'Man is for the woman made,' 'I'll sail upon the dog-star' and 'There's nothing so fatal as woman' to set any normal reader humming reminiscently. Yet it is only the chance selection of modern editors that has made these more popular than numbers of others. We find every type of song in these plays: popular ditties, elaborate declamation, love songs, coloratura arias, chromatic recitative and those curiosities of the period known as 'mad songs,' in which the phases of temporary insanity are represented by variations in tempo and style. Purcell's invention is here seen at its best. The pomp of pageantry, the pangs of love, the quips and oddities of rustic gossips,

dramatic situations and picturesque description—they are all here
to supplement the evidence of the 'operas.' There is material,
too, for the student of technique in the *da capo* arias in *Aureng-Zebe*
(1692?) and *Timon of Athens* (1694), in the rondo aria, 'Lucinda is
bewitching fair,' in *Abdelazer* (1695), and in that splendid example
of a ground bass, the song, 'Music for a while shall all your cares
beguile,' in *Œdipus* (1692?), which I am inclined to consider,
apart from Dido's lament, the most satisfying, in technique and
expression, that Purcell ever wrote, if only because of the continual
re-creation of energy in the bass:

There is no doubt that Purcell was fortunate in his librettists. Several of them were poets of distinction, who did not regard theatrical composition as an excuse for relaxing their standards. The modern reader may get a little tired of the succession of love-sick swains and shyly consenting maids, the praises of Celia's eyes and Climene's charms, and may feel at the end of a long perusal the need for something less artificial than the conceits that masked, or rather revealed, the sensuality of the age. But the verses are nearly always charmingly polished and offer the musician excellent material for the exercise of his skill. When Southerne in *The Maid's Last Prayer* (1693) provided Purcell with such a neatly turned trifle as this:

> Though you make no return to my passion,
> Still, still I presume to adore;
> 'Tis in love but an odd reputation,
> When faintly repulsed to give o'er.
> When you talk of your duty,
> I gaze on your beauty,
> Nor mind the dull maxim at all;
> Let it reign in Cheapside
> With a citizen's bride,
> It will ne'er be received at Whitehall [1]

what could he do but respond with a melody no less neatly turned? (Note, by the way, the jeer at the *bourgeoisie* in the last three lines, a sure way of raising a laugh from the aristocratic audience that attended the playhouse.) This is the type of verse and music that conquered the town when Gay introduced them in his *Beggar's Opera* as a counterblast to the popularity of the Italian opera. The tradition persisted in the comic operas of the late eighteenth century and was gloriously revived in the nineteenth —though with an extra drop of satirical acid—by Gilbert, whose wit has been immortalized in Sullivan's ingenious settings. In all its essentials this is a typically English genre; indeed, unkind foreign observers and pessimists at home have been known to

[1] This is the text as it appears in Purcell's setting; the version in the printed edition of the play has some minor variants.

urge that this is the only form of opera that the Englishman ought to cultivate.

Sometimes in his adoption of a popular cast of melody Purcell comes very near to folksong, as in this pleasant jogging tune [1] from *The Mock Marriage* (1695):

In similar vein are those semi-pastoral duets, in which two humble people exchange homely sentiments in $\frac{6}{4}$ time, on the model of the Corydon and Mopsa duet in *The Fairy Queen*; or it may be the squawking controversy of rival trollops, as in *The Canterbury*

[1] Used later by Gay for the song, 'In pimps and politicians,' in *Polly* (1729).

Guests (1694), where the two wives are the forerunners of Polly Peachum and Lucy Lockit in *The Beggar's Opera*. More serious, though not more sophisticated, are those passionate duets in which Purcell confesses his admiration for the Italian operatic style. In 'No, no, resistance is but vain' from *The Maid's Last Prayer* (1693), and more particularly 'My dearest, my fairest' from *Pausanias* (1695), the influence of Monteverdi's mature style and the work of his successors is apparent. The opening of the second may be compared with the duet between the Valletto and the Damigella or the duets between Nero and Poppæa in Monteverdi's *L'incoronazione di Poppea* (1642).

Purcell

Italian influence is to be seen, too, in the songs with trumpet obbligato, such as 'To arms, heroic prince' in *The Libertine* (1692?), in the bustling orchestral 'Preludio' in *The Virtuous Wife* (1694–5?),[1] and in the use of coloratura in arias and declamatory passages. Sometimes this is adopted for some picturesque and dramatic effect, as in the magician Montesmo's accompanied recitative in the first part of *Don Quixote* (1694) (*see page* 157). But often it has no other purpose than to give the singer an opportunity to display his skill. A striking example of this declamatory style is to be seen in the song 'Whilst I with grief,' in *The Spanish Friar* (1694–5), which was inspired by Mrs. Bracegirdle's singing in the second part of *Don Quixote*. The later arias show the same development in style that we have already noted in *The Tempest*, particularly in the structure of their basses. The end of 'Ah! how sweet it is to love,'[2] in *Tyrannic Love* (1694?), is an illuminating instance of melodic organization dominated by the bass—a product, in fact, of the *basso continuo*:

Pains of love are sweet er far Than all, all, all, all
o ther plea sures are.

Of choral music in these plays there is very little. 'Britons, strike home,' in *Bonduca*, is similar in tonality and in its square-cut vigour to 'Come if you dare' in *King Arthur*, and the well-known

---

[1] For my arguments for this date see p. 273.

[2] I consider this to be an earlier version than the instrumental 'Song Tune' in *The Virtuous Wife*. See p. 273.

'In these delightful pleasant groves' in *The Libertine* will supply us with another example of the 'fa-la-las' which appeared in *Dido and Æneas*. A more spacious manner is to be found in the massive chorus, 'Who can resist such mighty charms?' in *Timon of Athens,* which would not be out of place in a Handelian oratorio, so solid and dignified is the style (*see page* 159). The brief dominant pedal on the last syllable of 'disarms' is extra- ordinarily effective. Notice, too, the use made of the basses' top notes and particularly the sonorous unison with the tenors in the fourth and fifth bars.

In addition to the songs in the plays Purcell wrote a large number of secular songs and duets for private performance. Solo singing had been a popular diversion in the reigns of James I and Charles I and during the Commonwealth, and it lost none of its popularity under Charles II, by which time the practice of singing madrigals had declined. The earliest solo songs of the seventeenth century were issued with lute accompani- ment, which had originally represented the missing parts of a polyphonic composition but before long assumed an independent character of its own. The value of these lute accompaniments to the student of the period is that every note is represented by a specific letter in the tablature, so that there is no doubt about the accidentals or any detail of the harmony. In the course of the century lute tablature gave place to the *basso continuo*, which had been imported from Italy. This consisted simply of the bass of the harmony printed in staff notation, with figures added to denote any deviations from the root positions of common chords or any accidentals not in the key signature. The *basso continuo* was associated particularly with the keyboard instrument of the period, the harpsichord, but it was still permissible to accompany these songs on the lute. The result, however, was bound to be less exact than that produced by the tablature, since the disposition of the chords and the sequence of parts in the accompaniment was left to the choice of the performer.

The introduction of the *basso continuo* was accompanied by the cultivation of what I have called the declamatory style, in which the rhythm of the words was considered more important than formal structure. Among the composers who laboured to adapt this rather pedantic principle to English words Henry Lawes won particular renown and was honoured by Milton's approval. He was a close acquaintance of John Cooper—an English musician who had studied in Italy and returned to England disguised as Giovanni Coperario—and so naturally contributed to the infiltration of new methods from abroad. To the modern ear Lawes's settings are apt to sound dull, partly because we no longer welcome the principle as a novelty and partly because Lawes himself was not a composer of the front rank.

The adoption of this principle did not kill the old type of air. Symmetry is too obvious and necessary a factor in musical design to be defeated by theory, and Lawes himself could write simple metrical settings when the passion for 'just note and accent' was less exacting. Solo song was closely bound up with the masques of the period. A work like *Cupid and Death* (1653), set by Matthew Locke and Christopher Gibbons, shows plainly the influence of new methods, not only in the use of the rather inchoate type of melody favoured by Lawes, but also in the attempt to achieve expression by means of *fioriture* or vocal embellishments. The masque also influenced song through its dance movements. The regular pulse of the *coranto* had its counterpart in the swinging rhythm of the strophic song, which was also fertilized by the traditions of popular folksong.

The subject-matter of Restoration song was still largely determined by the predominant passion of Renaissance art—to recreate the spirit of the ancient world. It was only natural that the poets of the Italian courts should derive their inspiration from Vergil and Theocritus and delight to sing in their own tongue the idyllic loves and heart-rending sorrows of nymphs and shepherds. So in the earliest operas the union of Orpheus with Eurydice and his final apotheosis were celebrated in song and spectacle by a rustic chorus, and Tityrus recumbent under his beech tree inspired the dramatic pastoral. The persistence of this tradition can be seen in Purcell's semi-operas, in *Dioclesian,* in *King Arthur* and in *The*

Fairy Queen. Solo song could not remain immune from this prevalent infection; and even when the pastoral setting was laid aside, the manner and attitude remained. It was an age when poets and musicians revelled in the languorous accents of sophisticated passion; and so universal was the theme that the same conceits and, in music, the same melodic and harmonic progressions did duty equally for love-songs and elegies. Musicians found, too, that the clichés of pathetic expression could be applied to sacred verse. The whole temper of the times was subjective. The lover, the mourner, the penitent—each was deeply conscious of his personal relationship towards the object of his passion, his tears or his worship; and whether the theme was the cruelty of a reluctant mistress, the bitterness of inexorable fate or man's humility before God, the single fount of melody and harmony supplied them all.

There was also a lighter side. When the poets relaxed, they could forget coy Silvia and lamenting Strephon and discuss the relationships of the sexes in less self-conscious, less pretentious strains. The result was a frankness that often went beyond the bounds of legitimate plain-speaking.

> In vain we dissemble, in vain do we try
> To stifle our flame and check our desire,

sang the author of one of Purcell's songs. But the truth was that there was really very little dissembling, and desires were as often fulfilled as checked. When Pelham Humfrey set a poem beginning,

> Of all the brisk Dames, *Misselina* for me;
> For I love not a woman unless she be free,[1]

he was helping to propagate a sentiment that accorded all too well with the habits of Restoration society. To the musician these songs offered the opportunity of matching the words with light-hearted, irresponsible melodies. There was nothing inconsistent with refinement in being associated with the lowest type of verse. Purcell, composer in ordinary to the king and organist

[1] *Choice Ayres, etc.,* book i, p. 23.

of Westminster Abbey, had no hesitation in lending his art to such sordid trifles as *Love is now become a trade.*

A large number of secular songs of all kinds were issued in the second half of the seventeenth century by John Playford, a staunch champion of British music at a time when the superiority of the foreigner was loudly proclaimed. Manifestos in praise of native musicians were not uncommon at this time; but no one put the case more forcibly than Playford in the third book of his collection of *Choice Ayres, Songs and Dialogues* (1681). Introducing a further instalment of songs by English composers, he wrote:

I need not here commend the Excellency of their Composition, the ingenious Authors Names being printed with them, who are Men that understand to make *English* Words speak their true and genuine Sence both in good humour and Ayre; which can never be performed by either *Italian* or *French,* they not so well understanding the Proprieties of our Speech. I have seen lately published a large Volum of *English* Songs, composed by an *Italian* Master, who has lived here in *England* many Years; I confess he is a very able Master, but being not perfect in the true *Idiom* of our Language, you will find the Air of his Musick so much after his Country-Mode, that it would sute far better with *Italian* than *English* Words. But I shall forbear to censure his Work, leaving it to the Verdict of better Musical Judgments; only I think him very disingenious and much to blame, to endeavour to raise a Reputation to himself and Book, by disparaging and undervaluing most of the best *English* Masters and Professors of Musick. I am sorry it is (in this Age) so much the Vanity of some of our *English* Gentry to admire that in a Foreigner, which they either slight, or take little notice of in one of their own Nation; for I am sure that our *English* Masters in Musick (either for Vocal or Instrumental Musick) are not in Skill and Judgment inferiour to any Foreigners whatsoever, the same Rules in this Science being generally used all over *Europe*.[1]

Playford's remarks on the peculiar difficulties of setting English words need no commendation; and his claim that this was a task for English composers was amply justified in Purcell's own work.

[1] The Italian master referred to in this extract is plainly Reggio, who had published a volume of songs with a provocative preface in the previous year. See p. 93.

No composer has shown a greater care or precision in accentuation or a greater care for the inflexions of the poet's text. It may be said that this is a minor detail of the composer's technique. That is true; and it is equally true that just accentuation and respect for poetry do not in themselves produce great music, as any one can see by examining the early Florentine operas. But the ability to reconcile his musical invention with the just demands of poetry is none the less indispensable to a composer who aims at good song-writing; and Purcell's skill in achieving this reconciliation is not the least of his virtues. In passages like this, from *Ah! cruel nymph, you give despair*:

But charm - ing, air y, hu · morous and gay

or this, from *Corinna is divinely fair* (1692) [1]:

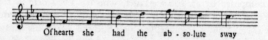

Of hearts she had the ab · so · lute sway

the music seems to fit the words like a glove and yet retain its independence. That Purcell's gifts as a song-writer were fully recognized by his contemporaries is evident from Henry Playford's preface to the second edition of the first volume of *Orpheus Britannicus* (1706):

The First Edition of this Work having been so well received, and the real Value each Piece carries along with it, has Encourag'd the Reprinting of this our *British Orpheus*, which I may venture to say, does Excell any Collection of *Vocal Music* yet Extant in the *English Tongue*, and may Vie with the best *Italian Compositions*.

The Author's extraordinary Tallent in all sorts of *Music*, is sufficiently known; but he was particularly admir'd for his *Vocal*, having a peculiar Genius to express the Energy of *English Words*, whereby he mov'd the Passions as well as caus'd Admiration in all his Auditors.

Even if we discount some of the enthusiasm natural to a publisher

[1] The dates given for the songs are those of publication.

this still remains an eloquent tribute to the enduring popularity of Purcell's songs.

In his earliest songs, such as *When Thirsis did the splendid eye* (1675) or *Cease, O my sad soul* (1678), he was clearly influenced by Lawes, imitating the older composer's artificial freedom and studious avoidance of symmetry. But, like Lawes, he was also quite ready to adopt the easy rhythms and regular periods of popular melody. There are examples, for instance, of the rhythm ♩. ♪ ♩,[1] which was much in vogue at the time and was used frequently by composers like Humfrey, Locke and Robert Smith; and even at the end of his life Purcell was quite content to publish such a simple ditty as *Sawney is a bonny lad* (1694) for the amusement of the polite readers of the *Gentleman's Journal*. He also found scope for the use of his favourite device of a ground bass, notably in *Cease, anxious world* (1687), the two settings of *What a sad fate is mine* and the mature and finely imagined *O solitude, my sweetest choice* (1687).

The most fully developed and, in a sense, the most interesting of his songs are those in which he has taken as his model the Italian cantata, a popular form with composers in the second half of the seventeenth century. Here recitative (or declamation) and aria were found together within the confines of a single piece; the more elaborate examples consisting of several short movements, linked together by identity or connection of key and by an emotional significance common to the whole song. Carissimi, Rossi and Stradella were notable exponents of this form. Purcell shows considerable variety in his treatment, using *fioriture*, chromatic progressions or florid counterpoint between voice and bass as it suits his purpose. In the latter case the harpsichord ceases to be a merely supporting instrument and becomes a partner, as in the rumbustious opening of *Anacreon's Defeat* (1688) or *Love arms himself in Celia's eyes*, which begins with this boldly suggestive figure for the *continuo*:

---

[1] e.g. *I resolve against cringing* (1679) and *How I sigh when I think* (1681).

An expert player would have made a brilliant and dashing preamble of these two bars. Elsewhere the accompanist has to be content with providing a background while the voice develops alternately the resources of decoration and pathos. A quotation from the deeply expressive *The fatal hour comes on apace* will illustrate the method:

To the cantata type belong those lavish elegies in which, after the fashion of the times, the tragedy of loss was expressed in terms of pastoral symbolism. Such are the commemorations of John Playford and Thomas Farmer. Unique among these tributes is the Latin elegy on the death of Queen Mary, *Incassum, Lesbia, rogas* (1695), which without any undue extravagance or display remains a dramatic and impressive record of a subject's grief. The wandering modulations sing sorrow's strain as poignantly as in Dido's lament:

and later the sinking appoggiaturas recall more precisely the emotions of the earlier work.

The chamber duets cover much the same range as the solo songs. Here again, among the extended cantatas, the outstanding piece is an elegy on the queen, *O dive Custos Auriacae domus,* where Purcell makes no attempt to reproduce the Alcaic metre but sets the words with generous repetition in a manner that irresistibly suggests comparison with Bach's arias, however different the style and technique. The expressive possibilities of appoggiatura are exploited to the full:

and in the sliding chromaticism of the final bars is stored the whole essence of profound and genuine lamentation. Among several other examples of the pathetic vein one may mention particularly *Go tell Amyntas, gentle swain,* and, on a slighter scale, *Lost is my quiet for ever,* a tranquil and beautiful setting of sadly conventional words.

Here and there are to be found picturesque touches in Purcell's characteristic manner, such as the setting of the word 'morose' in *Nestor, who did to thrice man's age attain* (1689):

or the quaint suggestion of freezing in *I spy Celia*. And as a combination of daintiness and passion nothing could be neater than *Dulcibella, whene'er I sue for a kiss*:

where the interruption by the bass is contrived with the happiest and most sensitive art.

Nothing need be said here of Purcell's numerous catches. They are of some interest for the light they throw on the manners and history of the period and as an example of his dexterity in

Purcell

handling a popular form of the musician's craft; but they are too slight to have any permanent significance. It would be a mistake, however, to pass over the sacred songs, most of which were published in the two volumes of Playford's *Harmonia Sacra* in 1688 and 1693. The earlier examples in particular show an extraordinary faithfulness to the inflexions and sentiment of the words. There is no formal structure, in the ordinary sense of the word; the verse decides the progress of the music, which is rather declamation than song. The opening of *Great God and just* shows a peculiar sensitiveness to the suggestions of the text:

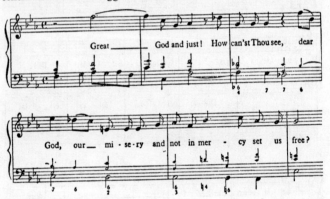

Sometimes the style recalls Bach's accompanied recitatives in its intensity, as at the end of *In the black dismal dungeon of despair*. Or again, as in the setting of Herbert's *With sick and famish'd eyes*, the combination of chromatic harmony in the accompaniment and appoggiaturas in the melody may produce an effect that is independent of epoch or environment:

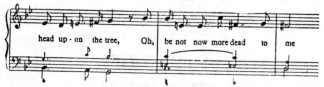

The later songs (as well as Cowley's *Awake and with attention bear* in the first book) are rather cantatas, with contrasted arias and recitatives. Here the Italian convention of coloratura is wholeheartedly and sometimes rather incongruously accepted. When Purcell writes in *Lord, what is man?*:

an over-nice judgment might object to the manner in which God's praises are sung; but that would be a harsh criticism of a composer who had every justification for moving with the times.

CHAPTER XIII

ODES AND CANTATAS

ONE of Purcell's duties as a court composer was the setting of complimentary odes for state occasions, such as birthdays, marriages and the king's return from holiday. Of these royal odes we have a complete series from 1680 to the death of Queen Mary in 1694. They may be divided into four sets:

(1) 5 welcome songs for Charles II (1680–4).
(2) 3 welcome songs for James II (1685–7).
(3) 6 birthday odes for Queen Mary (1689–94).
(4) 3 occasional odes for members of the royal family.

The earliest of the welcome songs for Charles II are for the most part dull and uninteresting. This is not to be attributed to the fact that they were written to order, nor to the pedestrian stodginess of the words. A good composer may quite well produce his best work on commission, and the inadequacy of Purcell's librettists does not seem to have hampered his inspiration on other occasions. The reason for the poor quality of these early odes is simply that Purcell was still learning his trade. In the string fantasias of 1680 we have a remarkable indication of how thoroughly he had mastered the old, traditional style. But the composition of these royal odes involved the acquisition of a more brilliant manner, for which Purcell's training had not fully prepared him. It was not until the 1683 ode, *Fly, bold rebellion,* that he began to get into his stride. This and its successor, *From those serene and rapturous joys,* are both mature and confident works in comparison with the awkward gait and pompous conventionality of the first three odes.

Not that these early works are insignificant. To a student of Purcell's development they are extremely interesting, but their interest lies rather in isolated details of technique or invention. Actual poverty of invention is comparatively rare. Purcell did not often sink to the platitudinous ineptitude of the chorus 'But your blest presence now,' in the 1680 ode, *Welcome, vicegerent.* The weakness of this section may possibly be the result not of a lack of ideas but of the deliberate attempt of a trained musician to adopt a simple and direct style. It may be that the breezy straightforwardness of some of Purcell's most popular songs and choruses was not the outcome of a natural talent for simplicity but the product of the hard labour of refinement. Occasionally in these odes we come across little songs that might have strayed from the theatre music, such as the graceful little duet 'When the summer in his glory,' in *Welcome, vicegerent,* or the tenor solo, 'Your Augusta he charms,' in *Swifter Isis, swifter flow* (1681). But in general mere tunefulness plays a minor part in these serious and rather consequential compositions.

In form the welcome songs may be described as choral cantatas. They are set for solo voices and chorus with four-part strings and continuo (sometimes with the addition of two flutes), and the vocal movements are interspersed with a number of instrumental symphonies. There is some similarity with the more elaborate of the anthems with string accompaniment, particularly in the use of solo and 'verse' sections. Of the solo songs the one outstanding example is the alto solo, 'These had by their ill usage drove,' from *The summer's absence unconcerned we bear* (1682), which in technique and inspiration is in a class by itself. Readers who have the vocal score of *Dido and Æneas* by them should compare the song 'Oft she visits this lone fountain,' which clearly owes not a little to the ideas already used here:

beau teous nymph long | since away, These | since a way,

Had she not, van - quished by your love,

Charmed, charmed in your soft_____ em

bra - ces lay, Had she not, van - quished

by _____ your love, Charmed in your soft_____

Apart from this song the principal interest of the odes of 1680, 1681 and 1682 is to be found in the instrumental symphonies and ritornelli, which are bold and assured in style and show a complete mastery of part-writing. Here again the importance of Purcell's peculiar talent for instrumental composition should not be missed. Sometimes he gives us more than a bold and clear outline and cunning inner parts. The ritornello after 'Let no sham pretences' in *The summer's absence unconcerned we bear* rises to heights of real eloquence. The most conventional of ground basses has here borne more than ordinary fruit.

The 1683 ode, *Fly, bold rebellion*, is a much more impressive work than its predecessors. The melodic invention of such songs as 'Rivers from their channels turned,' with its fascinating drooping figure in the second bar, or the tenor solo, 'But kings like the sun'—a spacious setting—shows a firmer grasp and a bolder imagination. Their attractiveness is enhanced by the method, already adopted in the previous odes, of repeating them on the strings, the part-writing offering a modern editor useful hints on how to treat the continuo of Purcell's songs. There is another anticipation of *Dido and Æneas* in the opening chorus, which, with its characteristic setting of the word 'victorious' to the rhythm ♩♩♩|♩ ♩, brings to mind the triumphing song and dance from the later work.

Contemporary Italian influence appears strongly in the 1684 ode, *From those serene and rapturous joys*, particularly in the relation be-tween chorus and orchestra in passages like the one quoted on p. 176, an example of a technique which Handel later exploited with some success. The florid bass solo, 'Welcome as soft refreshing

flowers,' which comes a little later, is of small interest except as a reminder of the exaggerated attention paid to vocal ornament at the time. A finer testimony to Purcell's artistry is the setting for tenor of the words:

> Welcome, more welcome does he come
> Than life to Lazarus from his drowsy tomb,
> When in his winding sheet at his new birth,
> The strange surprising word was said—Come forth!

The song is on a moving ground bass in E minor, and the whole feeling of the music suggests in some inexplicable way the atmosphere of a sepulchre. The final cadence lingers in the mind, and the violins repeat the melancholy strain. The duet that follows for alto and bass with violin obbligato includes a very attractive treatment of a dominant pedal. The rest of the ode lapses into that conventional jubilation into which Purcell was so often snared by the mere mention of trumpets. Two other royal odes also belong to the period 1680–4: a welcome song for the Duke of York, *What, what shall be done in behalf of the man?* (1682), which calls for no particular comment, and the wedding song for Princess Anne and Prince George of Denmark, *From hardy climes* (1683), in which the florid concerted style of the overture is particularly noteworthy.

The first of Purcell's three welcome songs for James II, *Why, why are all the Muses mute?* (1685), is peculiar in that the symphony is preceded by an introductory recitative, on a similar plan to the opening of Mendelssohn's *Elijah*. The first movement of the symphony, with its persistent trochaic rhythm, is very characteristic of the period. The work as a whole is disappointing. The music has an air of suave distinction, and the composer is clearly thoroughly at home with his material; but the fire of imagination burns fitfully. Only a few casual glints reward investigation such as the following passage in the final chorus, which is interesting for its treatment of a chromatically descending bass, with appoggiaturas in the upper part and a free counterpoint in the tenor (*see page* 178).

Ye tuneful Muses (1686), though in some respects a clumsier and less finished work, is interesting in several ways. We can afford to smile now at the ingenuous passage where the violins scrub over all four strings to illustrate the words 'Tune all your instruments,' and may raise our eyebrows at the persistent tonic and dominant bass that accompanies the solo and chorus, 'From the rattling of drums.' But the first would have seemed highly dramatic in an age when instrumental effects as we know them were in their infancy, while the second is insipid only to a taste that has long been nourished on the conventionalized tonality of the late eighteenth century; and no one can deny that Purcell has

178

solved his own problem very neatly. Earlier in the work he has incorporated a racy popular tune, 'Hey then, up go we':

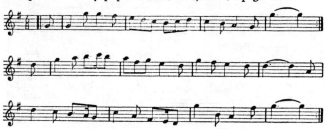

to accompany the verse:

> Be lively then and gay,
> All signs of sorrow chase away,
> Be cheerful as the patron of the day,
> After a gloomy night's gone by
> And not one cloud obscures the glorious sky.

The way in which the tune is used is most ingenious. First it forms the bass to the alto solo; then when the chorus enters it is transferred to the treble and heard on the violins; finally it is used again as a bass for the instrumental ritornello, with an entirely new counterpoint above. How elaborate Purcell's contrapuntal treatment is may be seen by an extract from the choral section:

Once again the most satisfying music of the work is to be found in the instrumental sections. The opening symphony contains a fugal *allegro* which is a model of fine craftsmanship, and there is a sober dignity in the ritornello that succeeds the elaborate alto solo on a ground, 'With him he brings the partner of his throne.'

The 1687 ode, *Sound the trumpet, beat the drum,* opens with pompous magnificence. The alto soloist imitates the first instrument, the bass the second; the chorus joins in, with that square-cut homophony popularized by the Italian composers, the strings interpolating lively figuration. The style suggests Handel in its breadth and splendour. The key is the only one possible--D major. The tenor solo that follows is built on one of Purcell's more daring ground basses, in which the first beat in the bar is persistently silent. Towards the end of the ode occurs that mighty chaconne, impressive for all its length and occasional heaviness, which was afterwards used as the 'First Music' in *King Arthur*. The plausible suggestion has been made that a dance took place here, since the length of the movement far exceeds the normal span of instrumental symphonies. As always with Purcell, the change to the minor brings a deepening of the emotional background. The last eight bars before the return to the original major are unmistakably stamped with his hall-mark. There is imagination, too, in the setting of the words, 'His fame, like incense, mounts the skies,' with the halting appoggiaturas in the strings and the typical mannerisms in the bass solo—the high E for the word 'skies' and the bottom D for 'the deep abyss below,' and the curiously regretful repetition of the word 'never' as in the last chorus of *Dido and Æneas*. We need no written testimony to the gifts of the Reverend John Gostling. If he could sing things like this he must have been a bass in a hundred. The final chorus is elaborate but unconvincing. The endless runs in oily thirds smell too much of the workshop.

The six birthday odes for Queen Mary (1689–94) show a firmer realization of the possibilities of a massive style of brilliantly accompanied choral writing, with which Purcell had already made some experiments. The solidly built opening chorus of *Now does the glorious day appear* (1689) has the rock-like determination commonly associated with Handel's choral works. The instrumental writing shows the same richness, and the use of strings in five parts, after Lulli's model, gives an added richness to the texture. In the first movement of the overture the old style of the French introduction is abandoned for a less severe, more obvious manner, based on the Italian sonata. Side by side with these newer developments we find the old declamatory style persisting, as in the setting for bass solo of the words: 'It was a work of full as great a weight.' Purcell had not yet completely reconciled the desire to satisfy the vocalist's ambition with the symmetry of the Italian aria form.

Purcell

182

Again in the 1689 ode we have one of Purcell's favourite D minor airs over a perpetually moving ground bass, carried out with the same sure smoothness and fretless ease, and a tenor solo in D major over a similar ground bass, which is more successful than his previous essays in the same style and key. But on the whole the chief impression in this ode is made by the choral writing, which in the finale in particular has a brilliant opulence. Here is the work of a composer who knew exactly what he wanted to do and did it without fumbling (*see page* 182).

The 1689 ode is surpassed, however, by its successor in the same key, *Arise my Muse* (1690), which begins with a symphony also associated with *King Arthur*. The atmosphere of festal pomp is even more skilfully suggested in this elaborate and imposing work. The use of trumpets for the first time in a royal ode adds magnificence. From the dazzling blaze of the D major opening we turn to an alto solo on a ground in the relative minor, a setting of the words:

> See how the glitt'ring ruler of the day
> From the cool bosom of the sea
> Drives, drives with speed away,
>   And does attending planets all
>   To wanton revels call,
> Who from the starry east and west
> To celebrate this day make haste,
> And in new robes of glory dressed
>   Dance in a solemn ball.

Purcell has seized on the suggestion offered by the last line and given to the whole song the atmosphere of a minuet. The atmosphere, not the form. The dance rhythm is not so much present to our ears as implicit in the background. The final cadence is exquisitely turned:

Dance in a so - lemn, dance in a so - lemn ball.

The duet that follows is cunningly based on a ground bass which omits the third of the key-note and so can equally well serve for major and minor—a convenience of which Purcell naturally takes full advantage. The concluding ritornello is a brilliant affair, with trumpets and oboes playing their part in the counter-point.

The most dramatic section of this ode is the finale, in which the plaints of Eusebia, representing the Anglican Church lamenting William's departure, are contrasted with Glory's injunction to the warrior king to pursue his chosen course. The alto solo, 'But ah, I see Eusebia drowned in tears,' is a fine example of Purcell's treatment of the pathetic style. The Queen Mary odes coincide with the fertile period of his theatre music, and his natural talent for the stage, once it had found its outlet in its proper sphere, could be used to intensify and vivify his concert works. A few bars of this solo must be quoted:

must not   let him   go

Glory's answer follows in D major in a vigorous ⁶⁄₄ time. The
movement has been subjected to amused comment, merely
because the words are a little ridiculous. The oddity of the
repeated command 'go on' should not blind us to the fine,
compelling sweep of the music. Twice the unhappy Eusebia
renews her plaints, but at last the chorus support the bass soloist
in repeating Glory's words, and with the same easy swing the ode
comes to an end.

Welcome, welcome glorious morn (1691) also has parts for trumpets
and oboes, but the strings are reduced again to four parts. The
opening solo and chorus are founded on a ground bass in C
major, similar, though not in rhythm, to that used for the last
chorus of *Dioclesian*. Otherwise the work is in no way remarkable and much of it is conventional. In *Love's goddess sure was
blind this day* (1692) Purcell turns aside from festivity and assumes
a more intimate manner, prompted no doubt by Sedley's text,
which is much superior to the average of these productions.
There are no trumpets in the score, and the introductory symphony
is allied in style to the contrapuntal overtures of the earlier odes,
though there are purely homophonic sections that show the
influence of modern methods. The key of the work is G minor,
which might seem a curious choice for a birthday ode if it were
not that Purcell frequently uses this key for songs suggesting the
emotions of love as well as the pangs of regret. The alto solo
that follows the symphony sets the tone for the whole work; it
has a courtly winning grace, which persists through the succeeding
ritornello. The celebrated soprano solo, the bass of which is

the popular melody 'Cold and raw,' would not have attracted any attention apart from the anecdote associated with it; it has too much the flavour of a counterpoint exercise. Indeed, on the face of it one would hardly expect a song-tune to make a good bass. More significant is the duet for two altos, 'Many such days may she behold,' constructed with a wealth of detail over a bass that suggests a distant kinship with Bach:

The duet reaches its climax, like so many of Purcell's songs over a moving bass, in the instrumental ritornello at the end. A chorus follows, in which the foundations of the English oratorio style can plainly be discerned:

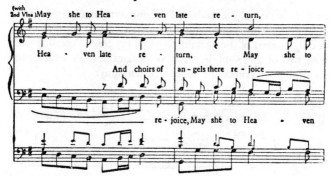

This will bear comparison with Handel. But the crown of the whole work is the reversion to the original minor key at the end, where the suggestion of the queen's eventual death draws from Purcell a note of plaintive regret, reminiscent of the end of *Dido and Æneas*. The short concluding section that follows should be compared with the chorus, 'With drooping wings,' in the opera.

With *Celebrate this festival*, the 1693 ode, Purcell returns to majesty and splendour. The principal key of the work is C major, which offers abundant scope for brilliant trumpet-writing. The overture is taken from the ode on St. Cecilia's Day written in the previous year, with little alteration beyond transposition. There are passages here and there in the work where the note of festivity strikes one as a little forced, and the trumpet obbligatos have lost the interest they had in a century when virtuosity on wind instruments commanded respect. But the baroque magnificence of the choral writing and the proud energy of the melodies make the work as a whole an imposing *pièce d'occasion*. Such solemn jubilee is proper to a queen's birthday. The advent of spring is hailed with an outburst of riotous and exuberant joy; and at the end trumpets, oboes, violins and voices unite in one of those swinging tunes that we rightly call Purcellian. Yet the excellence of the work is not confined to these festal strains. There is a quieter dignity in the mezzo-soprano solo, 'Crown the

altar, deck the bay,' with the unhurrying, yet unresting persistence
of its ground bass; and when the soprano soloist turns from the
pealing fanfares of the opening to plead for peace Purcell is ready
with one of those subtle pieces of declamation in which mere
vocalization becomes the servant of harmony:

But the finest of all the Queen Mary odes is the last, *Come ye
sons of art away* (1694). Once more trumpets are used, but simply
as concerted instruments, taking part on equal terms with strings
and voices. The overture, a solid and dignified piece, was also
used in *The Indian Queen* and has been mentioned already. In
the opening solo and chorus Purcell was faced with some very
clumsy verse, feeble in expression and metrically lopsided. But
difficulties of this kind, which might have depressed a man of
less imagination, merely stimulated him to livelier efforts. The
miserable words are set to a brisk dance rhythm, the tune, as in
the last movement of *Celebrate this festival,* being so constructed
that it can be played on the natural trumpet. It is first heard on
oboes and violins alternately, then sung by the alto soloist. The
effect, when all the voices and instruments enter, with the tune in
the alto and the sopranos singing a descant, is splendid. Among
the other delightful things in this ode are the duet 'Sound the
trumpet' (a lively and florid piece in which the first alto is required

to sing up to E on the fourth space of the treble stave), the soprano solo, 'Bid the virtues,' with its elaborate obbligato for solo oboe, and the pompous bass solo, 'These are the sacred charms,' a brilliant aria in the most up-to-date Italian manner, with a constantly repeated bass. The last six bars may serve as a specimen:

The work ends in a blaze of glory with another of those tremendously energetic trumpet tunes. Here is the entry of the chorus [1]:

[1] To save space I have given the voice parts only.

When the bold, unsubtle melody returns for the last time the whole world seems to be singing.

One other royal ode remains to be mentioned, *Who can from joy refrain?*, composed for the Duke of Gloucester's sixth birthday in 1695. Technically mature, it suffers from a want of imagination. Familiar processes are repeated without the driving force of new ideas. The extended chaconne at the end is the most interesting movement. Of Purcell's odes composed for other occasions four were written for the celebrations of St. Cecilia's day. The earliest of these are *Welcome to all the pleasures* and the Latin song, *Laudate Ceciliam,* both of which date from 1683. *Welcome to all the pleasures* is one of the best of Purcell's earlier works. The responsibility of providing a new piece for the Gentlemen of the Musical Society seems to have roused him to display all his musicianship. The overture, though short, is well constructed, and much of the vocal writing has a natural grace. The alto solo on a ground, 'Here the Deities approve,' was later issued as a harpsichord solo in the second part of *Musick's Hand-Maid* (1689). The final chorus is in the unusual key of E major, and the voices and instruments, instead of ending together, break off one by one until the basses alone are left singing 'Cecilia.' *Raise, raise the voice,* another St. Cecilia ode of uncertain date, also provided material for *Musick's Hand-Maid* in a little minuet in D minor. The work is lively and there are some curious harmonic experiments in the air on a ground, 'Mark, mark how readily the pliant string,' but the music has no outstanding originality. The style would suggest a date round about 1685.

The 1692 ode, *Hail, bright Cecilia,* is on a different plane. The conception is magnificent—a great hymn in praise of music and all its instruments; and though the achievement sometimes falls short of the intention, it is still possible to admire the glory of the attempt. The ode contains one of Purcell's most majestic, most ingenious and most inspired choral movements: the chorus 'Soul of the world.' These noble pages set the welkin ringing. After a tremendous introduction, in which the aspirations of humanity are heard above a prolonged pedal point and the discord of nature's atoms is represented by an abrupt diminished seventh and tremolandos for the strings, the voices break into a brilliant fugal movement in which Purcell is the undisputed peer, as he is the obvious predecessor, of Handel (*see page* 192). Thereafter voices and instruments compete in strenuous rivalry for a few bars before the contrapuntal thread is taken up again. There is a majestic peroration on a dominant pedal. Short as it is, this chorus shows perfect mastery of technique and imagination. The finale, where Purcell has clearly aimed at an even more impressive pageant of sound, is weakened by the conventional jubilation of the orchestral fanfares. But there is a splendid moment when the subject of the *fugato*—a theme reminiscent of a well-known chorale melody—is heard simultaneously in the bass in ponderous augmentation, with the counter-subject superimposed.

The instrumental writing is frequently elaborate. The second movement of the overture, a fugal canzona—later used in the 1693 Queen Mary ode—is an exhilarating adventure along the paths of instrumental counterpoint. In the third movement (*adagio*) there is a quietly expressive antiphony between strings and oboes; and in the duet, 'Hark, each tree,' Purcell has introduced a similar contrast, balancing the violins and basses against

three recorders (two trebles and a bass), the whole being constructed over a ground bass. The movement has advanced quite
a long way before it becomes apparent that the reason for this
alternation is to be found in the text, which celebrates the creation
of the rival instruments. While the bass soloist gambols indus-
triously to represent the 'sprightly violin,' the soprano sings the

praises of the flute in more sedate and more pathetic tones. When the poet speaks of the sympathy that drew the 'list'ning brethren' of the box and fir, the two voices unite in flowing coloratura. There is a further experiment in instrumentation in the opening chorus, where oboes alone are used to accompany the upper voices of the semi-chorus, the violins entering again with the full choir. Less successful is the picturesque setting of 'The fife and all the harmony of war,' where trumpets and timpani bear the burden—a rather conventional burden—of accompaniment. Of the songs the finest is the bass solo—a *da capo* aria on a ground—'Wondrous machine,' where the oboes maintain a persuasive commentary while the singer exults in the superlative majesty of the organ. One single piece of declamation has acquired a special notoriety—the alto solo ''Tis Nature's voice'—since this was the piece that Purcell sang himself at the first performance. Contemporary appreciation was expressed principally for the 'incredible graces' that encrust the voice part. Our own age, less interested in vocal exhibition, may find more to admire in the characteristic note of suffering associated with the idea of grief:

or in the delightful use of a pedal in an inner part at the words, 'At once it charms,' to suggest the captivating powers of nature's voice.

Three other occasional odes remain to be mentioned. *Celestial music*, a dignified work but in no way remarkable, was written for a private school performance in 1689. The overture is borrowed from the coronation anthem, *My heart is inditing*. *Of old when heroes*, better known as *The Yorkshire Feast Song*, belongs to the following year. There is a good deal of pomp and circumstance in the work—D major trumpets rejoicing in their strength, and the like—but on the whole it is stodgy and unadventurous. Perhaps Purcell's interest in London Yorkshiremen was not sufficient to stir him to the depths. The gentle serenity of the tenor solo, 'So when the glitt'ring queen of night,' is pleasing, but the two-bar bass on which it is founded is not fertile enough to support a whole movement; the continual return to the tonic is enervating. The ode written for Trinity College, Dublin, in 1694—*Great parent, hail*—also bears the marks of perfunctory interest. There is some vigorous counterpoint in the overture,

and some imaginative writing for the bass soloist, but not enough to compensate for several pages of barren pomposity. A fragment for bass and strings that shows a Handelian dignity and exuberance will represent this ode at its best (*see page* 194).

Purcell also left a number of chamber cantatas for two, three or four voices, with accompaniment for continuo and obbligato instruments. These are graceful specimens of his art, and the words—in some cases by Cowley—have a refinement absent from some of his more extended works. The end of *If ever I more riches did desire* is an exquisite example of his gift for portraying in music a lingering melancholy:

These cantatas contain some admirable writing for flutes and violins. The overture to *How pleasant is this flowery plain* indulges in the most frivolous syncopation between the flutes and continuo:

There is an amusing detail in *If ever I more riches did desire*. An optional low D for the bass soloist is specially marked 'Gostling.' We have heard much already of the feats of this reverend gentleman and of his exceptional *basso profundo*. The evidence of the autograph answers all the churlish suspicions of sceptical inquiry.

CHAPTER XIV

CHURCH MUSIC

PURCELL'S church music, indeed Restoration church music as a whole, seems to belong to a world of its own, however definite and obvious its relationship to the secular music of the period. The combination of political and musical circumstances that helped to shape its development resulted in a product so characteristic of its period that any revival gives a curiously incongruous impression. The political circumstances are well known. The ban imposed on church music by the Commonwealth government cut sharply across its natural development. The steady changes that would have taken place during the years 1640–60 are represented by a blank in musical history. When church music reappeared at the Restoration, there was much that had to be taken for granted, and hence a certain hesitancy and inconclusiveness in the new style. The pre-Commonwealth composers had already begun to develop a new type of anthem, in which the old vocal polyphony was partly replaced by music for solo voice or voices with instrumental accompaniment, whether for viols or organ. This type of composition was known as a 'verse' anthem, in contrast to the 'full' anthem, which was purely polyphonic in conception, even though certain sections might be sung by solo voices instead of by the whole choir. Byrd had already experimented with the new form, which was in full accordance with the growing tendency to give prominence to the solo voice, and it was carried still further by Orlando Gibbons. Gibbons's anthem, *This is the record of John,* with string accompaniment, is a familiar example of the application of the declamatory principle to English church music. Gibbons was also alive to the possibilities of *fioritura,* though he made only a limited use of them.

By the time the English church service was restored in 1660 the Italian declamatory style, with its characteristic effects of pathos and dramatic expression, had become familiar in England, with the result that it was naturally adopted for the solo sections of the anthems that composers were now called upon to write for cathedrals and the royal chapel. A further influence is discernible in the acclimatization of that lively homophonic style which Morley had introduced in his 'fa las' or ballets, published in 1595. Hence we find a composer like Child, who was born in the early years of James I's reign, writing the following at the end of his anthem, *O Lord, grant the king a long life,* which was composed for Charles II's restoration in 1660 [1]:

[1] Brit. Mus., Harl. 7338, fo. 86.

A further stage in the transformation of the anthem into a cantata was the introduction of instruments on an equal basis with the voices. Among the anthems sung at Charles II's coronation in 1661 was Cooke's *Behold, O Lord, our defender,* in which the choral sections were answered by an orchestra of strings and wind.[1] In the following year the innovation was made of regularly employing the band of twenty-four violins in the Chapel Royal.[2]

The application of the newer style to church music appears also to have been fostered by Charles II. Since he was a boy of ten when the Civil War broke out, he can have had very little chance of becoming acquainted with the older style of church music, which was even then in its decline. His musical education must have been influenced by the tastes of his mother, who was French, and by his residence during his exile in Paris, where he had opportunities of hearing the latest French and Italian music. His attitude towards English church music is described by Tudway in a passage that has often been quoted:

The Standard of Church Music begun by Mr. Tallis & Mr. Bird, &c. was continued for some years after the Restauration, & all Composers conform'd themselves to the Pattern which was set by them. His Majesty who was a brisk & Airy Prince, comeing to the Crown in the Flow'r & vigour of his Age, was soon, if I may so say, tyr'd with the Grave & solemn way, And Order'd the Composers of his Chappell to add symphonys &c. with Instruments to their Anthems; and therupon Establis'd [*sic*] a select number of his private music to play the symphonys & Retornellos which he had appointed.

The King did not intend by this innovation to alter any thing of the Establish'd way. He only appointed this to be done when he came himself to the Chappell, which was only upon Sundays in the Morning, on the great festivals, & days of Offerings. The old Masters of Music, viz. Dr. Child, Dr. Gibbons, Mr. Law [*sic*] &c., Organists to his Majesty, hardly knew how to comport themselves with these new fangl'd ways, but proceeded in their Compositions according to the old style, & therfore there are only some services & full Anthems of theirs to be found.

---

[1] Baker's *Chronicle*, p. 817.   [2] See p. 28.

In about 4 or 5 years time some of the forwardest & brightest Children of the Chappell, as Mr. Humfreys, Mr. Blow, &c. began to be Masters of a faculty in Composing. This his Majesty greatly encourag'd by indulging their youthfull fancys, so that ev'ry month at least, & afterwards oft'ner, they produc'd something New of this Kind. In a few years more severall others, Educated in the Chappell, produc'd their Compositions in this style; for otherwise it was in vain to hope to please his Majesty.

Thus this secular way was first introduc'd into the service of the Chappell, And has been too much imitated ever since by our Modern Composers. After the death of King Charles symphonys indeed with Instruments in the Chappell were laid aside; But they continu'd to make their Anthems with all the Flourish of interludes & Retornellos, which are now perform'd by the Organ.[1]

It is curious that Tudway, who was himself brought up as a choirboy under this régime, should show such prejudice against the new style. His suggestion that Charles II's individual tastes were solely responsible for altering the course of church music does not fit the facts. The new tendencies had already begun to appear before the Civil War, and the old masters whom Tudway praises were not quite so much behind the times as he would have us believe.

Put more moderately, the position is this. The older men were still inevitably linked with the pre-Commonwealth and hence ultimately with the Elizabethan traditions, whereas the younger generation of composers who were brought up by Cooke would naturally react directly to the latest modern developments. At the same time the cultivation of Elizabethan music was anything but extinct. The large number of anthems by Elizabethan and Jacobean composers in Clifford's *Divine Services and Anthems* (1663 and 1664) shows that, then as now, the music of England's Golden Age formed a substantial part of the repertory of cathedrals

---

[1] Brit. Mus., Harl. 7338, fo. 2ᵛ-3. I have modernized the punctuation and written 'the' in place of the detestable abbreviation 'yᵉ,' the retention of which in modern reprints gives an entirely false suggestion of quaintness; so also with 'wᶜʰ' and 'wᵗʰ.'

and the Chapel Royal. Tudway particularly emphasizes that the king only ordered instrumental symphonies to be used when he came to the chapel himself, and 'did not intend by this innovation to alter any thing of the Establish'd way.' The musical practice of the Chapel Royal was clearly more closely associated with the traditions of the past than has sometimes been supposed; and of course the work of Blow and Purcell shows a thorough familiarity with the older polyphonic style.

It will be noted that Pelham Humfrey is one of the composers mentioned by Tudway as encouraged by the king. He seems to have been a particular favourite. I have already mentioned how he was sent abroad at the king's expense, presumably for the purposes of completing his education by a closer study of foreign styles. It has often been assumed that he studied with Lulli, and the conclusion has been drawn that he absorbed the French operatic style (though Lulli had written only ballets at the time of his visit), transferred it to his church music, thereby giving the anthem a secular frivolity, and influenced Purcell in the same direction. This conclusion could only be accepted by those unacquainted with Humfrey's music. The dominant note of his anthems is not frivolity at all, but a serious and sometimes pathetic melancholy.[1] Such works as *Thou art my King, O God ; Haste Thee, O God; O Lord my God* and *Like as the hart,* all in minor keys and marked by a sober gravity, do not strike one as the product of a pioneer of frivolity. Humfrey, it is true, could write cheerful movements in dance rhythm, as in *O give thanks,* which is in B flat major, but even here the music has dignity and restraint.

The 'secularity' to which Tudway objected consisted in the introduction of instrumental symphonies, which were a novelty and therefore, to him, undesirable, since he remained an out-of-date admirer of the old school. In the same way Evelyn was shocked at the use of the band of violins, because he thought the instruments unsuitable to a sacred building. But once let it be accepted that instrumental music in church was admissible,

[1] Note, too, that the style of Lulli's church music is anything but frivolous.

and it is clear that the only style in which it could have been written was a secular style. There was no tradition of instrumental church music. To the Restoration composers instrumental music was simply instrumental music, without any qualification. It has too often been supposed that a secular style means a frivolous style, unsuited to the divine offices; whereas it should have been obvious that secular music can be, and often is, as sober and dignified as anything written expressly for the church. The whole objection to the innovation was, in fact, based on a false hypothesis.

Humfrey's influence on Purcell may be traced in the declamatory sections of his anthems, where he introduced, almost *ad nauseam,* those pathetic inflexions which he had learned in Italy. The use of augmented or diminished intervals in a descending passage was one of the clichés of the period. He may also by his own example have acquainted Purcell with the French type of instrumental overture. Blow, too, was obviously interested in Italian music, and his own enterprising though sometimes misguided originality may have served as a stimulus to his pupil's awakening genius. But it is probable that Purcell, like so many other great composers, learned most by his own experience. As a boy he must have sung church music of all kinds, old and new, and formed an ineradicable impression of conflicting styles. The old music evidently appealed to him strongly, since he wrote a number of 'full' anthems in the polyphonic tradition. These all belong to the earlier part of his career. But as time went on it was impossible for him to remain content with old formulas. He had to develop a style based on the new methods that were already beginning to dominate English music. To us, admiring the texture of the old masters, the change may seem unfortunate. To him it would have seemed a natural and obvious step forward.

It is not known when Purcell began writing church music. He was certainly already composing anthems for the Chapel Royal in 1679, as we learn from the letter written by his father to the Reverend John Gostling.[1] Nor is it quite certain where

[1] See Appendix E.

all his anthems were performed. It is clear that the anthems with instruments were written for the Chapel Royal, which alone had the necessary resources; but it cannot be proved that the others were composed for Westminster Abbey. Tudway's account shows that verse anthems with instruments were only performed when the king was present on Sundays and holy days. If anthems were sung on other occasions, as seems likely, the Chapel Royal would be the natural place for those elaborate 'full' works in several parts, since the choir was larger and better equipped than that at Westminster Abbey. The attempt has sometimes been made to divide Purcell's church music into a 'Westminster' period and a 'Chapel Royal' period, but this rests on an assumption that cannot be proved, and the use of the word 'Westminster' is misleading, seeing that Purcell remained organist of the abbey till the end of his life.

If Purcell wrote anthems as a boy they have not been preserved. The earliest anthems we possess already show an accomplished technique of part-writing, in spite of occasional clumsiness and an inclination to disregard tradition.[1] It is interesting to notice in one of his earliest anthems—the first setting of the funeral sentence *In the midst of life*—how he experiments with the traditional device of chromaticism to indicate the 'bitter pains of eternal death,' and also shows a characteristic disregard for euphony when the movement of the parts seems to him more important:

[1] The general chronology of Purcell's anthems, though not complete in detail, has been satisfactorily established by Nigel Fortune (Purcell Society's edition, vol. xxviii).

Equally suggestive is the end of the first version of *Hear me, O Lord*:

The influence of Humfrey may be detected in the occasional use of repetition at the end of a movement, as in *Bow down Thine ear*, where the final phrase, 'Praise Thy name for evermore,' is repeated with varied harmony. The cadences sometimes show a bold independence of normality, as in *Who hath believed our report?*, and the use of appoggiatura occasionally produces striking effects, as in the following example from *Bow down Thine ear*:

where the sudden emergence of the tenor on middle C gives a strange colouring to the discord. Elsewhere Purcell shows less concern about the resolution of a suspension. The day was past when these details of part-writing were guided by inexorable rules, though it was not long before the domination of modern tonality brought in its train a set of traditions no less rigid than the forgotten pedantry of the past, so that Burney, secure in the conventions of the eighteenth century, could look askance—and sometimes with justice—at Purcell's contempt for formality.

The early full anthems—some of them written in as many as eight parts—stand to the rest of Purcell's church music much as the string fantasias do to his later instrumental work. They represent, for all their skill and dignity, the artificial fostering of a tradition that was already out of date. Looking at them now with an eye for their intrinsic value rather than for their historical

significance we can appreciate them as noble examples of polyphony. But to Purcell's more advanced contemporaries they must
have had a slightly antiquated flavour. They are not, of course,
exclusively contrapuntal in style. Homophony, or the simul-
taneous movement of all the parts, is not despised any more than
it was by the Elizabethans. It is often used, as in the last section of
O God, Thou hast cast us out, to provide a contrast to the subsequent
dispersal of the voices in strict and close imitation; and sometimes, as in the second half of *O God, Thou art my God,* whole
sections are homophonic in character. Not even these full
anthems could remain free from the tendencies of the time. One
of the later examples, *I will sing unto the Lord,* which was written
before 1683, is not only mainly homophonic, but also shows the
influence of secular song which made itself felt so much more
strongly in the verse anthem. Of the purely polyphonic full
anthems one of the noblest, *Hear my prayer,* is unfortunately
incomplete; only the first movement survives. What remains is
a masterly example of the expressive value of counterpoint in the
hands of a skilled craftsman.

The days of the full anthem were numbered. For the development of Purcell's style as a composer for the church we must turn
to his verse anthems, with or without string accompaniment.
Here we find quite early not only an imitation of the declamatory
style adopted by Humfrey but also a tendency to copy the decora-
tive trimmings of Italian opera, as in the introductory bass solo
to *O Lord, Thou art my God* and in a three-part verse setting of the
word 'Hallelujah' later in the same work.

Declamation, it should be noted, is not confined to a single
voice, but in accordance with the custom of the period is often
divided among the separate parts.

The earliest of the anthems with string accompaniment are
My beloved spake and *Behold now, praise the Lord.* Both of them
already show the typical characteristics of the form: an instrumental introduction, similar in style to the Italian and French
opera overtures, sections for individual singers with organ accompaniment, verses for groups of solo voices and a jubilant choral

finale. The style of the instrumental writing is not yet mature and the old harmonic traditions still linger, giving to the music what seems to the modern listener a pleasant suggestion of antiquity, but in breadth and dignity these overtures and symphonies already foreshadow Purcell's later achievements. The epithet 'secular' has generally been applied with damning implication to these movements by people who can never have heard them performed. Here, as in the great majority of Purcell's anthems in this style, the instrumental symphonies are closely linked up with the general structure of the music; it is a great mistake to regard them as irrelevant. The vocal writing also remains attached to some extent to the older traditions; but *My beloved spake* also contains an example of the new homophonic style in which all the joyousness of secular song is brought into the service of the church's hymn of praise and thanksgiving:

The form of the Purcellian anthem with strings is similar to that of the royal welcome songs, though the variety of subject-matter results in something different from the pomposity of those tributes to a patron. The whole manner and execution of these elaborate offerings to God is akin to the spirit of Renaissance architecture. It is impossible to feel that they are intended solely for the glory of God. They are there also to be noted and approved by man; there is an element of ostentatious magnificence that is wholly absent from the church music of the Elizabethans. Restoration church music, like the secular music of the time, came into line with the changes that had already taken place in Italy, where all the splendours of elaborate choral and orchestral forces had for long been used by the Venetian masters to sing God's praises, in much the same way as the scene-painter and the engineer put forth all their energies to win the favour of their ducal employers. 'In Quires and Places where they sing,' says the 1662 Prayer Book after the third collect, 'here followeth the Anthem'; and for enthusiastic amateurs like Pepys it was no less an important part of the service than the sermon. In days when public concerts were still a comparative novelty the Chapel Royal, like the Theatre Royal, was regarded as a place where one could hear good music performed by some of the best musicians in the kingdom.

The majority of Purcell's verse anthems appear to be not later than 1685. One or two are dated 1687 and 1688 and three belong to the last three years of his life. If we remember that practically the whole of his best work in other fields of composition falls in the reign of William III and Mary—that is to say, between the years 1689 and 1695—we shall not be surprised to find that most of the verse anthems are inferior works. The reason for this is the same as for the tentative experimentation that marks the earlier welcome odes. Purcell had broken with the old style, in which he had produced some memorable music, and the full mastery of the new style was necessarily a slow and laborious business. It is obvious, too, from an inspection of these anthems, that he had views on the character of music intended for the church. He hardly ever uses the ground bass, which is such a familiar feature in his other work, and there is practically nothing to correspond to the set arias, with their fresh and genial flow of melody, that we find in the odes and the dramatic music. The principal object of the anthem was to provide an adequate musical setting of the words and to enable worshippers to appreciate the significance of the Psalmist's text, which incidentally was much easier to follow in the new style than in the old, where the meaning was often obscured by the interlacing of the parts.

Purcell's dramatic talent had little scope in the anthem, because he was dealing with words, not with a situation. An exception is the coronation anthem, *My heart is inditing,* where the magnificence of the ceremony clearly appealed to his imagination and led to the production of a piece that must have matched the splendour of the scene. He has often been extravagantly praised for his just accentuation of words, but this was not his peculiar virtue. The whole essence of the monodic ideal which had helped to produce opera and oratorio and swept Europe in triumph was faithful adherence to the text. Purcell would not have been a child of his time if he had done differently. So too with those rather naïve musical illustrations of particular words, such as 'high,' 'down,' 'storm' and the like. Picturesque tone-painting of this kind was as old as the madrigalian period, and Purcell's examples are in no way remarkable.

This preoccupation with the text and a natural conception of the dignity of church music precluded anything like a transference to his anthems of the style that he was developing in his secular music. The so-called 'secular' character of Purcell's verse anthems derives from a secularization, if it may be called so, that had already taken place abroad—in Italy. The cult of monody and the rise of the virtuoso singer had induced Italian church composers to introduce into their works the style that was dominating secular music, but not without regard for propriety. What we regard as 'frivolous' would more properly have been described as 'brilliant.' Those long roulades, those endless passages in thirds, those brisk, mercurial choruses that we find in Carissimi were no less serious in intention than the declamatory pathos to which they provided a natural antithesis. What is striking about Purcell's verse anthems is not that they are 'frivolous,' but that so many of them are dull—dull with the unthinking acceptance of stereotyped formulas. The endless trios for counter-tenor, tenor and bass, the continual successions of thirds, both in the major and the minor keys, and the frequently meandering recitative combine to produce a kind of grey uniformity. The acceptance of modern tonality brought with it a more rigid system of harmonic progressions, and the 'audacities' of the earlier period disappeared in favour of a conventional respectability.

This development in the style of Purcell's anthems is naturally gradual. In the earlier examples the instruments play an important part, not only in the symphonies, which are sometimes repeated in the course of an anthem, but also in accompanying the voices. In O *praise God in His holiness,* for instance, we find a violin obbligato to the bass solo, 'Praise him on the well-tuned cymbals,' and at the four-part verse, 'Let every thing that hath breath,' two string parts are added above the voices, producing free imitation in six parts. In his choral writing he shows a growing appreciation of the massive style of the Venetians, in which impressiveness is obtained not by ingenuity of part-writing but by the full weight of a mass of voices or the suggestive antiphony of contrasted groups. There is a good example in *Praise the Lord, O my soul, and all that is within me,* where the upper voices are answered by the lower, the strings reply and the whole of the six voices answer.

The finest example of this massive style is the anthem for James II's coronation, *My heart is inditing of a good matter.* On this occasion Purcell had the use of two choirs and could write on a lavish scale. The voices are in eight parts, with string accompaniment. Though the work is technically a verse anthem, Purcell also falls back in places—particularly in the stately opening —on the old polyphonic style of the full anthem, enriching it with string accompaniment. The elaborate part-writing is sometimes in his earlier manner, in which the free movement of the voices results in thick and occasionally curious successions of chords, as in the following extract, the opening of which is in the antiphonal style (*see opposite page*).

The instrumental writing in this anthem has a noble breadth and dignity. The ritornello of the section 'Instead of thy fathers

Massive Antiphony

thou shalt have children' has something of the same irresistible
sweep that characterizes the opening of Bach's St. Matthew
Passion. Best of all is the finale, in which the voices and
instruments answer each other like the tolling of some magnificent peal of bells. The effect in performance of this
tremendous climax must have been overwhelming. It begins
simply:

and increases in intensity as it proceeds. Before long the bells become more insistent, and the minims break into joyful crotchets. The new motion spreads through the whole ensemble of voices and instruments, till the very building seems to be singing 'Allelujah':

The concluding bars triumphantly set the seal on all that has gone before, with the basses plunging dramatically to a low E.[1]

These repeated 'allelujahs' are a typical mannerism of the

[1] See the reproduction of this passage in plates between pp. 84 and 85.

period. I have already quoted an example from William Child. The effect, it must be admitted, is apt to be perfunctory; but often the simple repetition is given an added significance, as here, by the introduction of suspensions. It should be remembered, too, that the organist probably sustained these chords and provided a solid background to the choral ejaculations. Sometimes the 'alle-lujahs' are divided between solo voices, as in *In Thee, O Lord, do I put my trust,* which belongs to the same period as *My heart is inditing*:

This is certainly not an inspired setting; but its weakness lies not in the 'frivolity' of the vocal parts but in the unfruitful stodginess of the ground bass.

In the midst of much that is conventional in these anthems there are moments when a more personal expression is introduced, when the light of day, so to speak, is allowed entrance into the cathedral atmosphere. Such, for instance, is the characteristic setting of the words 'sorrow and mourning' in *Awake, awake, put on thy strength* or this poignant fragment of recitative from *Praise the Lord, O my soul, and all that is within me*:

are __ but dust, He remem - b'reth that __ we are but dust.

Sometimes a harmonic progression is used to add picturesqueness, in the Italian manner, as in *Let God arise*, an early verse anthem without orchestra, where Purcell introduces the juxtaposition of the apparently unrelated chords of A major and C minor—a dramatic device that had already been used with great effect by Peri and Monteverdi.[1] Or again, in *Blessed is he that considereth the poor*, one of the later anthems, we have a curiously suggestive example of the effect that can be achieved by independent move- ment of the parts:

The Lord com - fort him, when he li - eth sick __ up - on his bed

Continuo

Compare the strangely modern effect of the following, from the dramatic anthem, *Why do the heathen rage?*:

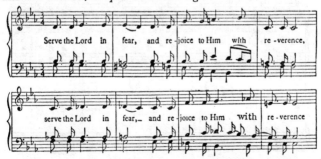

Serve the Lord in fear, and re - joice to Him with re - verence,

serve the Lord in fear, __ and re - joice to Him with re - verence

---

[1] See my paper, *The Originality of Monteverdi*, in the Proceedings of the Musical Association, 1933–4, pp. 5–6 and 14–16.

Of florid writing there is an abundance, or rather a superfluity. That was the penalty Purcell paid for living in an age when 'graces' were thought to be an inseparable constituent of the singer's art.

The anthem that marks his most whole-hearted adoption of what may be called the Italian oratorio manner, foreshadowing Handel's later achievements, is *O sing unto the Lord,* which dates from 1688. Here the solemnity typical of the 'French' overture is replaced by the simpler, more direct style of the Italian sonata. The vocal writing not only shows a mastery of the homophonic style and the contrast of voices and instruments, as in the following example (where the bass already has the contours characteristic of the early eighteenth century):

but also the new polyphony, instrumental in origin, in which the movement of the parts is conditioned by the harmonic frame-

216

work, in contrast to the old contrapuntal style in which the part-writing largely determined the harmony.

The solos in these verse anthems are generally for counter-tenor, tenor and bass, though one or more soprano parts are occasionally introduced. The anthem *My song shall be alway of the lovingkindness* (1688?) was published for soprano solo by Playford but in the best manuscript scores is for bass. It is unlikely that there was a boy at the Chapel Royal capable of doing justice to this elaborate solo, since if there had been Purcell would not have hesitated to provide for him in other anthems. If the work was in fact written for a soprano, the soloist must have been a visitor, perhaps the eunuch Siface.[1] His introduction into the Chapel Royal would have been an irregularity, but not impossible under a Roman Catholic king, and the fact that Purcell commemorated his departure from England in a little harpsichord piece seems to point to an intimate acquaintanceship. It is perhaps significant that the solo as printed is actually for a mezzo-soprano, the compass being from B below middle C to E on the fourth space. The most remarkable of the solos in the verse anthems are those for bass. Here Purcell had the opportunity of writing for an exceptional singer, and used it to the full. A passage like the following, from *I will give thanks unto thee, O Lord*, is not to be attempted by any ordinary bass:

and there are trials more exacting, though of a less severe compass, than this. A visit to the Chapel Royal on Sunday must have been worth while if only to hear the Reverend John Gostling negotiate such prickly obstacles.

Similar in style to the English anthems are the two Latin psalms—*Beati omnes qui timent Dominum,* with its florid final 'Hallelujah,' and the stately *Jehovah, quam multi.* The settings of non-Bible words, generally referred to as 'hymns,' are in quite a different category. The texts are in many cases taken from Patrick's metrical versions of the psalms. In these pieces, which were probably intended for private devotional use, there is an intimacy of approach and an intensity of personal expression that we rarely meet with in the anthems. The extraordinary opening of *Plung'd in the confines of despair*—a striking use of chromaticism and the diminished fifth—is typical of the composer's imaginative sincerity and technical freedom. The harmonic progressions seem to be the product of a desire to extract every ounce of pathos from the words, to create in sound a true outlet for emotion

Here too, as in the anthems, there are humdrum things; but the best of the 'hymns'—such as *Lord, I can suffer, O, I'm sick of life,* and in particular the subtle and intricate *Ah! few and full of sorrow* —have a rare beauty, a flavour curiously remote from what we are accustomed to call Purcellian. Unique among these works is the dramatic scena, *In guilty night,* which was published by Playford in the second book of *Harmonia Sacra.* This is in effect a miniature oratorio for three voices on the subject of Saul's visit to the Witch of Endor, a solitary example of a genre that Purcell nowhere else attempted. The piece is remarkable for its occasional suggestion of an atmosphere commonly supposed to be the product of nineteenthcentury romanticism, as in the setting of the introductory narrative (*see page* 218) and again in the wild desolate echo of the final farewell.

Of Purcell's services only one complete setting survives—the *Morning and Evening Service* in B flat major, which includes all the alternative canticles as well as the Kyrie and the Nicene Creed. The date is before 1683, and the style, though largely homophonic, is founded on the old sober traditions of church music. At the same time there are signs of a more uptodate inclination—for example, in the setting of 'sing, rejoice and give thanks' in the *Cantate Domino,* and in an occasional freedom of harmonic development. At the words, 'Thy saving health among all nations,' in the *Deus Misereatur,* the independent chromatic movement of the parts produces a curiously acid progression. In general this service is a finely dignified piece of work and one of the best examples of Purcell's early church music. The effects are often achieved in the simplest way, by the alternation of upper and lower voices; but the music flows so smoothly and is so aptly fitted to the words that the result is far more impressive than many a more pretentious work. A passage like the setting of 'Let the sea make a noise' shows plainly enough Purcell's inheritance of the old ecclesiastical tradition. There are also a number of ingenious canons—pure music, not crabbed puzzles—to delight the craftsman's heart. In the G minor *Magnificat and Nunc Dimittis,* a separate work, Purcell relaxes the austerity of the severe style to give an oddly nostalgic turn to the final 'Amen' of the second canticle[1]:

The D major *Te Deum and Jubilate*, written for the celebration of St. Cecilia's Day, 1694, is one of Purcell's essays in the grand manner. It was much admired by Tudway and subsequently by Burney,[2] and for many years enjoyed the popularity accorded to a recognized masterpiece. It cannot be denied, however, that its plush and gilt have faded with the passage of time. The reiteration of the chord of D major, however glorious the choir and however magnificent the trumpet-playing, no longer excites us as it did Purcell's contemporaries and the audiences of the eighteenth century, to whom such magnificence was still novel and striking. The weakness of the *Te Deum and Jubilate* is not merely its reliance on largely superficial effects but also the disconnected structure of the whole. The continual succession of short movements—some very short indeed—destroys any impression of unity. The most striking moment in the work is not the jaunty trumpet solo that introduces the *Jubilate* nor the sonorous

---

[1] In a manuscript found in the Song School at York the *Gloria* of this *Nunc Dimittis* is attributed to 'Mr. Rosengrave junior.'

[2] Brit. Mus., Harl. 7342, fo. 12; Burney, vol. iii. pp. 484–6 *bis*.

tutti on 'Holy, holy, holy' that induced such rapture in Tudway, but the setting for soprano and alto of 'We are his people, and the sheep of his pasture':

Not pride in man's achievement but the humility of God's creation is the key-note of this searching dialogue.

CHAPTER XV

INSTRUMENTAL WORKS

PURCELL'S importance as an instrumental composer has already been mentioned. Practically all his orchestral music is associated with the stage or forms part of his odes and anthems; and the few independent pieces that survive—which may, indeed, have belonged originally to larger works now lost—do not call for particular mention. What remains to be discussed is the chamber music: works for two or more instruments and solos for harpsichord and organ. The concerted chamber music falls into two clear-cut divisions. On the one hand we have the fantasias for strings, which appear to have been written in 1680, on the other the two sets of sonatas for two violins, bass and continuo, published in 1683 and 1697 respectively. The fantasias, like the 'full' anthems, represent Purcell's early attachment to the old traditions; the sonatas are typical of his study of the latest Italian style.

The fantasia, or 'fancy' as it was generally called in England, had enjoyed great popularity at the end of the sixteenth and throughout the seventeenth century. Unlike those madrigals which for convenience were published as 'apt for viols and voices,' it was purely instrumental music, even though in origin it may have been associated with the old vocal polyphony. Its name sufficiently describes its style and purpose. The composer was not tied to a plainsong *canto fermo,* as in the type of composition known as 'In Nomine,' but could give free rein to his imagination. The essence of the style was imitation. A simple thematic fragment would be developed by means of all the devices known to the contrapuntists of the time. Canon, augmentation, inversion and diminution were employed in ingenious combination; and when the possibilities of the first theme had been exhausted, a second would take its place, so to speak, in the ring. These imitative sections of the fancy were the forerunners of the eighteenth-century fugue. They were at once a challenge to the composer's technique and to his imagination, and it is not surprising that many who could answer the first demand were unequal to the second.

Like the madrigal, the fancy was music that appealed first and foremost to the performers; the prime delight was to be found in pursuing a single part with the ever-present consciousness of the rival association of the others. So potent, so enduring was this delight that the form survived the turmoils of the Civil War, continued to be practised during the Commonwealth and still had a following in the early years of the Restoration. It could not, however, survive the intrusion of the new concerted style from abroad. With the introduction of the French and Italian instrumental music it fell out of fashion. By the eighteenth century the fancy, with its kindred forms, had become an antique. The paper on which the once popular pieces were written might be useful for making kites or stoking the kitchen fire, but hardly any one but a conscious antiquarian would have dreamed of playing them.[1]

The contributory causes of change were the decline of the consort of viols and the adoption of the *basso continuo*. During the early part of the seventeenth century the violin, though it was already known in England and established at court, had not yet conquered the amateur circles for which instrumental chamber music was primarily composed. The instrument of the ordinary music-lover was the viol, and it was for the consort of viols that fancies and similar pieces were written. It was customary to accompany the viols on a chamber organ, but the player did not originally improvise his own accompaniment from a figured bass, as in the new music that was coming over from Italy; he was given a special organ part to play from.[2] About the middle of the century the violin began to gain ground, and even the most conservative musicians were induced to consider its possibilities. Anthony Wood, a keen chamber-music player, who had hitherto

[1] North, *Musicall Gramarian*, pp. 12–13.
[2] North, *Musicall Gramarian*, p. 28, *Autobiography*, p. 69; Mace, *Musick's Monument* (1676), pp. 234 and 242.

confined his attention to the viol, started teaching himself the violin and tuned it in fourths by analogy; but it was not long before he began to study it with a competent teacher.[1] The technical skill of men like Baltzar and Mell also helped to encourage the popularity of the violin among amateurs. Meanwhile in Italy the old instrumental music in several parts had been supplanted by a simpler form, in which a keyboard instrument took the place of what had been the middle parts of the polyphony. The new violin literature not only demanded an adequate technique from string players; it also involved the skilled co-operation of the accompanist, who had to interpret the shorthand of the figured bass.

With these new developments fancies for the viols were already at the Restoration a survival from a past age. Indeed Purcell's fantasias are the last known examples of the form. Attempts have been made recently to show that consort music was written for the violin family, and that Purcell's pieces are illustrations of this practice.[2] But the evidence is very meagre, and the proved examples so rare that they may be regarded as exceptions. Thomas Mace, writing in Charles II's reign, speaks of 'whole' consort music as viol music, without any qualification.[3] He allows the music-lover to add to his chest of viols 'a *Pair* of *Violins,* to be in Readiness for any *Extraordinary Jolly,* or *Jocund Consort-Occasion,*' but he refuses to admit them as normal members of the consort, and objects to them in general on the ground that they upset the balance of parts.[4] It is true that Matthew Locke's *Little Consort* in three parts (written in 1651 and published in 1656) was issued for viols or violins; but that seems to have been merely an attempt to make the best of both worlds, and players had the choice between performing them alone or with theorbos and harpsichord.

[1] Wood, *Life and Times,* vol. i, pp. 173, 178, 181, 212.

[2] Hayes, *Musical Instruments,* vol. ii, pp. 193–4; Holland, *Henry Purcell,* p. 138.

[3] A 'whole' consort was one composed of instruments of the same family. A combination of strings and wind was known as a 'broken' consort.

[4] *Musick's Monument,* pp. 236 and 246.

Even in the new concerted violin music the bass part was quite commonly played not on the cello but on the bass viol.[1]

The theory that Purcell's fantasias were written for a violin consort involves the assumption that the old tenor violin (tuned a fourth below the viola) was used, since in the seventh of the four-part pieces the third instrument of the quartet descends to B, a semitone below the viola's bottom string; and equally the second part, which frequently goes below the violin G, would have to be played by the viola. But no evidence has been produced to show that the tenor violin—the 'true' tenor, as it is called by enthusiasts—was normally used in England at this time. Playford, in the 1687 edition of his *Introduction to the Skill of Musick*, gives the name 'tenor' to what we call the viola, and makes no mention of any instrument between this and the bass; and Anthony Wood speaks of only three kinds of violin—treble, tenor and bass.[2] All Purcell's four-part orchestral music is written for the string quartet as we know it; when he wrote in five parts, as in the Queen Mary odes for 1689 and 1690, he added either a third violin or a second viola. For want of any specific evidence to the contrary we may assume that the fantasias were written for viols, and that the four-part pieces were played on two trebles, a tenor and a bass. In the second four-part fantasia the lowest string of the bass-viol must be tuned down to C, which was quite a customary procedure in consort music.[3] Otherwise the parts lie within the normal compass of the instruments. Arguments from style have been adduced in support of the violin theory, but they prove very little. It would be quite natural for viol music to be affected by violin technique, much as modern organ music shows the influence of the pianoforte.[4]

[1] Playford's advertisement of Purcell's *Sonatas of III Parts* in *Choice Ayres, Songs and Dialogues*, book v (1684), describes them as written 'for two *Violins* and *Bass-Viol*.'

[2] *Life and Times*, vol. i, p. 212 (January 1657).

[3] Dolmetsch, *The Interpretation of the Music of the Seventeenth and Eighteenth Centuries*, p. 449.

[4] In transcribing the four-part fantasias for string quartet, Peter Warlock was compelled to interchange the second and third parts

Purcell's fantasias are contained in an autograph volume of his compositions now in the British Museum.[1] There are three in three parts, nine in four parts, and one in five parts. In addition there are two in six and seven parts respectively, which are actually 'In Nomines.' It is clear, however, from the large number of pages left blank that Purcell intended a much more comprehensive collection of pieces. The importance he attached to his work may be gathered not only from the scrupulously careful scores, but also from the fact that every one of the four-part fantasias is dated with the year, month and day. The fragment of a tenth four-part fantasia, dated three years later (1683), suggests that he had some idea of completing his scheme; but there is nothing to show that he wrote more than what we actually possess.

In structure the fantasias are traditional. The expert handling of all the problems of contrapuntal imitation proves that Purcell at twenty-one had already fully mastered the art of writing in the old style. But in intensity of expression they are far in advance of the average compositions of this kind, and the idiom is both modern and personal. Purcell has used a traditional form not simply as a bony framework on which to erect an equally bony structure but as a vehicle for a warm and vivid imagination. The simplest passages, like this little canon at close quarters in the ninth fantasia, are charged with feeling:

Purcell employs the most complicated devices with perfect ease. The following example from the first fantasia is typical. The subject is heard in augmentation in the third part, after the fashion

whenever the second goes below the compass of the violin. This was a pity, as it spoils the independence of the parts; the pieces could easily have been issued for violin, two violas and cello, with alternative parts for occasions when two violas are not available.

[1] Add. 30930.

of a *canto fermo*, while the other instruments make play with it above and beneath, first in direct imitation and then by inversion:

By contrast there are sections where the writing is more homo-phonic in character, and here the opportunity is taken to introduce the most subtle harmonic progressions. The short section marked 'Drag' in the eighth fantasia is an illuminating example of Purcell's art of colour:

Purcell

The tonality shifts like the gentle gradations of pastel shades merging one into another. In a similar section in the first fantasia he employs a bolder transition, starting on B flat and running through a whole series of keys before coming to rest on a chord of D major.

In the five-part *Fantasia upon One Note* Purcell has set himself a more severe problem. The fourth part consists solely of middle C, repeated in every bar, round which the other four instruments weave a cunning embroidery, first in minims and then in increasing note-values until scurrying semiquavers are heard dancing above and below the still-repeated monotone. In the six-part and seven-part fantasias he has used the traditional plainsong on which the old composers constructed their 'In Nomines.' Here the style is severe and dignified; the end of the seven-part fantasia is a noble piece of polyphony, the dark colour of the bass instruments contrasting with the more brilliant trebles (the repeated D's in the third part are the end of the *canto fermo*):

The same manuscript also contains a four-part chaconne—or, as Purcell calls it, a chacony—in G minor, and a pavan in the same key, in which the four instruments discourse with exquisite gravity; the close imitation over a chromatic bass is beautifully managed:

In the two sets of sonatas Purcell turns from the traditional technique of the viol consort to the new concerted style that had grown up in Italy. This style is both polyphonic and harmonic; the string parts indulge in imitation and fugue, while the keyboard instrument—organ or harpsichord—supplies the chordal background. This new polyphony was constantly cultivated by composers throughout the latter half of the seventeenth and the early part of the eighteenth century and reached its climax in the astonishing virtuosity of Bach's concertos and cantatas. Purcell's first set is entitled *Sonatas of III Parts,* the second, *Sonatas of IV*

Parts—a confusing system of nomenclature which has been known to puzzle even professed students of the composer's work. The truth is that there is no difference whatever in the forces employed. Both sets have string parts for two violins and bass (whether bass viol or cello) and both were issued with figured-bass parts for the accompanist. Either set might equally well be called *Sonatas of III Parts* or *Sonatas of IV Parts*. In the first set, for instance, the string bass part is by no means identical with the figured bass throughout, and in the *largo* of the fifth sonata a whole section is in four parts, the lowest being provided by the continuo. In his preface Purcell explains that he had not originally intended to have the figured bass engraved—a very curious observation in view of this and similar passages.

Earlier in the preface, which I have quoted in full on page 47, he claims that he has 'faithfully endeavour'd a just imitation of the most fam'd Italian Masters; principally, to bring the seriousness and gravity of that sort of Musick into vogue, and reputation among our Country-men, whose humor, 'tis time now, should begin to loath the levity, and balladry of our neighbours.' The second half of this sentence is supposed, quite reasonably, to refer to the French. But it is impossible not to feel that Purcell's remark is a little too self-righteous. It is true that the French had no instrumental music to compare with the Italian; but 'levity and balladry' are quite unjustifiably hard terms to use of French music, which was often characterized by great dignity and serious-ness. As for levity, Purcell himself has left us a sufficient amount of frolicsome music to give a flavour of hypocrisy to his charge, and on occasion he was even capable of descending to balladry.[1]

There has been quite unnecessary speculation as to the models Purcell took for these sonatas. Unnecessary, since he answered the question himself: his models were 'the most fam'd Italian Masters.' He did not have to go very far afield. The Italian musicians who had made London their home would naturally

[1] It is quite possible that the preface to these sonatas was written for Purcell by Playford, just as the dedication to *Dioclesian* was written by Dryden (see p. 69, n. 1). But in both cases the composer may be presumed to have endorsed the sentiments expressed.

bring over quantities of new manuscripts from Italy, and wealthy music-lovers were eager to import the latest novelties for their private practice.[1] A manuscript in the British Museum,[2] dated 1680 and bearing the name of its owner, Sir Gabriel Roberts, contains a whole set of twenty-two Italian sonatas; and in the following year Playford was able to inform his clients that he had in stock 'a large Collection of the new Instrumental Musick for two Trebles and Bass,'[3] which may quite plausibly be held to include such importations from abroad. Long before this English composers had written music for violins and continuo. John Jenkins is credited with the publication of twelve sonatas for two violins, bass and continuo in 1660, and William Young's, published at Innsbruck in 1653, anticipated Purcell's by thirty years.[4] It is not without interest that Young returned to England at the Restoration or earlier and became a member of the king's band of violins.[5]

There were two types of sonata in the seventeenth century: the *sonata da chiesa* or church sonata, and the *sonata da camera* or chamber sonata. The first, as its name implies, was supposed to be more severe in style, though naturally it could not remain immune from secular influences and soon became a purely secular form itself. The second consisted of a succession of dance movements, which were theoretically excluded from the church sonata, though dance rhythms were not infrequently found there. The *sonata da chiesa* was the ancestor of the classical sonata, while the *sonata da camera* was associated rather with the development of the suite. The typical examples of both forms are to be found in the work of Purcell's Italian contemporary, Arcangelo Corelli. Purcell's sonatas belong to the first type; the *largo* movements, like Corelli's, sometimes recall the rhythm of the sarabande, but they are not specifically dance movements. As standardized in Italy the *sonata*

---

[1] North, *Memoirs*, p. 105. [2] Add. 31431.

[3] Advertisement in *Choice Ayres, Songs and Dialogues*, book iii (1681).

[4] A modern edition, by W. G. Whittaker, is published by the Oxford University Press.

[5] *King's Musick*, p. 123, etc.

da chiesa had four movements, arranged in two contrasted pairs: a slow introduction, an *allegro,* a *largo,* and a brisk finale. This scheme, however, was not exclusively followed. Thus the sixth sonata of Corelli's Op. 3 begins with a *vivace,* followed by a *grave,* and then continues with two allegros, separated merely by two bars of *adagio.* Purcell's sonatas show a great variety of structure. The first sonata of the first set, for example, has a fifth movement—a *largo* in sarabande rhythm—after the normal four; in the fifth sonata of the same set three slow movements are sandwiched between two quick ones, and so on. One exceptional sonata—the sixth of the second set—is in one movement, an extended chaconne. Among the allegros we frequently find a canzona, the name given to a brisk fugal movement, in which the counter-subject sometimes appears simultaneously with the subject. Purcell's dramatic music contains examples of the same form.

Dr. Alfred Einstein has said of the *sonata da chiesa* that 'it recalls the heroic atmosphere and elegiac mood of Poussin's landscapes.'[1] The comparison is brilliantly apt and may well be applied to Purcell's sonatas in particular. It is the formal beauty that strikes the listener most, the interplay of voices, the pattern of contrasts, the mingling of fine craftsmanship with a clear-sighted imagination. Emotion there is in plenty; Purcell, like his contemporaries, was well aware of the poignant effect of chromaticism and knew better than most of them how to give harmony those unexpected turns that wring the heart and enchant the ear. But emotion never breaks down the bounds of a classic restraint; there is no wallowing in self-surrender, no parade of self-revelation. This is pure music in the sense that it makes no pretence of telling a story. Associations there must have been in the composer's mind and may well be in ours. But that is a matter for individual fantasy; the music is what matters.

Superficially the sonatas of 1683 may seem to be a complete break with the old tradition, but a close inspection will show many minor points of resemblance with the fantasias. The

[1] *A Short History of Music* (English trans.), p. 90.

technique is different in its reliance on the *basso continuo* and in the use of a less rigid system of imitation, but details here and there unmistakably recall the older manner. The opening of the first sonata is a clear echo of the earlier style:

By contrast the next movement is an uncompromising imitation of the Italian sonata:

The influence of Italian composers is to be seen too in such details as successions of sixths and skips for the violins, of which the following passage from the second sonata supplies examples:

and in the adoption of what are sometimes described as 'neutral' subjects for fugal movements.

In general the quick movements are the more severe in style; the principal interest is in the neat handling of the counterpoint. The opening of the sixth sonata, where there is a canon by twofold augmentation in the fifth and octave above, has often been quoted. Here is another example, less complex but no less delightful, from the tenth sonata:

Neat joinery of this kind seems so inevitable that one is apt to ignore the necessity for working at it in the first place. Even in the quick movements Purcell exploits chromaticism. In the canzona of the seventh sonata he introduces a new chromatic counter-subject half-way through and ingeniously combines it with his diatonic subject. But the slow movements are the chief glory of these sonatas. The tranquil gravity and rich colouring of the largos and adagios make them a noble contribution in themselves to the literature of chamber music. More than once the magnificent repose of Purcell's cadences recalls the slow arias of Handel's operas. A passage like this, from the eighth sonata, is like a bridge between the work of two masters:

The second set of sonatas, published by Mrs. Purcell two years after her husband's death, contains some examples that show a riper mastery and a further development of technical resources,

while others seem in mood and idiom more akin to the first
set. It is quite possible that the sonatas of this set were composed
at different times and finally reassembled for publication. An
autograph fair copy of several of them is in the British Museum
manuscript already mentioned, but this gives no clue to their date.
Here, too, the slow movements contain a wealth of fine music.
One may mention particularly the lovely B minor *largo* of the
first sonata and the *adagio* of the ninth (known for some reason as
the 'Golden' Sonata), both of which are built up on successions
of appoggiaturas treated with consummate skill and imagination.
Splendid, too, in its breadth and dignity is the G minor chaconne
that forms the whole of the sixth sonata; nothing in it is more
effective than the entrance of the *ostinato* in canon on the violins
above its untiring repetition in the bass. In the more mature
sonatas Purcell seems to plunge boldly into the eighteenth century
with a fine gesture of anticipation. The end of the opening
adagio of the second sonata:

is curiously similar in mood to a passage from 'He was despised' in
Handel's *Messiah*. Compare, too, this figure from the same sonata:

with the texture of Bach's organ Fugue in D major. Beside these
sonatas we may fitly place the single sonata for violin and continuo in G minor, a mature work in Purcell's unmistakable
manner.

It is sometimes said that Purcell's trio sonatas are not typically violin music, the implication being that he was imperfectly acquainted with the instrument. Attention is drawn to the absence of any material for exercising the virtuoso's skill and to the limited compass employed. This opinion is quite unfounded. Purcell's trio sonatas are just as much—or as little—violin music as Corelli's. In Corelli's Op. 3, for instance, only one of the sonatas, the twelfth, has anything higher than D (third position on the E string), and only in this sonata is there anything that would appeal particularly to the virtuoso—and that in spite of the fact that Corelli was one of the foremost players of the day. The truth is that the trio sonata was primarily chamber music, not a vehicle for the virtuoso's skill. If Purcell had wanted to write virtuoso violin music he could easily have done so. Whether he played the instrument himself is quite beside the point. He must have heard Matteis and other eminent players, and his position as composer for the king's violins gave him ample opportunity for learning all there was to be known about the technique of violin playing. The difference between Purcell's and Corelli's trio sonatas is not so much in the style of writing for the instruments as in mood. In so far as one can generalize, it may be said that Corelli's movements have a greater fluidity, a more genial suavity than Purcell's, the suggestion, as it were, of a more generous clime. Perhaps something of this was in Roger North's mind when he spoke of Purcell's 'Noble set of Sonnatas, which however clog'd with somewhat of an English vein—for which they are unworthily despised — are very artificiall and good Musick.'[1] For English listeners and players that 'English vein' is one of Purcell's principal attractions.

Purcell's compositions for keyboard instruments are relatively unimportant. The organ voluntary on the *Old Hundredth* (the tune of 'All people that on earth do dwell') is interesting as an early example of the chorale prelude, but does not represent

[1] *An Essay of Musicall Ayre* (Brit. Mus., Add. 32536, fo. 78ᵛ). North is probably referring to the first set. 'Artificiall' has the same meaning as the German *kunstvoll*, i.e. 'full of craftsmanship.'

Purcell at his best; and the same may be said of the other organ pieces (if indeed they are his), which in the fashion of the time are concerned mostly with brilliant excursions. Of the harpsichord pieces the most important are the little suites published by Mrs. Purcell with a dedication to Princess Anne in 1696. These consist of dance movements in the manner already established in *Melothesia* (1673), a miscellaneous collection of suites by Locke and other composers. Purcell's examples are slight and sometimes inconclusive, as though he had become uncertain of his direction; but the best of them are worthy predecessors of Bach's French and English suites. Here we have the rambling, quasi-improvisatory prelude, with imitation between right and left hand, the easy-flowing allemande, the lively courante, with its little subtleties of rhythm, and the grave sarabande. These are the principal movements, but there are also examples of the hornpipe and the minuet. The link that binds the seventeenth to the eighteenth century can be clearly seen in this allemande from the eighth suite:

which should be compared with the similar movement in the same key in the fourth of Bach's English Suites.

Mrs. Purcell added to her collection five shorter pieces, of which four are arrangements from the dramatic music. Several more pieces were published by Playford in Purcell's lifetime in the second part of *Musick's Hand-Maid* (1689), and a number of others have been collected in our own day from various sources. These too include arrangements from the dramatic music as well as settings of popular songs. There is nothing here of any great significance, though a handful of these gay and dainty movements will pleasantly while away an odd half-hour or so at the keyboard. The most ambitious movement is the A major Toccata, a dashing virtuoso piece that calls for a fully developed technique. Whether it is really by Purcell is another matter. In one manuscript [1] it is attributed to Michele Angelo Rossi, and certainly the style is curiously different from that of the rest of Purcell's keyboard works.

[1] Brit. Mus., Add. 24313, fo. 16[v].

CHAPTER XVI

STYLE AND DEVELOPMENT

PURCELL has been called a child of his age. The phrase is a platitude. What great composer has not been a child of his age? Bach, Handel, Mozart, Beethoven—to go no further—each was a phenomenon inseparable from the time in which he lived. We sometimes hear talk about the music of the future. But the music of the future is not written by the great composers; they are too busy making the most of the present. It is the restless, self-conscious, second-rate composers who are constrained to conceal the poverty of their invention by adopting the deceptive mask of novelty. The great composer may be bold—as Wagner was in *Tristan,* and Beethoven in the last quartets—but he does not step outside the frame of his period; and it follows naturally that the great composers are admired and appreciated by their contemporaries. Not, perhaps, by all their contemporaries; but there is nothing surprising in that. There are always people who are too stupid to see greatness even when it is put in front of their noses—or perhaps just because it is put in front of their noses. Granted, however, that our phrase about 'the child of his age' is a platitude, it is none the less a useful one. It is one of the commonest errors of ill-informed criticism to mistake the common-places of a period for individual mannerisms. Thus turns of phrase are quite commonly called 'Mozartian' which are nothing but the stock-in-trade of the late eighteenth century. It is not until some comparison has been made with a great man's contemporaries that we get any very clear idea of the measure of his own genius.

This casual application of a label has more than once bred misunderstanding of Purcell's achievement. Admirers of his

work have been quick to hail as characteristic the lineaments
they most admire, without reflecting whether, after all, the progressions and sequences that held their fancy were peculiar to a
single composer. More serious still has been the perverted
Jingoism which has proclaimed Purcell as a typically English
composer, bravely carrying on the almost defunct tradition of the
Elizabethan age and holding the fort till it fell before the assaults
of Handel and Italian opera. This attitude is not only ridiculous
in itself but has had the natural effect of making us appear ridiculous in the eyes of our neighbours. It is evident that Purcell's
vocal music is 'English,' in the sense that the just setting of
English words will naturally have a flavour different from that
of French or Italian song; and this is the point of Addison's
note that

the *Italian* Artists cannot agree with our *English* Musicians, in admiring
Purcell's Compositions, and thinking his Tunes so wonderfully adapted
to his Words; because both Nations do not always express the same
Passions by the same Sounds.[1]

It is easy enough, too, to trace in his work the influence of
English folksong and dance and to point here and there to some
breezy movement or jolly melody that seems to reflect the spirit
of the English nation and character. There is also the influence
of his immediate predecessors; and I have already quoted (page
236) North's remarks on the 'English vein' in the trio sonatas.

But all this does not justify the acceptance of Purcell as the
champion of a native art. A treacherous champion, if so! Not
only do his works confess his emulation of foreign styles; he is
convicted out of his own mouth. The preface to the *Sonatas of
III Parts* (1683), in which he claimed to have imitated 'the most
fam'd Italian masters,' was followed eight years later by a similar,
though less provocative, gesture in the introduction to the full
score of *Dioclesian*.[2] In the latter he says quite frankly that
music in England is in a backward state. He adds that it is 'now

---

[1] *Spectator*, No. 29 (3rd April 1711).
[2] Quoted on p. 69.

learning *Italian*, which is its best Master,' and so far abandons the stiffness of his earlier address as to commend its studying 'a little of the *French* Air, to give it somewhat more of Gayety and Fashion.' Then, commenting on the growing inclination for refinement, he notes the disposition 'to distinguish betwixt wild Fancy, and a just, numerous Composition,' which is a plain advocacy of the symmetrical structure of the latest Italian music, both vocal and instrumental, in contrast to the looser rhapsodies of the older school of English composition.[1]

The direction in which Purcell was moving—a pioneer among his countrymen—was appreciated by his contemporaries. North speaks of 'the Orfeus Brittanicus Mr. H. Purcell, who unhappily began to shew his Great skill before the reforme of musick al Italliana, and while he was warm in the pursuit of it, Dyed, but a greater musical genius England never had.'[2] The implication of this rather muddled sentence, which at first sight may seem to involve a *non sequitur*, is clear. North had an abounding admiration for the old style of music, but he was also full of enthusiasm for the newer products from abroad. To him Purcell was England's greatest composer in spite of the fact that the Italian style did not completely dominate English music in his lifetime. If we agree that the words 'while he was warm in the pursuit of it' underestimate Purcell's achievement, the opinion, clumsy as it is, still points to an understanding of Purcell's aim. The first historians—Hawkins and Burney—had a more definite idea of Purcell's relation to the Italian composers of his time. Hawkins declared roundly that the explicit language of the prefaces to the sonatas and *Dioclesian* was 'enough to silence for ever those, who, knowing nothing either of him or his works, assert that the music of Purcell is different from the Italian, and entirely English';[3]

[1] 'Numerous' means 'measured, rhythmical.' Cf. Milton, *Paradise Lost*, v. 149–50:
'Such prompt eloquence
Flowd from thir lips, in Prose or numerous Verse.'

[2] *Musicall Gramarian*, p. 33.   [3] Hawkins, p. 759, n.

and Burney was careful to indicate his connection with such composers as Carissimi and Stradella.

French influence, which Burney was inclined to exaggerate, appears principally in Purcell's orchestral music—in the over-tures to anthems, odes and plays, where the so-called Lullian model is generally followed—and in several of his dance move-ments, which reproduce the elegant gaiety of the French *ballet de cour*. The production of Lulli's *Cadmus et Hermione* in London in 1686 [1] probably helped to familiarize him with French methods, though there had also been earlier opportunities. But the domi-nant influence in his work—and particularly in his vocal music—is Italian. A writer of the early eighteenth century thus sums up some of the differences between the French and Italian styles:

> The *French* in their Airs aim at the Soft, the Easie, the Flowing, and Coherent; the whole Air is of the same Tone, or if sometimes they venture to vary it, they do it with so many Preparations, they so qualifie it, that still the Air seems to be as natural and consistent as if they had attempted no change at all; there is nothing bold and adventurous in it, it's all equal, and of a Piece. But the *Italians* pass boldly, and in an Instant from *b* Sharp to *b* Flat, and from *b* Flat to *b* Sharp; [2] they venture the boldest Cadences, and the most irregular Dissonance; and their Airs are so out of the way that they resemble the Compositions of no other Nation in the World. [3]

This is a just distinction, if we allow some exceptions, as we must to every generalization; and to any one at all familiar with Purcell's music, it will supply yet another pointer to where his affinity lay. 'Bold' and 'adventurous,' not to mention 'irregular,' are words that can aptly be applied to innumerable passages in his works; and we may even go further and add, with Burney, 'licentious,' a favourite eighteenth-century epithet for anything that showed impatience of orthodoxy.

[1] On the question of French opera and ballet in London see Chapter IX.

[2] i.e. from major to minor, and vice versa.

[3] F. Raguenet, *A Comparison between the French and Italian Musick and Operas* (1709), p. 14.

The distinction between the two styles is not weakened by the fact that Lulli, the leading French composer of the seventeenth century, was himself an Italian by birth and had a practical acquaintance with Italian methods. Roger North says, rather ambiguously, that he 'had influenced the french style by infusing a great portion of the Italian harmony into it, whereby the ayre was exceedingly improved.' [1] But infusion is one thing, trans-formation another. French opera in Lulli's hands remained an entirely national and characteristic form of art, largely, as Addison saw,[2] through the peculiar exigencies of the French tongue. A language that has no tonic accent clearly demands a particular kind of musical setting; and this peculiarity has helped to give French vocal music at all times the smoothness and coherence of which Raguenet speaks. It is true of French song more than of any other national art that an intimate knowledge of the language—not merely an academic knowledge but a personal acquaintance with its inflexions—is a necessary step to apprecia-tion. So thoroughly did Lulli recognize the essential difference of style that he could himself portray in song the distinctive genius of each country. In his *Ballet de la Raillerie* (1659), written fourteen years before his first opera, *Cadmus et Hermione*, there is an instructive dialogue between 'La Musique italienne' and 'La Musique française,' each singing not only in the correct language but in the appropriate style. The little scene is an epitome of national idiosyncrasies.[3]

A comprehensive survey of Purcell's style would include not only a comparison, illustrated by a profusion of musical examples, between his work and that of his foreign contemporaries and predecessors, but also a thorough examination of the trend of music before his time and during the Restoration period in general; and that would be followed by a more precise investigation into

[1] *Memoirs*, p. 102.

[2] *Spectator*, loc. cit. For a detailed discussion of the relation between Lulli and contemporary Italian music see Prunières, *L'Opéra italien en France avant Lulli*, pp. 362–70.

[3] It is printed in Prunières, op. cit., musical example No. v.

the individual characteristics of his art, a more curious study of
what happened when he deserted the well-trodden path and
followed his own diversions. It needs no wild imagination to
see that all this would involve a separate volume; indeed, a Swiss
scholar has devoted a moderately substantial book to the style of
Purcell's anthems alone.[1] Here we have only a chapter in which
to compress a whole host of generalizations; and since that is a
practical impossibility, there is nothing to be done but throw out
a few hints and underline some of the more important characteristics. Certain things will strike at once the most casual
student of Purcell's music—the use of a syncopated rhythm in
$\frac{3}{4}$ time (as in 'Fear no danger to ensue' in *Dido and Æneas*);
the dancing trochees (♩ ♪ ♩ ♪) that do duty for triumph,
victory, storm and the like; the fondness for melting appoggiaturas,
particularly if the piece is vocal and the word 'soft' is there to prompt
imagination. All these were the stock-in-trade of seventeenth-
century composers, and if Purcell used them more than others, it
was because they satisfied some natural whimsy in his own mind.

So too with other technical devices. The ground bass was
one of the delights of the period, a perpetual conundrum for the
composer to solve. We all know what happened when he
failed to solve it—those dreary *ostinati* recalling inexpert con-
versationalists whose only and repeated topic is the weather. It
is easy to see why the ground bass had such a fascination. The
introduction of the *basso continuo* had thrown tremendous emphasis
on the bass of a composition; it was no longer something that
appeared and retreated, spoke and was silent. The thorough-
bass or *continuo* was true to its name; it was thorough and continuous. And since this new continuity imposed a heavy burden
on the composer's imagination, it was natural to solve one problem
and set another by repeating a phrase of a few bars throughout the
composition. It might be merely the notes of a descending scale
or some less obvious pattern—it mattered little; above this multi-
plied foundation a structure could be erected. Purcell revelled

[1] Fritz de Quervain, *Der Chorstil Henry Purcell's* (1935).

in the device. Sometimes it ran away with him, and the ground bass would go on repeating itself mechanically like a gramophone record when the needle has stuck in a groove. More often he held it in strict control and so far subdued it to his will that he could use it to produce the miracle of Dido's lament. An examination of almost any one of his songs on a ground will show a most ingenious subtlety in circumventing the dangers of the form: the introduction of an occasional rest to give the ground breathing-space or the placing of the beginnings of the vocal phrases at points that do not coincide with the entry of the fundamental formula, so that the regular segments are there on paper but do not advertise themselves to the ear.

Purcell's harmony is of its time in the sense that it shows a progress from freedom to a regularity no less free. Or, to exchange paradox for technicalities, we may say that it begins by inheriting the multiple tonality of the modes and ends by accepting the single system of our modern major and minor, in the development of which the *basso continuo* had played such a significant part. Writing music in a single key, with the choice of major or minor and respect for the relationship of tonic and dominant, seems at the present day a sign of simplicity, even of naivety. Progress, as we call it, in modern music has consisted in relaxing the bonds of a diatonic system, in weakening its tyranny by the introduction of chromaticism and finally by the abandonment of key and the reign of licence. In the seventeenth century progress, or rather change, moved in the reverse direction. Modern tonality as we know it was something that was achieved as a norm only by persistent struggle and experiment. It had long been familiar in the restricted melodies of folksong as one of a number of possible modes. But its establishment in harmonized and developed music and the rejection of alternative systems was something new. The music of the transitional period shows composers fumbling awkwardly to express themselves within a convention that was not yet, so to speak, in their bones; and Purcell's early works, such as the string fantasias and the anthems of his youth, still exhibit traces of this transition.

One consequence of the free tonality of the madrigalian period had been that composers readily introduced chromaticism as a means of heightening expression. The absence of an absolute necessity for remaining within a single key-system made it possible for the music to embark on curious excursions through adjacent semitones; and the polyphonic habit of writing, in which the motion of the parts tended to condition the harmony, resulted sometimes in progressions that to the modern listener, trained in a different school of historical development, often appear outlandish or before their time. The check on wild modulation was to be found in the composer's instinct for proportion and relevancy. It was only when this instinct was capricious or imperfectly trained that it led to extravagance, as in Gesualdo's madrigals.

Chromaticism passed from the madrigal to the lute song and solo song with figured bass. It was used by the early opera composers — Peri, Caccini and Monteverdi — and naturally adopted by those Englishmen who followed in the wake of the Italians. The *basso continuo* gave a slightly modified aspect to chromaticism by supplying a more definite chordal progression beneath the changing semitones, but it naturally made no difference to its melodic character. A simple example from Locke's *Psyche* (1675) will illustrate a conventional type of treatment:

(The choice of Locke is not entirely fortuitous. Several details of resemblance suggest that Purcell owed to his friend some part of his acquaintance with Italian methods.) In so far as poly-phony was still kept alive in the anthem and choral ode and in instrumental music, chromaticism in several parts also continued to appear. Purcell handled it with his customary disregard for incidental harshness. If the progress of the parts sometimes led to oddities, they were only temporary, and it was the idea of combined movement that would remain uppermost in the hearer's mind.

This principle of independent movement colours a good deal of Purcell's part-writing for voices and instruments, particularly in his early work. Sometimes in his youthful anthems it pro-duced mere clumsiness, as Burney did not hesitate to point out. It has become the fashion nowadays to poke fun at Burney. Writers who have not a tithe of his musicianship or literary skill amuse themselves by ridiculing his opinions because they are supposed to be out of date. This is a tedious pastime. It is true that Burney was apt to apply the accepted rules of com-position a little too rigidly to the music he was examining; but no one had a more whole-hearted admiration for Purcell's genius, and only a vapid and uncritical taste could welcome some of the obstinate polyphony that appears in the pages of Restoration com-posers. The principle of independent movement must be judged, like most principles in aesthetics, by the result. In his youth Purcell sometimes wrote 'bold' contrapuntal solutions merely because he had not the experience or would not take the trouble to find alternatives.

A frequent, and in general a successful, application of the principle in simple harmonization is one that may be described as 'overlapping.' Two alternative solutions of a cadence present themselves, and the opportunity afforded by several parts, whether vocal or instrumental, induces the composer to use both sim-ultaneously. The curious reader has only to turn over the pages of the preceding chapters to find a number of examples of this practice. Here an obvious instance dating from

Purcell's maturity—the chorus of 'Full fathom five' in *The Tempest* (1695):

The harmonic and melodic structure of these two bars is most interesting. Even if we take only the soprano and bass we have an example of independent movement. The bass of the second bar is not the natural complement of the tune; it is a repetition of the pattern set in the first bar, irrespective of the different melodic conditions above. The simple, unadorned bass would be a minim G, which is actually present in the alto part. The additions provided by the remaining parts—the tenor and the second violin—are merely an enrichment of the soprano and bass. The tenor moves in sixths with the soprano, and the second violin in thirds with the bass. The result is the curious chord on the third quaver, where four successive notes of the scale are heard at the same time.

One of the commonest forms of independent progression is the use of both the flat and the sharp seventh in different parts, either simultaneously or in succession. This is found particularly in Purcell's earlier works, but he never abandoned it entirely and it is still to be met with in *The Fairy Queen* (1693), the festal *Te Deum* (1694) and the music to *The Married Beau* (1694). A particularly elaborate and striking example is at the end of the coronation anthem, *My heart is inditing* (1685), which I have quoted on page 213. Here is a simpler one from *The Yorkshire Feast Song* (1690):

This type of cadence is not peculiar to Purcell. Blow, for instance, combines the flat seventh with a six-four chord on the dominant in his anthem, *Behold, O God our Defender*:

and in his *Rules for playing of a Through Bass* [1] gives the following example of a 'half cadence':

This juxtaposition of adjacent semitones, whether in the same chord or merely in the same bar, is a survival of Elizabethan practice. The flat seventh is the normal constituent of several of the old modes, but it has to be sharpened by 'chromatic alteration' in order to produce the 'leading note.' [2] Thus—to

---

[1] Brit. Mus., Add. 34072; printed in F. Arnold, *The Art of Accompaniment from a Thorough-Bass* (1931), pp. 163–72.

[2] The extension of this licence helped to break down the modal system. When the seventh of the Mixolydian was sharpened it became temporarily identical with the Ionian—our modern major—in which

take an example from the Mixolydian mode—if the final cadence consists of a chord of G followed by a chord of C, whichever part moves upward from B to C—whether soprano, alto or tenor— must have B natural, while the other parts are free to use B flat as a normal step in the melodic progress. This compromise, as it seems to us, was not confined to cadences. Anywhere in the composition the need might be felt to give particular shape to an individual part by employing the sharp seventh where the flat seventh was proper to the mode. The result of this conjunction of two tonalities in a small space is known as a 'false relation,' though actually it was not until modern tonality was firmly established that there was any 'true' standard to which the relation could be 'false.'

It is one of the poses of pretentious scholarship to chortle with glee whenever these clashes occur. This is extravagant. It is

---

the sharp seventh was normal. Hence the distinction between the two tended to diminish, and as the attraction of a permanent leading note grew stronger the Mixolydian declined and eventually disappeared, leaving the Ionian in possession of the field. In the case of the Æolian and Dorian modes, which gave us our modern minor, the solution was less simple. In fact the minor still employs chromatic alteration by sharpening its leading-note without incorporating the accidental in the key-signature. At the same time it retains the flat seventh common to the Æolian and Dorian modes and also uses at will the flat sixth of the former and the sharp sixth of the latter. Purcell was quite ready to introduce all four—the two sixths and the two sevenths—in close proximity, as in this example from the welcome song, *Sound the trumpet* :

right to insist that a modern reprint should make no attempt to whitewash the original. But it is ridiculous to pretend that all passages of this kind have a divine loveliness. The 'false relation' was merely a technical device of the period, in which the logical progress of independent parts was considered more important than euphony. The effectiveness of a false relation depends on the disposition of the parts—on the distance and difference between the lines that clash and on the behaviour of the complementary voices. A false relation can be striking if there is a contrast between the two opposing strands—between a soprano and tenor, or a violin and voice; but if the clash occurs in the same octave between voices or instruments of the same timbre, the result can be hideous; and no amount of reverence for the past should deter us from saying so.

I have embarked on this digression—as it may appear—because many people who study Purcell's music without a sufficient idea of the sources of his art may be puzzled by these progressions, and all the more if they see authoritative writers gloating over things that they themselves find distasteful. The chief interest of Purcell's use of false relations is that it shows him, like some of his contemporaries, still attached to older traditions. It would be possible to quote a large number of examples, but we must be content here with a single illustration, from the 'Echo Dance' in *Dido and Æneas,* which I have selected because it is instructive in other ways:

The significance of this extract is not confined to the clash between E flat and E natural, which passes so quickly that it is hardly noticed. The behaviour of the second violin is also curious. Of the two statements of the passage the second—the 'echo'—seems the more natural, since there the A which I have

marked with an asterisk may be regarded as a suspension from the
previous chord. It may be that Purcell wrote this version first,
and then, liking the effect of the A, transferred it without immediate resolution to the first statement. But more probably the
whole thing is a characteristic example of his sometimes dis-
concerting directness in harmonic progression, another form of
independent movement. There is, in fact, almost no end to the
surprises he is prepared to spring on the listener. Harmonic
progressions that seem quaint and even uncouth to us often
occurred in music of the period as a result of a polyphonic mode
of thought. But Purcell goes beyond his predecessors and contemporaries in the 'boldness' of his progressions, the end in view
being more important to him than the mere transition.[1] He is
even prepared to accept the dreaded bogy of consecutive fifths,
if his fancy is strong enough to override pedantry.

One final characteristic of his harmony may be mentioned. It
consists in the use of irregularly resolved suspensions. When, for
instance, in a succession of sixths a melody note was held over
from a previous chord, the orthodox procedure was to allow it
to sink to the next note below, thus:

But adventurous composers developed the licence of letting the
suspended note drop to a lower note in the next chord, as a means
of intensifying expression. Here is an example from Purcell's
song, *What can we poor females do?*:

What can we, what can we poor, poor fe - males do?

[1] There is an interesting and fully illustrated summary of Purcell's
harmonic methods in his chamber music in Professor Whittaker's
article, 'Some Observations on Purcell's Harmony,' *Musical Times*,
October 1934.

This device, which was naturally popular in opera and became domesticated in songs and church music, was associated closely with the development of the *basso continuo,* since if the suspension was irregularly resolved the accompanist had to supply the missing note. Purcell was particularly attracted by the emotional possibilities of this type of suspension, and used it again and again in different forms.

It would be a mistake to suppose that a catalogue of Purcell's 'irregularities'—which, in any case, has not been attempted here—implies that he was inadequately fitted for his task. No one can spend even an afternoon with his scores without seeing that here was a man who had mastered the whole art of composition. Mr. Holland has well said that he was an 'immensely professional composer.' How much he valued the technique of writing we can see not only from his many ingenious canons and solutions of similar problems but also from his careful revision of Playford's *Introduction to the Skill of Music,* where the most scrupulous attention is devoted to instructing the student in all the essential elements of the art, including the complexities of fugue.[1] There is a danger, too, in paying too close a regard to individual progressions or cross-sections of a musical composition. We should heed the parable of Browning's grammarian, 'dead from the waist down.' The man who examines a score with a microscope may sometimes miss essentials that are apparent to a less inquisitive, less scholarly observer. A study of details is of no value unless it helps us to appreciate the whole. In the long run it is not such and such a progression that matters in the work of any composer, but the way it is introduced, its relation to what has gone before and what is to come, its place in the general plan and the service it renders to imagination.

---

[1] North, in his *Essay of Musicall Ayre* (Brit. Mus., Add. 32536, fo. 84ᵛ), speaks pityingly of 'poor old Playford's Introduction, of which may be truely sayd that it is but just (if at all) better then None.' It is impossible to know which edition he is referring to, and no one else seems to corroborate this contemptuous opinion. North was an amateur.

Hence it is Purcell's sense of form that should engage our final attention, first in the limited span of melody and then on a larger scale. As a melodist he was and is supreme. I have suggested elsewhere that his mastery of formal proportion and inevitable grace may well have been due to constant effort, to a persistent desire to polish and adjust. The spontaneity of his tunes conceals the art that has formed them. It is sometimes supposed— generally by persons who have no experience of composition —that it is easy to write a good tune. Nothing could be farther from the truth. Every one of us could probably write one good tune, by the grace of God and the light of our own imagination. But the regular production of good tunes is a matter either for laborious effort or genius—and a familiar definition of the latter equates the two. Melody may bubble from some unseen fount in the mind of genius, but even that spontaneity is the result of previous reflection, of a certain habit of mind and of a creative grasp of the principles of melody in general. The most remark able thing about Purcell's tunes is their length. They spread in spacious curves, depending for their symmetry less on repetition than on an ingenious equilibrium of contrasted elements. The singer or listener who exclaims after one of Purcell's songs: 'What a perfect melody,' would do well to study more closely the basis of that perfection—how range and rhythm are adjusted to the temper of the words and how skilfully passing notes are used to smooth the way.[1]

Towards the end of his life Purcell adopted the formal prin ciples of the Italian aria, and showed that he could handle the conventions of the *da capo* form as easily and naturally as Scarlatti. These arias and the chaconnes, whether vocal or instrumental, are the most extended examples of his use of larger forms. He has sometimes been reproached for not working on a bigger canvas; his music has been called 'shortbreathed.' But one might with as much or as little justice complain because Wagner did not write miniatures. The *concerto grosso* and the fully developed

[1] For an acute analysis of one of Purcell's songs see Professor Dent's article, 'Binary and Ternary Form,' *Music and Letters*, October 1936.

contrapuntal choral style did not reach their maturity till after Purcell's death. He was content to use the forms that lay ready to hand and to do his best with them, though even so there are frequent anticipations of a later style. We may regret that he was tied to the court, the church and the theatre; but limitations of this kind were common to all composers during the period of aristocratic patronage. It is easy to confuse restricted scope with restricted imagination. The history of music makes it abundantly clear that though local circumstances may provide the framework for the musician's art, they do not condition his inspiration. If we criticize Purcell, it must not be for using limited forms, but for using them imperfectly, for yielding to triviality, as he sometimes did, and accepting convention for want of ideas.

Modern research has made it possible to assign a date—either definite or approximate—to practically everything that Purcell wrote. The result is curious. In a comparison between the anthems and the dramatic music it will be noticed that, whereas the majority of the extant anthems belong to the early part of his career, the bulk of the dramatic music dates from the last five years of his life. A general survey of both departments of his work consequently reveals not only such differences in style as one might expect to find between music for the church and music for the theatre but also two different stages of development. For a continuous evidence of progress we must turn to the royal odes, which cover a period of fifteen years, from 1680 to 1695. Though these do not exhibit every side of Purcell's talents, they show convincingly enough the strengthening of the feeling for tonality, with the consequent simplification—as it seems to us—of the harmonic texture, and the growth of a stronger, purer melodic invention. If we sum up Purcell's development in terms of Italian art, we may say that it is a progress from Monteverdi to Scarlatti, the names standing as types of particular styles rather than as specific objects of imitation.

Technical analysis can tell us a good deal about a composer, but it does not tell us everything. It sometimes happens that the poet sees more than the scholar, that intuition reveals more than empirical research. English scholarship has paid a splendid tribute to the inspiration of Purcell's art. If I end this chapter with a reference to one who never pretended to be more than an admirer, it is with no implied disrespect to that scholarship or ingratitude for its achievements. It is merely that Gerard Manley Hopkins's sonnet on Purcell seems to me to sum up better than any critical account I know the fundamental reasons for admiration. The poetry is obscure and sometimes, it may seem, perverse, but the imagery and imagination are tremendous. The core of the poem is in the second quatrain:

> Not mood in him nor meaning, proud fire or sacred fear,
> Or love or pity or all that sweet notes not his might nursle:
> It is the forgèd feature finds me; it is the rehearsal
> Of own, of abrupt self there so thrusts on, so throngs the ear.

'The forgèd feature'! Could anything better express the stubborn individuality of a great artist? We may be touched by Purcell's melancholy, revel in his exuberance, take fire from this or that expression of emotion. But these things are not peculiar. Gaiety and grief are not the prerogative of any one composer. We do not admire Bach's suites because they are lively or pay homage to the St. Matthew Passion because it touches the springs of sorrow. It is Bach himself who wins our unresisting suffrage. And so with Purcell. Who cares, after all, whether we know much or little of his life? The man himself is in his music, and that insistent evidence of personality digs us out of complacency, compels attention and holds our love. The measure of our affection for a composer is not our estimate of his music but the invisible bond that draws us back to it again and again. With this compulsion we can remember if we will that every great artist was at times unworthy of himself—remember it and then forget.

Judgments of Purcell's art have differed according to individual reactions. Some have found it feminine and yielding, others have been struck by its boisterous energy. In art as in religion we are apt to discover what we hope to find, to judge the source by the extent to which it supplies our own thirst. What no one will fail to find in Purcell at his best is a spring of life, a vitality that glows with the effort of the whole man. To listen is to share an experience, to catch some of his glancing fire and to have a part in his aching regret. He was a man of changing moods and sympathies, ready to boast, to worship, to sigh and to lament. He could bid the trumpets sound for majesty, or seeking flight from love's sickness find the fever in himself.

APPENDICES

APPENDIX A

CALENDAR

(Figures in brackets denote the age reached by the person mentioned during the year in question.)

Year	Age	*Life*	*Contemporary Musicians*
1659		Henry Purcell born, between June and Nov. 20, in London (?), son of Thomas Purcell, musician (later gentleman of the Chapel Royal, musician for the lute, viol and voice, composer for the violins, groom of the robes, and musician in ordinary in the private music).	Bernabei (G. A.) born (approx.); Porter (*c.* 64) dies, Nov.; Scarlatti (A.) born.

Akeroyde aged *c.* 9; Aldrich 12; d'Anglebert 31; Bai *c.* 9; Banister 29; Benevoli 57; Bernabei (G. E.) *c.* 39; Biber 25; Blow 11; Bontempi *c.* 32; Buxtehude 22; Cambert 31; Carissimi 54; Cavalli 57; Cesti 36; Chambonnières 39; Charpentier 25; Child 53; Colasse 10; Cooke *c.* 44; Corelli 6; Crüger 61; Draghi *c.* 19; Foggia 55; Froberger *c.* 42; Gibbons (C.) 44; Grabu *c.* 24; Hammerschmidt 47; Humfrey 12; Jenkins 67; Jewett 56; Kerl 31; Krieger (A.) 25; Krieger (J. P.) 10; Krieger (J.) 7; Lalande 2; Lanier 71; Lawes (H.) 63;

Year	Age	Life	Contemporary Musicians
			Legrenzi *c.* 34; Locke 37; Lully 27; Marais 3, Moreau 3; Muffat (sen.) *c.* 14; Pachelbel 6; Pasquini 22; Piggott *c.* 4; Pitoni 3; Reinken 36; Rogers 45; Rosenmüller *c.* 40; Schütz 74; Selle 60; Simpson *c.* 49; Steffani 5; Stradella *c.* 15; Strungk 19; Theile 13; Tunder 45; Turner 8; Vitali (G. B.) *c.* 15; Wilson 64.
1660	1		Ariosti born (approx.); Campra born, Dec. 4; Clarke born (approx.); Fux born; Kuhnau born.
1661	2		Böhm born; Perti born, June 6.
1662	3		Desmarets born; Lawes (H.) (66) dies, Oct. 21.
1663	4	Birth of Daniel Purcell (approx.).	Eccles born (approx.); Murschhauser born, June; Selle (64) dies, July 2.
1664	5	Death of P.'s uncle (?), Henry Purcell, gentleman of the Chapel Royal, musician for the lute and voice, senior lay clerk and master of the choristers of Westminster Abbey.	
1665	6		Vitali (T. A.) born (approx.).
1666	7		Krüger (A.) (32) dies, June 30; Lanier (78) dies, Feb.; Montéclair born (approx.); Rebel born, April.

Year	Age	Life	Contemporary Musicians
1667	8	Three-part song, *Sweet tyranness*, published in Playford's *Musical Companion* (possibly by the elder Henry Purcell).	Froberger (*c.* 50) dies, May 7; Humfrey (20) becomes a gentleman of the Chapel Royal; Lotti born; Pepusch born; Tunder (53) dies, Nov. 5.
1668	9		Blow (20) appointed organist of Westminster Abbey; Couperin born, Nov. 10; Gasparini born, March 5.
1669	10	(?) P. becomes a chorister at the Chapel Royal, where Cooke (*c.* 54) is master of the children.	Clari born (approx); Simpson (*c.* 59) dies.
1670	11	(?) Composes a birthday ode for Charles II (40).	Caldara born (approx.); Chambonnières (50) dies (approx.); Vivaldi born (approx.).
1671	12		
1672	13	Comes under the tuition of Humfrey (25), who is appointed master of the children of the Chapel Royal in succession to Cooke (*c.* 57).	Benevoli (70) dies, June 17; Bononcini born; Cooke (*c.* 57) dies, July 13; Destouches born (approx.); Schütz (87) dies, Nov. 6.
1673	14	P.'s voice breaks and he leaves the choir of the Chapel Royal. Appointed assistant to John Hingston, keeper of the king's instruments.	
1674	15	On the death of Humfrey, P. comes under the tuition of Blow (26), who is appointed master of the children of the Chapel Royal. He becomes organ tuner at Westminster Abbey.	Albinoni born (approx.); Carissimi (69) dies, Jan. 12; Humfrey (27) dies, July 14; Keiser born, Jan. 9; Wilson (79) dies, Feb. 22.

Purcell

Year	Age	Life	Contemporary Musicians
1675	16	Song, *When Thirsis did the splendid eye*, published in *Choice Ayres*, book i.	Abaco born, July 12; Hammerschmidt (63) dies; Jewett (72) dies, July 3; Lœillet born (approx.).
1676	17	Copies some organ parts for use at Westminster Abbey.	Cavalli (*c.* 77) dies, Jan. 14; Gibbons (*c.* 61) dies, Oct. 20.
1677	18	Appointed composer in ordinary for the violins, Sept. *Elegy on the death of his worthy friend, Mr. Matthew Locke* (published in *Choice Ayres*, book ii, in 1679).	Locke (55) dies, Aug.
1678	19	Songs published in *New Ayres and Dialogues*.	Croft born, Dec.; Jenkins (86) dies, Oct. 27.
1679	20	Appointed organist of Westminster Abbey. Songs published in *Choice Ayres*, book ii.	Banister (49) dies, Oct. 3.
1680	21	Four-part fantasias for strings, June to Aug. Welcome song for Charles II (50), *Welcome, vicegerent*, Sept. Music for Nathaniel Lee's (*c.* 27) tragedy, *Theodosius*.	Geminiani born.
1681	22	(?) P. marries. Welcome song, *Swifter Isis, swifter flow*, for the return of Charles II (51) from Windsor, Aug. Music for Nahum Tate's (29) tragedy, *King Richard II*, and D'Urfey's (28) comedy, *Sir Barnaby Whigg*. Songs published in *Choice Ayres*, book iii.	Astorga born, Dec. 11; Telemann born, March 14.
1682	23	Welcome song, *What, what shall be done?* for the return of the Duke of York (49, later	

Year	Age	Life	Contemporary Musicians
		James II) from Scotland. P. is appointed one of the organists of the Chapel Royal, July. Death of Thomas Purcell, July. Son, John Baptista, born, Aug. (?) Music for Beaumont and Fletcher's tragedy, *The Double Marriage.* Death of son, Oct.	
1683	24	*Sonatas of III Parts* published, June, with dedication to Charles II (53). Ode, *From hardy climes and dangerous toils of war,* for the marriage of Princess Anne (18) to Prince George of Denmark, July. Welcome song after the frustration of the Rye House Plot, *Fly, bold rebellion,* Sept. (?). Odes for St. Cecilia's Day, *Welcome to all the pleasures* and *Laudate Ceciliam,* Nov. P. appointed organ maker and keeper to the king in succession to Hingston, Dec. Songs published in *Choice Ayres,* book iv.	Rameau born, Sept.
1684	25	Competition between two organ builders, Bernard Smith (c. 54) and Renatus Harris, at the Temple Church. P. plays for the former, whose instrument is eventually chosen; Harris's organ is played by Draghi (c. 44). Welcome song,	Dagincourt born; Dandrieu born; Durante born, March 15; Rosenmüller (c. 65) dies, Sept. 10–11.

Year	Age	Life	Contemporary Musicians
		From those serene and rapturous joys, for the return of Charles II (54) from Winchester, Sept. Songs and duets published in *Choice Ayres,* book v.	
1685	26	Song on the death of Charles II (55), *If prayers and tears.* Coronation of James II (52) at Westminster Abbey, April 23, for which P. has composed the anthem, *My heart is inditing.* P. appointed to the king's private music, Aug. Welcome song after Monmouth's (36) rebellion, *Why, why are all the Muses mute?* Oct. (?) Music for Nathaniel Lee's (c. 32) tragedy, *Sophonisba.* Songs and duets published in the *Theater of Music,* books i and ii. Duets and catches published in *Catch that catch can.*	Bach born, March 21; Handel born, Feb. 23; Scarlatti (D.) born, Oct. 26; Veracini born (approx.).
1686	27	Birth and death of a son (?), Thomas, Aug. Welcome song, *Ye tuneful Muses,* for James II (53), Oct. Duets and catches published in *Pleasant Musical Companion,* book ii.	Marcello born, July 31/Aug. 1; Porpora born, Aug. 19.
1687	28	Birth of a son, Henry, June. Petition to the king for payment as keeper of the organs and harpsichords, June. Death of son, Sept. Welcome song, *Sound the trumpet,*	Graupner born, Feb.; Lully (55) dies, March 22; Senaillé born, Nov. 23.

Year	Age	Life	Contemporary Musicians
		performed on James II's (54) birthday, Oct. 14. Elegy on the death of John Playford (64) to words by Nahum Tate (35). Songs and duets published in the *Theater of Music* book iv, and other collections. Anthems, *Behold I bring you glad tidings*; *Praise the Lord, O my soul*; *Thy way, O God, is holy*; *Sing unto God.*	
1688	29	Anthem, *Blessed are they that fear the Lord,* composed for a day of thanksgiving for the queen's pregnancy, Jan. 15. Music for D'Urfey's (35) comedy, *A Fool's Preferment,* which is hissed off the stage. Birth of a daughter, Frances, May. Sacred songs published in *Harmonia Sacra*, part i. Songs and duets published in the *Banquet of Music*, books i and ii. Anthems, *O sing unto the Lord* and *The Lord is King.*	Fasch (J. F.) born, April 15; Foggia (84) dies, Jan. 8.
1689	30	Coronation of William III (39) and Mary (27) at Westminster Abbey, April 11. P. is compelled by the dean and chapter to hand over money received for admitting visitors to the organ loft. Ode, *Now does the glorious day appear,* for the queen's birthday, April 30, the words by Thomas Shadwell (*c.* 47). P. appointed to the	

Purcell

Year	Age	Life	Contemporary Musicians

king's private music, July.
Ode, *Celestial music,* performed at Louis Maidwell's
school, Aug. 5. Birth of a
son, Edward, Sept. (?) *Dido
and Æneas,* libretto by
Nahum Tate (37), per-
formed at Josias Priest's
school at Chelsea. Song and
duets published in *Comes
Amoris,* book iii. Harpsichord pieces (including
Sefauchi's Farewell, written on
the departure of Siface, 36)
published in *Musick's Hand-
Maid,* part ii.

1690 31 *Yorkshire Feast Song,* words
by D'Urfey (37), performed
in London, March 27. Ode,
Arise my Muse, for the
queen's (28) birthday, April
30, words by D'Urfey.
Music for *Dioclesian,* adapted
by Thomas Betterton (55)
from Beaumont and
Fletcher's *The Prophetess*;
Dryden's (59) comedy,
Amphitryon; Elkanah Settle's
(42) tragedy, *Distressed Innocence*; Thomas Southerne's
(30) comedy, *Sir Anthony
Love*; and Nathaniel Lee's
(c. 37) tragedy, *The Massacre
of Paris.* Ode to the queen
for solo voice, *High on a
throne of glittering ore.* Elegy
on the death of Thomas
Farmer, *Young Thirsis' fate.*

Babell born (approx.);
Carey born (approx.);
Legrenzi (c. 65) dies, July
26; Muffat (jun.) born,
April; Vinci born.

266

Appendix A—Calendar

Year	Age	Life	Contemporary Musicians
1691	32	Score of *Dioclesian* published, March. Ode, *Welcome, welcome, glorious morn*, for the queen's (29) birthday, April 30. Music for Dryden's (60) *King Arthur*; an anonymous comedy, *The Gordian Knot Untied*; *The Indian Emperor*, tragedy by Dryden and Howard; and Southerne's (31) comedy, *The Wives' Excuse*. Duets published in the *Banquet of Musick*, book v.	D'Anglebert (63) dies.
1692	33	Ode, *Love's goddess sure was blind*, for the queen's (30) birthday, April 30, words by Sir Charles Sedley (53). Music for Dryden's (61) tragedy, *Cleomenes*; *The Fairy Queen*, adapted by Settle (?) from Shakespeare's *Midsummer Night's Dream*; D'Urfey's (39) comedy *The Marriage-Hater Matched*; John Crowne's tragedy, *Regulus*; (?) Shadwell's comedy, *The Libertine*; Mountfort's (?) tragedy *Henry II*; (?) Dryden's tragedy *Aureng-Zebe*; *Œdipus*, a tragedy adapted from Sophocles by Dryden and Lee (c. 39). Ode for St. Cecilia's day, *Hail, bright Cecilia*, performed at Stationers' Hall, Nov. 22, P. singing the counter-tenor solo. Songs published in	Tartini born, April 8; Vitali (G. B.) (c. 48) dies, Oct. 12.

267

Year	Age	Life	Contemporary Musicians
		the *Gentleman's Journal* and the *Banquet of Musick,* book vi.	
1693	34	Ode, *Celebrate this festival,* for the queen's (31) birthday, April 30, words by Nahum Tate (41). Music for Congreve's (23) comedy, *The Old Bachelor;* D'Urfey's (40) comedy, *The Richmond Heiress;* Southerne's (33) comedy, *The Maid's Last Prayer;* a comedy, *The Female Virtuosos,* adapted by Thomas Wright from Molière's *Les Femmes savantes;* Congreve's comedy, *The Double Dealer;* Shadwell's comedy, *Epsom Wells;* (?) Fletcher's comedy, *Rule a Wife and Have a Wife.* Birth of a daughter, Mary, Dec. Anthem, *O give thanks.* Songs published in the *Gentleman's Journal* and *Comes Amoris,* book iv. Sacred songs published in *Harmonia Sacra,* part ii.	Kerl (65) dies, Feb. 13; Locatelli born; Sammartini (G.) born (approx.).
1694	35	Performance at Dublin of the ode, *Great parent, hail,* for the centenary of Trinity College, Jan. 9. Ode, *Come ye sons of art away,* for the queen's (32) birthday, April 30. P. revises the twelfth edition of John Playford's *Introduction to the Skill of Musick.* He contri-	Daquin born, July 4; Leo born, Aug. 5.

butes, with Eccles (*c.* 31), to
the incidental music to
D'Urfey's (41) *Don Quixote,*
parts i and ii. Music for
Dryden's (63) tragi-comedy,
Love Triumphant; Crowne's
comedy, *The Married Beau;*
Southerne's (34) play, *The
Fatal Marriage;* Edward
Ravenscroft's comedy, *The
Canterbury Guests;* Shakespeare's tragedy, *Timon of
Athens;* Dryden's tragi-
comedy, *The Spanish Friar,*
and tragedy, *Tyrannic Love;*
and (?) D'Urfey's comedy,
The Virtuous Wife. Anthem,
*The way of God is an un-
defiled way,* Nov. *Te Deum
and Jubilate* in D for St.
Cecilia's Day, Nov. Songs
published in the *Gentleman's
Journal, Thesaurus Musicus,*
book ii, and *Comes Amoris,*
book v.

1695 36   Anthem, *Thou knowest, Lord,*   Grabu (*c.* 60) dies (approx.);
composed for the funeral   Greene born.
service of Queen Mary (d.   Abaco aged 20; Akeroyde
Dec. 28, 1694) on March 5.   *c.* 45; Albinoni 21; Aldrich
Two elegies on the queen's   48; Ariosti *c.* 35; Astorga
death. Ode, *Who can from*   14; Babell *c.* 5; Bach 10;
joy refrain? for the birthday Bai *c.* 45; Bernabei (G. A.)
of the Duke of Gloucester   *c.* 36; Biber 51; Blow 47;
(6), son of Princess Anne   Böhm 34; Bononcini 23;
(30), July 24. Music for   Bontempi *c.* 68; Buxtehude
Aphra Behn's tragedy, *Ab-*   58; Caldara *c.* 25; Campra
delazer; Bonduca, a tragedy 35; Carey *c.* 5; Charpentier
adapted from Beaumont and   61; Child 89; Clari *c.* 26;

Year	Age	Life	Contemporary Musicians

Fletcher; Thomas Scott's comedy, *The Mock Marriage*; Gould's tragedy, *The Rival Sisters*; Southerne's (35) tragedy, *Oroonoko*; (?) Shakespeare's *The Tempest,* adapted by Shadwell (c. 53); *The Indian Queen,* by Dryden and Howard; Norton's tragedy, *Pausanias*; D'Urfey's (42) comedy, *Don Quixote,* part iii. Songs published in *Deliciae Musicae,* books i and ii, and *Thesaurus Musicus,* book iii.

Purcell dies in London, Nov. 21, and is buried in Westminster Abbey, Nov. 26.

Clarke c. 35; Colasse 46; Corelli 42; Couperin 27; Croft 17; Dagincourt 11; Dandrieu 11; Daquin 1; Desmarets 33; Destouches c. 23; Draghi c. 55; Durante 11; Eccles c. 32; Fasch (J. F.) 7; Fux 35; Geminiani 15; Graupner 8; Handel 10; Keiser 21; Krieger (J. P.) 46; Krieger (J.) 43; Kuhnau 35; Lalande 38; Leo 1; Locatelli 2; Lœillet c. 20; Lotti 28; Marais 39; Marcello 9; Montéclair c. 29; Moreau 39; Muffat (sen.) c. 50; Muffat (jun.) 5; Murschhauser 32; Pachelbel 42; Pasquini 58; Pepusch 28; Perti 34; Piggott c. 40; Porpora 9; Purcell (D.) c. 32; Rameau 12; Rebel 29; Reinken 72; Rogers 81; Sammartini (G.) c. 2; Scarlatti (A.) 36; Scarlatti (D.) 10; Senaillé 8; Steffani 41; Strungk 55; Tartini 3; Telemann 14; Theile 49; Turner 44; Veracini c. 10; Vinci 5; Vitali (T. A.) c. 30; Vivaldi c. 25.

APPENDIX B

THE Roman numerals in brackets refer to the volumes of the Purcell Society's edition. The distinction between 'verse' and 'full' anthems is explained on page 197. The conventional abbreviations for voices are employed, but it should be noted that S. includes parts written in the mezzo-soprano clef and that A. should be interpreted as counter-tenor rather than alto. Choruses are for S.A.T.B. unless otherwise stated and strings in four parts with continuo. Anthems for which no instrumental accompaniment is specified are with organ. The dates assigned to the dramatic works are based on W. Barclay Squire's article, *Purcell's Dramatic Music,* in *S.I.M.G.*, iv, p. 489. The approximate chronology of the anthems follows that suggested by Nigel Fortune in the Purcell Society's edition, vol. xxviii. The dates given for songs are those of publication, unless otherwise stated; dates are given only for those which appeared in Purcell's lifetime. Flutes = recorders.

DRAMATIC WORKS

Operas

Dido and Æneas. Opera (Tate). 1689 (?). (III.)

Fairy Queen, The. Opera with dialogue (adapted from Shakespeare's *Midsummer Night's Dream*). 1692. (XII.)

Indian Queen, The. Opera with dialogue (Dryden and Howard). 1695. (XIX.)

King Arthur, or the British Worthy. Opera with dialogue (Dryden). 1691. (XXVI.)

Prophetess, or the History of Dioclesian, The. Opera with dialogue (adapted from Fletcher and Massinger by Betterton). 1690. (IX.)

Tempest, or the Enchanted Island, The. Opera with dialogue (adapted from Shakespeare by Shadwell). 1695 (?). (XIX.)

Plays with Incidental Music and Songs

Abdelazer, or the Moor's Revenge. Tragedy (Aphra Behn). 1695. (XVI.)

Amphitryon, or the Two Sosias. Comedy (Dryden). 1690. (XVI.)

Aureng-Zebe. Tragedy (Dryden). 1692 (?). (XVI.)

Bonduca, or the British Heroine. Tragedy (adapted from Beaumont and Fletcher). 1695. (XVI.)

Canterbury Guests, or a Bargain Broken, The. Comedy (Ravenscroft). 1694. (XVI.)

Circe. Tragedy (Charles D'Avenant). 1690 (?). (XVI.)

Cleomenes, the Spartan Hero. Tragedy (Dryden). 1692. (XVI.)

Distressed Innocence, or the Princess of Persia. Tragedy (Settle). 1690. (XVI.)

Don Quixote, The Comical History of. Comedy (D'Urfey). Parts i and ii, 1694. Part iii, 1695. (XVI.)

Double Dealer, The. Comedy (Congreve). 1693. (XVI.)

Double Marriage, The. Tragedy (Beaumont and Fletcher). 1682–5 (?). (XVI.)

Epsom Wells. Comedy (Shadwell). 1693. (XVI.)

Fatal Marriage, or the Innocent Adultery, The. Play (Southerne). 1694. (XX.)

Female Vertuosos, The. Comedy (adapted from Molière's *Les Femmes savantes* by Thomas Wright). 1693. (XX.)

Fool's Preferment, or the Three Dukes of Dunstable, A. Comedy (adapted from Fletcher's *Noble Gentleman* by D'Urfey). 1688. (XX.)

Gordian Knot Untied, The. Comedy. 1691. (XX.)

Henry II, King of England. Tragedy (? Mountfort). 1692. (XX.)

Indian Emperor, The. Tragedy (Dryden and Howard). 1691. (XX.)

King Richard II, The History of (The Sicilian Usurper). Tragedy (adapted from Shakespeare by Tate). 1681. (XX.)

Libertine, The. Comedy (Shadwell). 1692 (?). (XX.)

Love Triumphant, or Nature will Prevail. Tragi-comedy (Dryden). 1694. (XX.)

Maid's Last Prayer, or Any rather than Fail, The. Comedy (Southerne). 1693. (XX.)

Marriage-Hater Matched, The. Comedy (D'Urfey). 1692. (XX.)

Married Beau, or the Curious Impertinent, The. Comedy (Crowne). 1694. (XX.)

Massacre of Paris, The. Tragedy (Lee). 1690. (XX.)

Mock Marriage, The. Comedy (Thomas Scott). 1695. (XX.)

Œdipus. Tragedy (Dryden and Lee). 1692 (?). (XXI.)

Old Bachelor, The. Comedy (Congreve). 1693. (XXI.)

Oroonoko. Tragedy (Southerne). 1695. (XXI.)

Pausanias, the Betrayer of his Country. Tragedy (Norton). 1695. (XXI.)

Regulus. Tragedy (Crowne). 1692. (XXI.)

Richmond Heiress, or a Woman once in the Right, The. Comedy (D'Urfey).
1693. (XXI.)

Rival Sisters, or the Violence of Love, The. Tragedy (Gould). 1695.
(XXI.)

Rule a Wife and Have a Wife. Comedy (Fletcher). 1693. (XXI.)

Sir Anthony Love, or the Rambling Lady. Comedy (Southerne). 1690.
(XXI.)

Sir Barnaby Whigg, or No Wit like a Woman's. Comedy (D'Urfey).
1681. (XXI.)

Sophonisba, or Hannibal's Overthrow. Tragedy (Lee). 1685 (?). (XXI.)

Spanish Friar, or the Double Discovery, The. Tragi-comedy (Dryden).
1694–5. (XXI.)

Theodosius, or the Force of Love. Tragedy (Lee). 1680. (XXI.)

Timon of Athens. Tragedy (adapted from Shakespeare by Shadwell).
1694. (II.)

Tyrannic Love, or the Royal Martyr. Tragedy (Dryden). 1694. (XXI.)

Virtuous Wife, or Good Luck at Last, The. Comedy (D'Urfey).
1694(?).[1] (XXI.)

---

[1] The play was first performed in the autumn of 1679, but Purcell's
music cannot have been written for this production for the following
reasons: (1) Downes expressly states that the music to *Theodosius* (1680)
was Purcell's first work for the theatre; (2) the music of *The Virtuous
Wife* is in the style of his maturity; (3) the 'Song Tune' is an instrumental version of 'Ah! how sweet it is to love' from *Tyrannic Love*, the
music to which was probably written for a revival at the end of 1694.
On these grounds I suggest 1694 or 1695 as the date for the music to
The Virtuous Wife, though there does not appear to be any record of a
revival at that time. If we adopt an earlier date for the music to
Tyrannic Love, which in any case cannot be earlier than 1690 (Squire,
op. cit., p. 560), the date of *The Virtuous Wife* can be advanced ac-
cordingly.

Purcell

Wives' Excuse, or Cuckolds make Themselves, The. Comedy (Southerne). 1691. (XXI.)

[The music to *Macbeth,* often attributed to Purcell, is probably by Leveridge. Catches from *The English Lawyer* and *The Knight of Malta* are printed in vols. xvi and xx respectively, but it is not certain that they were written for productions of these plays. They are listed below under 'Catches.' For a list of the individual solo songs in the plays and operas see Appendix F.]

ODES AND WELCOME SONGS

Arise my Muse. Ode for Queen Mary's birthday (D'Urfey). A.A.T.B. soli, chorus, flutes, oboes, trumpets, strings (5 parts). 1690. (XI.)

Celebrate this festival. Ode for Queen Mary's birthday (Tate). S.S.A.T.B. soli, chorus (S.S.A.A.T.T.B.B.), flutes, oboes, trumpets, strings. 1693. (XXIV.)

Celestial music. Ode performed at Louis Maidwell's school, words by one of his pupils. S.A.T.B. soli, chorus, flutes, strings. 1689. (XXVII.)

Come ye sons of art away. Ode for Queen Mary's birthday. S.A.A.B. soli, chorus, flutes, oboes, trumpets, timpani, strings. 1694. (XXIV.)

Fly, bold rebellion. Welcome song for Charles II. S.S.A.A.T.B.B. soli, chorus, strings. 1683. (XV.)

From hardy climes. Ode for the marriage of Prince George of Denmark and Princess Anne. S.S.A.T.B. soli, chorus, strings. 1683. (XXVII.)

From those serene and rapturous joys. Welcome song for Charles II (Flatman). S.S.A.T.B. soli, chorus, strings. 1684. (XVIII.)

Great parent, hail. Ode for the centenary of Trinity College, Dublin (Tate). S.A.T.B. soli, chorus, flutes, strings. 1694. (XXVII.)

Hail, bright Cecilia. Ode for St. Cecilia's Day (Brady). S.A.A.T.B. soli, chorus (S.S.A.A.T.B.), flutes, bass flute, oboes, trumpets, timpani, strings. 1692. (VIII.)

Laudate Ceciliam. Ode for St. Cecilia's Day. A.T.B., violins, continuo. 1683. (X.)

Light of the world (Prior). 1694. The music has not survived.

Appendix B—Catalogue of Works

Love's goddess sure was blind. Ode for Queen Mary's birthday (Sedley). S.A.A.T.B. soli, chorus, flutes, strings. 1692. (XXIV.)

Now does the glorious day appear. Ode for Queen Mary's birthday (Shadwell). S.A.T.B.B. soli, chorus, strings (5 parts). 1689. (XI.)

Of old when heroes. Yorkshire Feast Song (D'Urfey). A.A.T.B.B. soli, chorus (S.S.A.T.B.), flutes, oboes, trumpets, strings. 1690. (I.)

Raise, raise the voice. Ode for St. Cecilia's Day. S. and B. soli, chorus (S.T.B.), violins, continuo. (X.)

Sound the trumpet. Welcome song for James II. A.A.T.T.B.B. soli, chorus, strings. 1687. (XVIII.)

Swifter Isis, swifter flow. Welcome song for Charles II. S.S.A.T.B. soli, chorus, flutes, oboe, strings. 1681. (XV.)

The summer's absence unconcerned we bear. Welcome song for Charles II. S.S.A.A.T.B.B. soli, chorus, strings. 1682. (XV.)

Welcome to all the pleasures. Ode for St. Cecilia's Day (Fishburn). S.S.A.T.B. soli, chorus, strings. 1683. (X.)

Welcome, vicegerent of the mighty King. Welcome song for Charles II. S.S.A.T.B. soli, chorus, strings. 1680. (XV.)

Welcome, welcome, glorious morn. Ode for Queen Mary's birthday. S.A.T.B.B. soli, chorus, oboes, trumpets, strings. 1691. (XI.)

What, what shall be done in behalf of the man? Welcome song for the Duke of York. S.S.A.T.B. soli, chorus, flutes, strings. 1682. (XV.)

Who can from joy refrain? Ode for the Duke of Gloucester's birthday. S.S.A.A.T.B. soli, chorus (S.S.A.T.B.), oboes, trumpet, strings. 1695. (IV.)

Why, why are all the Muses mute? Welcome song for James II. S.S.A.T.B.B. soli, chorus (S.S.A.T.B.), strings. 1685. (XVIII.)

Ye tuneful Muses. Welcome song for James II. S.S.A.A.T.B.B. soli, chorus, flutes, strings. 1686. (XVIII.)

SECULAR CANTATAS

(including duets with instrumental *obbligati*)

Hark, Damon, hark. S.S.B., violins, flutes, continuo. (XXVII.)

Hark how the wild musicians sing. T.T.B., violins, continuo. (XXVII.)

How pleasant is this flowery plain. S.T., flutes, continuo. Published 1688. (XXII.)

Purcell

If ever I more riches did desire (Cowley). S.S.T.B., violins, continuo. (XXVII.)

In a deep vision's intellectual scene (Cowley). S.S.B., continuo. (XXVII.)

Oh! what a scene. S.B., flute, continuo. (XXII.)

See where she sits (Cowley). S.B., violins, continuo. (XXII.)

Soft notes and gently raised (Howe). S.B., flutes, continuo. Published 1685. (XXII.)

We reap all the pleasures. S.T.B., flutes, continuo. Incomplete. (XXVII.)

When night her purple veil. B., violins, continuo. (XXI.)

CHURCH MUSIC

Anthems

Awake, put on thy strength. Verse, A.A.B., [chorus,] strings. Incomplete. *c.* 1682–5. (XIV.)

Be merciful unto me. Verse, A.T.B. and chorus. Before 1683 (?). (XXVIII.)

Behold, I bring you glad tidings. Verse, A.T.B., chorus, strings. 1687. (XXVIII.)

Behold now, praise the Lord. Verse, A.T.B., chorus, strings. *c.* 1680. (XIII.)

Blessed are they that fear the Lord. Verse, S.S.A.B., chorus, strings. 1688. (XXVIII.)

Blessed be the Lord my strength. Verse, A.T.B. and chorus. Before 1683. (XXVIII.)

Blessed is he that considereth. Verse, A.T.B. and chorus. *c.* 1688 (?). (XXVIII.)

Blessed is he whose unrighteousness is forgiven. Verse, S.S.A.T.T.B. and chorus. *c.* 1680–2. (XIII.)

Blessed is the man that feareth the Lord. Verse, A.T.B. and chorus. *c.* 1688 (?). (XXVIII.)

Blow up the trumpet in Sion. Full, S.A.A.T.T.B.B. and S.S.S.A.T.T.B. (with verse, S.S.S.A.T.T.B.). 1681. (XXVIII.)

Bow down Thine ear. Verse, S.A.T.B. and chorus. *c.* 1680–2. (XIII.)

Give sentence with me, O God. Incomplete. (XXXII.)

Hear me, O Lord, and that soon. Verse, S.A.T.B. and chorus (S.S.A.T.B.). Two versions of the opening verse. *c.* 1680–2. (XIII.)

Hear my prayer, O God. Verse, A.T.B. and chorus. Incomplete. Before 1683. (XXVIII.)

Appendix B—Catalogue of Works

Hear my prayer, O Lord. Full, S.S.A.A.T.T.B.B. Incomplete. *c.* 1680–2. (XXVIII.)

I was glad when they said. Verse, A.T.B., chorus, strings. 1682–3. (XIV.)

I will give thanks unto the Lord. Verse, T.B.B., chorus, strings. *c.* 1680–2 (?). (XXVIII.)

I will give thanks unto Thee, O Lord. Verse, S.S.A.T.B., chorus, strings. *c.* 1682–5. (XVII.)

I will love Thee. Verse, B. and chorus. (XXVIII.)

I will sing unto the Lord. Full, S.S.A.T.B. (with verse). Before 1683. (XXVIII.)

In the midst of life. Full, S.A.T.B. (with verse). Two versions, both before 1682. (XIII, XXIX.)

In Thee, O Lord, do I put my trust. Verse, A.T.B., chorus, strings. *c.* 1682. (XIV.)

It is a good thing to give thanks. Verse, A.T.B., chorus, strings. *c.* 1682–5. (XIV.)

Let God arise. Verse, T.T. and chorus. Before 1683. (XXVIII.)

Let mine eyes run down with tears. Verse, S.S.A.T.B. and chorus. *c.* 1682. (XXIX.)

Lord, how long wilt Thou be angry? Full, S.S.A.T.B. (with verse, A.T.B.). *c.* 1680–2. (XXIX.)

Lord, who can tell? Verse, T.T.B. and chorus. *c.* 1677. (XXIX.)

Man that is born of a woman. Full, S.A.T.B. (with verse). *c.* 1680–2. (XXIX.)

My beloved spake. Verse, A.T.B.B., chorus, strings. Before 1683. (XIII.)

My heart is fixed. Verse, A.T.B., chorus, strings. *c.* 1682–5. (XIV.)

My heart is inditing. Verse, S.S.S.A.T.B.B.B., chorus (S.S.S.A.T.B.B.B.), strings. 1685. (XVII.)

My song shall be alway. Verse, B., chorus, strings. 1688 (?). (XXIX.)

O consider my adversity. Verse, A.T.B. and chorus. (XXIX.)

O give thanks unto the Lord. Verse, S.A.T.B. and chorus. 1693. (XXIX.)

O God, the King of Glory. Full, S.A.T.B. Before 1685. (XXIX.)

O God, they that love Thy name. Incomplete. (XXXII.)

O God, Thou art my God. Full, S.A.T.B. (with verse, S.S.A.T.B.). *c.* 1680–2. (XXIX.)

O God, Thou hast cast us out. Full, S.S.A.A.T.B. (with verse). *c.* 1680–2. (XXIX.)

Purcell

O Lord God of hosts. Full, S.S.A.A.T.T.B.B. (with verse, S.S.A.A.T.B.). *c.* 1680–2. (XXIX.)

O Lord, grant the king a long life. Verse, A.T.B., chorus, strings. 1685. (XXIX.)

O Lord our Governor. Verse, S.S.S.B.B. and chorus. Before 1683. (XXIX.)

O Lord, rebuke me not. Verse, S.S. and chorus. (XXIX.)

O Lord, Thou art my God. Verse, A.T.B. and chorus. *c.* 1680–2. (XXIX.)

O praise God in His holiness. Verse, A.T.B.B., double chorus (S.A.T.B., A.T.B.B.), strings. *c.* 1682–5. (XIV.)

O praise the Lord, all ye heathen. Verse, T.T. and chorus. *c.* 1685. (XXXII.)

O sing unto the Lord. Verse, S.A.T.B.B., chorus, strings. 1688. (XVII.)

Out of the deep. Verse, S.A.B. and chorus. *c.* 1680 (?) (XXXII.)

Praise the Lord, O Jerusalem. Verse, S.S.A.T.B., chorus (S.S.A.T.B.), strings. *c.* 1688 (?). (XVII.)

Praise the Lord, O my soul, and all that is within me. Verse, S.S.T.T.B.B., chorus, strings. *c.* 1682–5. (XIV.)

Praise the Lord, O my soul, O Lord my God. Verse, A.B., chorus, strings. 1687. (XVII.)

Rejoice in the Lord alway. Verse, A.T.B., chorus, strings. *c.* 1682–5. (XIV.)

Remember not, Lord, our offences. Full, S.S.A.T.B. *c.* 1680–2. (XXXII.)

Save me, O God. Full, S.S.A.T.T.B. (with verse). *c.* 1680–2. (XIII.)

Sing unto God. Verse, B. and chorus. 1687. (XXXII.)

The Lord is King, be the people. Verse, S.S. and chorus. (XXXII.)

The Lord is King, the earth may be glad. Verse, B. and chorus. 1688. (XXXII.)

The Lord is my Light. Verse, A.T.B., chorus, strings. *c.* 1682–5. (XIV.)

The way of God is an undefiled way. Verse, A.A.B. and chorus (S.S.A.A.T.T.B.). 1694. (XXXII.)

They that go down to the sea in ships. Verse, A.B., chorus, strings. 1685. (XXXII.)

Thou knowest, Lord, the secrets of our hearts. Verse, S.A.T.B. Two versions, both before 1683. (*a*, XIII; *b*, XXIX.)

Appendix B—Catalogue of Works

Thou knowest, Lord, the secrets of our hearts. Full, S.A.T.B. with 'flatt trumpets.' 1695. (XXXII.)

Thy righteousness, O God, is very high. Incomplete. (XXXII.)

Thy way, O God, is holy. Verse, A.B. and chorus. 1687. (XXXII.)

Thy word is a lantern. Verse, A.T.B. and chorus. (XXXII.)

Turn Thou us, O good Lord. Verse, A.T.B. and chorus. (XXXII.)

Unto Thee will I cry. Verse, A.T.B., chorus, strings. *c.* 1682–5. (XVII.)

Who hath believed our report? Verse, A.T.T.B. and chorus. *c.* 1679–80. (XIII.)

Why do the heathen? Verse, A.T.B., chorus, strings. *c.* 1682–5. (XVII.)

Services

Magnificat and Nunc Dimittis in G minor. Full, S.A.T.B. (with verse, S.S.A.T.B.). (XXIII.)

Morning and Evening Service in B flat (including all alternative canticles). Full, S.A.T.B. (with verse, S.S.A.A.T.B.B.). Before 1683. (XXIII.)

Te Deum and Jubilate in D. Verse, S.S.A.A.T.B., chorus (S.S.A.T.B.), trumpets, strings. 1694. (XXIII.)

Hymns, Psalms and Canons (XXX and XXXII)

Ah! few and full of sorrow (Sandys). S.A.T.B.

Allelujah. Canon. S.S.A.T.B.

Beati omnes qui timent Dominum. Latin psalm. S.S.A.B.

Early, O Lord, my fainting soul (Patrick). S.S.A.B.

Gloria Patri (G minor). Canon. S.A.B.

Gloria Patri (C minor). Canon. S.A.T.B.

Gloria Patri (G minor). Canon. S.A.T.B.

Glory be to the Father. Canon. S.A.T.B.

God is gone up. Canon. 7 v.

Hear me, O Lord, the great support (Patrick). A.T.B.

In guilty night. Scena. S.A.B.

Jehovah, quam multi. Latin psalm. S.S.A.T.B.

Laudate Dominum. Canon. S.A.B.

Lord, I can suffer (Patrick). S.S.A.B.

Lord, not to us (Patrick). A.T.B.

Purcell

Miserere mei. Canon. S.A.T.B.
O all ye people (Patrick). S.S.T.B.
O happy man (Patrick). S.S.A.B.
O, I'm sick of life (Sandys). A.T.B.
O Lord our Governor (Patrick). S.S.A.B.
Plung'd in the confines of despair (Patrick). T.T.B.
Since God so tender a regard (Patrick). T.T.B.
When on my sick bed (Flatman). A.T.B.

Also a hymn-tune, *Burford,* and various chants.

SACRED SONGS

(for one or two voices with continuo)

(XXX)

Awake and with attention hear (Cowley). B. 1688.
Awake, awake, ye dead (Tate). B.B. 1693.
Begin the song (Cowley). B. 1693.
Close thine eyes and sleep secure (Quarles). S.B. 1688.
Full of wrath his threatening breath (Taylor). S.
Great God and just (Taylor). S. (with chorus, S.S.B.). 1688.
Hosanna to the highest. B. (with chorus, A.B.).
How have I strayed (Fuller). S. (with chorus, S.B.). 1688.
How long, great God? (Norris). S. 1688.
In the black dismal dungeon of despair (Fuller). S. 1688.
Let the night perish (Taylor). S. (with chorus, S.B.). 1688.
Lord, what is man? (Fuller). S. 1693.
Now that the sun hath veiled his light (Fuller). S. 1688.
Sleep, Adam. S. 1683.
Tell me, some pitying angel (Tate). S. 1693.
The earth trembled (Quarles). S. 1688.
Thou wakeful shepherd (Fuller). S. 1688.
We sing to Him whose wisdom formed the ear (Ingelo). S. (with chorus, (S.B.) 1688.
With sick and famish'd eyes (Herbert). S. 1688.

280

Appendix B—Catalogue of Works

Catches

(XXII, unless otherwise marked)

A health to the nut-brown lass (Suckling). 4 v. 1685.

An ape, a lion, a fox and an ass. 3 v. 1686.

As Roger last night. 3 v.

At the close of the evening. 3 v. (B.B.B.). Possibly interpolated in Beaumont and Fletcher's *The Knight of Malta*. 1691. (XX.)

Bring the bowl and cool Nantz. 3 v. *c.* 1693–4.

Call for the reckoning. 3 v.

Come, let us drink (Brome). 3 v. with continuo.

Come, my hearts. 3 v. 1685.

Down, down with Bacchus. 3 v. 1693.

Drink on till night be spent (Ayres). 3 v. 1686.

God save our sovereign Charles. 3 v. 1685.

Great Apollo and Bacchus. 3 v.

He that drinks is immortal. 3 v. 1686.

Here's a health, pray let it pass. 3 v.

Here's that will challenge (*Bartholomew Fair*). 3 v. *c.* 1680.

I gave her cakes. 3 v. 1690.

If all be true that I do think. 3 v. 1689.

Is Charleroy's siege? 3 v. *c.* 1693–4.

Joy, mirth, triumphs. 4 v.

Let the grave folks go preach. 3 v. 1685.

Let us drink to the blades. 3 v. *c.* 1693–4.

My lady's coachman, John. 3 v. 1687.

My wife has a tongue. 3 v. Words from Ravenscroft's *The English Lawyer*. 1685. (XVI.)

Now England's great council. 'A catch made in the time of Parliament, 1676.' 3 v. 1685.

Now, now we are met. 3 v. 1687.

Of all the instruments that are. 3 v. 1693.

Once in our lives. 3 v. 1686.

Once, twice, thrice I Julia tried. 3 v.

One industrious insect (Tomlinson). 3 v.

Pale faces, stand by (Taverner). 3 v. 1688.

Pox on you for a fop. 3 v.

Purcell

Prithee be n't so sad and serious (Brome). 3 v.
Room for th' express. 3 v.   Words written, 1694.
Since the Duke is returned. 3 v. 1685 (words written, 1682).
Since time so kind to us does prove. 3v.
Sir Walter enjoying. 3 v.
Soldier, soldier, take off thy wine. 4 v.
Sum up all the delights. 3 v. 1687.
The Macedon youth (Suckling). 4v. 1686.
The surrender of Limerick. 3 v.   Words written, 1694.
'Tis easy to force. 4 v. (B.B.B.B.). 1685.
'Tis too late for a coach. 3 v. 1686.
'Tis women makes us love. 4 v. 1685.
To all lovers of music (Carr). 3 v. 1687.
To thee and to a maid. 3 v. 1685.
True Englishmen drink. 3 v.   Words written, 1689.
Under a green elm. 4 v. 1686.
Under this stone. 3 v. 1686.
When V and I together meet. 3 v. 1686.
Who comes there? 3 v. 1685.
Wine in a morning (Tom Brown). 3 v. 1686.
Would you know how we meet? (Otway). 3 v. 1685.
Young Colin cleaving (D'Urfey). 3 v. 1691
Young John the gardener. 4 v. 1683.

Three-part Songs with Continuo (XXII)

A poor blind woman. S.S.B. Authenticity uncertain.
Sweet tyranness, I now resign. S.S.B. 1667. (Possibly by the elder Henry Purcell; see p. 8.)
'Tis wine was made to rule the day. S.S.B. (with S. solo).
When the cock begins to crow. S.S.B.

Duets with Continuo

[For duets with instrumental *obbligati* see 'Secular Cantatas.']

A grasshopper and a fly (D'Urfey). S.B. 1686. (XXV.)

(The following are in XXII)

Above the tumults of a busy state. S.B.
Alas, how barbarous are we (Katherine Philips). S.B.
Come, dear companions. S.B. 1686.

Come, lay by all care. S.B. 1685.

Dulcibella, when e'er I sue for a kiss (Henley). S.B. 1694.

Fair Cloe my breast so alarms (Glanvill). S.B. 1692.

Fill the bowl with rosy wine (Cowley). S.B. 1687.

Go, tell Amynta, gentle swain (Dryden). S.B.

Has yet your breast no pity learned? S.B. 1688.

Haste, gentle Charon. B.B.

Hence, fond deceiver. S.B. 1687.

Here's to thee, Dick (Cowley). S.B. 1688.

How great are the blessings (Tate). S.B. 1686.

How sweet is the air and refreshing. S.B. 1687.

I saw fair Cloris all alone (Strode). S.B. 1686.

I spy Celia, Celia eyes me. S.B.

In all our Cynthia's shining sphere (Settle). S.B.

In some kind dream (Etherege). S.B. 1687.

Julia, your unjust disdain. S.B.

Let Hector, Achilles and each brave commander. S.B. 1689.

Lost is my quiet for ever. S.B. 1691.

Nestor, who did to thrice man's age attain. S.B. 1689.

O dive Custos Auriacae domus (Parker). S.S. 1695.

Oft am I by the women told (Cowley). S.B. 1687.

Saccharissa's grown old. S.B. 1686.

Silvia, thou brighter eye of night. S.B.

Silvia, 'tis true you're fair. S.B. 1686.

Sit down, my dear Silvia (D'Urfey). S.B. 1685.

There ne'er was so wretched a lover as I (Congreve). S.B.

Though my mistress be fair. S.B. 1685.

Trip it, trip it in a ring. S.B. Two-part version of a song in *The Fairy Queen.*

Underneath this myrtle shade (Cowley). S.B. 1692.

Were I to choose the greatest bliss. S.B. 1689.

What can we poor females do? S.B. (Also as a solo song in XXV.)

When gay Philander left the plain. S.B. 1684.

When, lovely Phyllis, thou art kind. S.B. 1685.

When Myra sings (Lord Lansdowne). S.B. 1695.

When Teucer from his father fled (Kenrick). S.B. 1686.

While bolts and bars my day control. S.B.

While you for me alone had charms (Oldham, after Horace). S.B.

Why, my Daphne, why complaining? S.B. 1691.

Purcell

Solo Songs with Continuo (XXV)

[For songs in the plays and operas see Appendix F.]

A thousand several ways I tried. 1684.

Ah! cruel nymph, you give despair.

Ah! how pleasant 'tis to love. 1688.

Ah! what pains, what racking thoughts (Congreve). Voice part only.

Amidst the shades and cool refreshing streams. 1687.

Amintas, to my grief I see. 1679.

Amintor, heedless of his flocks. 1681.

Anacreon's defeat. See *This poet sings*.

Ask me to love no more (Hammond). 1694.

Bacchus is a power divine.

Beneath a dark and melancholy grove. With S.B. chorus. *c.* 1681.

Bess of Bedlam. See *From silent shades*.

Beware, poor shepherds. 1684.

Cease, anxious world (Etherege). 1687.

Cease, O my sad soul (Webbe). 1678.

Celia's fond, too long I've loved her. 1694.

Corinna is divinely fair. 1692.

Cupid, the slyest rogue alive. 1685.

Draw near, you lovers (Stanley). With S.B. chorus.

Farewell, all joys. 1685.

Farewell, ye rocks (D'Urfey). With S.B. chorus. 1685.

Fly swift, ye hours. 1692.

From silent shades (*Bess of Bedlam*). 1683.

Gentle shepherds, you that know (Tate). Elegy on the death of John Playford. With S.B. chorus. 1687.

He himself courts his own ruin. 1684.

Hears not my Phyllis? (*Knotting Song*) (Sedley). 1695.

High on a throne of glittering ore (D'Urfey). Ode to Queen Mary. With S.B. chorus. Words printed, 1690.

How delightful's the life.

How I sigh when I think. 1681.

I came, I saw, and was undone (Cowley).

I envy not a monarch's fate. 1693.

I fain would be free. Voice part only.

I love and I must (Bell Barr).

I loved fair Celia (B. Howard). 1694. The music is identical with *We now, my Thyrsis*.

Appendix B—Catalogue of Works

I resolve against cringing. 1679.
I saw that you were grown so high. 1678.
I take no pleasure in the sun's bright beams. 1681.
If grief has any power to kill. 1685.
If music be the food of love (Heveningham). First setting. 1692.
If music be the food of love. Second setting. 1693.
If music be the food of love. Third setting. 1695.
If prayers and tears (*Sighs for our late Sovereign King Charles II*).
In Chloris all soft charms agree (Howe). 1684.
In vain we dissemble. 1685.
Incassum, Lesbia, rogas (Herbert). Elegy on the death of Queen Mary. 1695.
Leave these useless arts in loving. Solo version of a two-part song in Shadwell's *Epsom Wells.*
Let each gallant heart (Turner). 1683.
Let formal lovers still pursue. 1687.
Let us, kind Lesbia, give away. With S.B. chorus. 1684.
Love arms himself in Celia's eyes.
Love is now become a trade. 1685.
Love, thou canst hear tho' thou art blind (R. Howard). 1695.
Love's power in my heart shall find no compliance. 1688.
Lovely Albina's come ashore. 'The last song that Mr. Henry Purcell sett before he dy'd.'
More love or more disdain I crave (Webbe). 1678.
Musing on cares of human fate (D'Urfey). With S.B. chorus. 1685.
My heart, whenever you appear. 1685.
No, to what purpose should I speak? (Cowley). With S.B. chorus.
No watch, dear Celia, just is found. 1693.
Not all my torments can your pity move.
O! fair Cedaria, hide those eyes.
O how happy's he (Mountfort). 1694 (?). Voice part only.
O solitude, my sweetest choice (Katherine Philips). 1687.
Olinda in the shades unseen.
On the brow of Richmond Hill (D'Urfey). 1692.
Pastora's beauties when unblown. 1681.
Phyllis, I can ne'er forgive it. 1688.
Phyllis, talk no more of passion. 1685.
Pious Celinda goes to prayers (Congreve). 1695.
Rashly I swore I would disown. 1683.

Purcell

Sawney is a bonny lad (Motteux). 1694.

Scarce had the rising sun appear'd. 1679.

See how the fading glories of the year. With S.B. chorus. **1689.**

She loves and she confesses too (Cowley). 1683.

She that would gain a faithful lover. 1695.

She who my poor heart possesses. 1683.

Silvia, now your scorn give over. 1688.

Since one poor view has drawn my heart. 1681.

Since the pox or the plague. With S.B. chorus. 1679.

Spite of the godhead, powerful love (Wharton). 1687.

Stript of their green our groves appear (Motteux). 1692.

Sweet, be no longer sad (Webbe). 1678.

Sweet tyranness, I now resign. Solo version of the three-part song listed above. 1678.

The fatal hour comes on apace.

They say you're angry (Cowley). 1685.

This poet sings the Trojan wars (*Anacreon's defeat*). 1688.

Through mournful shades and solitary groves (Duke). 1684.

Turn then thine eyes. Solo version of two-part song in *The Fairy Queen.*

Urge me no more.

We now, my Thyrsis, never find (Motteux). 1693. (Cf. *I loved fair Celia.*)

What a sad fate is mine. First setting.

What a sad fate is mine. Second setting.

What can we poor females do? 1694. (For two-part version see above.)

What hope for us remains now he is gone? With S.B. chorus. Elegy on the death of Matthew Locke. 1679 (presumably written 1677).

When first Amintas sued (D'Urfey). 'A new song, to a Scotch tune. Set by Mr. Henry Purcell.' 1687.

When first my shepherdess and I. 1687.

When her languishing eyes said 'love.' 1681.

When I a lover pale do see. 1678.

When my Acmelia smiles.

When Strephon found his passion vain. 1683.

When Thirsis did the splendid eye. 1675.

While Thirsis, wrapt in downy sleep. 'A pastoral coronation song.' 1685.

Whilst Cynthia sung, all angry winds lay still. 1686.

Who but a slave can well express?

Who can behold Florella's charms? 1695.

Why so serious, why so grave? (Flatman). Voice part only.

286

Ye happy swains, whose nymphs are kind. 1685.

Young Thirsis' fate ye hills and groves deplore. Elegy on the death of Thomas
Farmer.   With S.B. chorus.   *c.* 1690.

INSTRUMENTAL WORKS
(XXXI, unless otherwise marked)
Strings
(*a*) *Without continuo*

Chaconne in G minor.   4 parts.
3 Fantasias.   3 parts.   1680 (?).
9 Fantasias.   4 parts.   1680.
Fantasia upon one note.   5 parts.
In Nomine.   6 parts.
In Nomine.   7 parts.
Pavan in G minor.   4 parts.
4 Pavans in 3 parts.
Prelude for violin (or flute).

(*b*) *With continuo*

Fantasia on a ground in D major.   4 parts.
3 Overtures.   (1) G major, 4 parts (a version of the introduction to
   Swifter Isis, swifter flow), (2) D minor, 4 parts, (3) G minor, 5 parts.
12 *Sonatas of III Parts.*   2 violins, bass, continuo. Published 1683. (V.)
10 *Sonatas of IV Parts.*   2 violins, bass, continuo. Published 1697. (VII.)
Sonata in G minor.   Violin and continuo.
Suite in G major.   4 parts (incomplete).   The fourth movement is from
   Distressed Innocence, the last from *Ye tuneful Muses.*

Wind

March and Canzona for four 'flatt trumpets.'   The former adapted from
   a movement in Shadwell's *The Libertine.*   1695.

Wind and Strings

Sonata in D major for trumpet, strings (4 parts) and continuo.

Harpsichord
(VI, unless otherwise marked)

A Choice Collection of Lessons for the Harpsichord or Spinet (published 1696
   and 1699).   Contents: 8 Suites (G major, G minor, G major, A

Purcell

minor, C major,[1] D major, D minor,[2] F major), March (C major),[3] Trumpet Tune (C major),[4] Chaconne (G minor),[5] Jig (G minor),[6] Trumpet Tune (*Cibell,* C major), Trumpet Tune (C major).[7]

Musick's Hand-Maid, part ii (published 1689) includes: 2 Song Tunes (C major),[8] 2 Marches (C major),[9] A New Minuet (D minor), 3 Minuets (2 in A minor, 1 in D minor[10]), A New Scotch Tune (G major), A New Ground (E minor),[11] A New Irish Tune (*Lilliburlero,* G major), Rigadoon (C major), *Sefauchi's Farewell* (D minor), Suite (C major).[12]

Other pieces:[13] 2 Airs (D minor,[14] G major [49]), Corant (G major) [48], Ground (G major) [33], Minuet (G major) [51], *The Queen's Dolour* (A minor),[14] 2 Suites (A minor,[15] B flat major[16]).

Transcriptions:[13] 3 Airs (D minor [37, 41], G minor [58]),[17] Canary (A major),[18] 2 Grounds (C minor [39, 51]),[19] 3 Hornpipes (B flat major,[20] D minor [38],[21] E minor [47[22]]), 4 Overtures (C minor, D major, D major, G minor [56].[23]

Organ (VI) [13]

Verse (F major) [36], 4 Voluntaries (C major [35], D minor [61], D minor [64], G major [53]), Voluntary on the Old 100th (A major) [59].

---

[1] The Corant and Saraband also in the Suite in *Musick's Hand-Maid.* [2] The Hornpipe from *The Married Beau.* [3] From *The Married Beau.* [4] From *The Indian Queen.* [5] From *Timon of Athens.* [6] From *Abdelazer.* [7] From *Dioclesian.* [8] No. 1=*Ah, how pleasant 'tis to love*; No. 2 (not in VI: in *Musick's Hand-Maid,* ii, ed. T. Dart)=*Silvia, now your scorn give over.* [9] No. 1 called 'Lesson' in VI. [10] From *Raise the Voice.* [11] From *Welcome to all the pleasures.* [12] In Dart, *op. cit.*; Almond in VI. 33 (Air); for Corant and Saraband see n. 1. [13] Numbers in square brackets refer to pages in VI. [14] Not in VI. [15] Prelude and Saraband (Lesson) in VI. 40 & 35; Almond and Corant in *Old English Composers for the Virginal and Harpsichord,* ed. E. Pauer. [16] In Pauer, *op. cit.* [17] No. 1 from *The Indian Queen*; No. 2 from *The Double Dealer*; No. 3 from *Abdelazer.* [18] From *The Indian Queen*; not in VI. [19] No. 1 from *Ye tuneful Muses*; No. 2 possibly by Croft. [20] From *Abdelazer*; not in VI. [21] From *Abdelazer*; called 'Rondo' in VI. [22] From *The Old Bachelor.* [23] Nos. 1–3 in Pauer, *op. cit.* No. 1 from *The Indian Queen,* No. 2 from *The Fairy Queen,* No. 3 from *Timon of Athens,* No. 4 from *The Virtuous Wife.*

APPENDIX C

Abell, John (1650–1724), counter-tenor singer and lutenist, sworn gentleman of the Chapel Royal, of which he may have been a chorister, in 1679. Married Frances Knollys, sister of the Earl of Banbury, travelled much abroad, was intendant at Cassel in 1698–9 and returned to England as a stage singer. Published some collections of songs.

Albrici, Bartolomeo (born *c.* 1630), Italian organist and composer, was organist at the court church of Dresden until 1663 and composer to Charles II from 1664, together with his brother Vincenzo (1631–90).

Baltzar, Thomas (*c.* 1630–63), German or Swedish violinist, came to England in 1655 and appointed one of the king's twenty-four violins in 1661.

Banister, John (1630–79), violinist and concert promoter in London, sent to France by Charles II and appointed leader of the king's band in 1662. Composed music for Charles D'Avenant's (q.v.) tragedy, *Circe,* and contributed songs to various collections.

Barnard, John, musician and minor canon at St. Paul's Cathedral, published the first printed collection of English cathedral music in 1641.

Bassani, Giovanni Battista (*c.* 1657–1716), Italian violinist and composer, organist at Ferrara and later in charge of the cathedral music at Bologna, returned to Ferrara as cathedral organist in 1685. He composed three oratorios, published six operas and brought out a large number of church and instrumental works. Corelli was probably his pupil.

Behn, Aphra (1640–89), dramatist and novelist, daughter of a barber named Johnston (?) at Canterbury, is said to have gone to Surinam with a relative named Amis, who was governor there and whom she called father. Although he died on the voyage, she is supposed to have stayed there and become acquainted with the slave Oroonoko, afterwards the subject of one of her novels. In 1658 she married

Purcell

Behn, a Dutch merchant in London, but was left a widow at the age of twenty-six. She became attached to the court and went to Antwerp as a political spy. Afterwards produced many plays in London and published a number of novels, poems and pamphlets.

Betterton, Thomas (c. 1635–1710), actor, made his first appearance at the theatre in Blackfriars in 1660 and played in D'Avenant's (q.v.) opera, *The Siege of Rhodes,* the following year. Opened the New Playhouse in Lincoln's Inn Fields with Congreve's *Love for Love* in 1695, but retired soon after.

Boyce, William (1710–79), composer and organist, boy chorister at St. Paul's Cathedral and later pupil of Maurice Greene, whom he succeeded in 1755 as master of the king's band. Organist of the Chapel Royal from 1758. Published a collection of English *Cathedral Music,* 1760–78.

Bracegirdle, Anne (c. 1674–1748), actress, pupil of Betterton (q.v.), made her first appearance in 1680 and later became a great exponent of Congreve, to whom she was said to be secretly married.

Bryan, Albert (born c. 1621), organist and composer, organist of St. Paul's Cathedral from 1638 and again after the Restoration. After the fire of London in 1666 he became organist of Westminster Abbey, a post in which he was succeeded by Blow in 1668, in which year he may have died.

Cambert, Robert (c. 1628–77), French composer, whose *Pomone,* produced in 1671, was the first French opera. He learnt the harpsichord from Chambonnières, was organist at the church of Saint-Honoré in Paris and superintendent of the queen's music. He was ousted by Lulli and went to live in London in 1672. Most of his work is lost.

Caproli (or Caprioli), Carlo, Italian violinist and composer, whom Cardinal Mazarin brought to Paris, where he produced the opera, *Le nozze di Peleo e Teti,* in 1654. Playford (q.v.) published two songs of his in the *Scelta di canzonette* in 1679, and he composed the oratorio, *Davide prevaricante,* in 1683.

Carissimi, Giacomo (1605–74), Italian composer who cultivated the forms of oratorio and cantata in their early stages. He was *maestro di cappella* at Assisi about 1624–8, then went to Rome, where he held a similar post at the church of San Apollinare attached to the German college. He remained there to the end of his life.

Appendix C—Personalia

Cavalli, Pietro Francesco (1602–76), Italian composer and one of the first masters of opera. He became a singer under Monteverdi at St. Mark's, Venice, in 1617, second organist at that church in 1640, first organist in 1665 and *maestro di cappella* in 1668. His first opera was *Le nozze di Teti,* produced in 1639, and in 1660 he was called to Paris to perform his *Serse* at the celebration of Louis XIV's marriage. In addition to the numerous operas written for the five theatres in Venice, he composed church music.

Cazzati, Maurizio (c. 1620–77), Italian composer who held successive posts at Mantua, Ferrara, Bergamo and Bologna, and composed secular vocal and instrumental music as well as works for the church.

Cesti, Pietro Antonio (1623–69), Italian composer, pupil of Carissimi (q.v.), became a member of the papal choir in Rome in 1660, after having been *maestro di cappella* at Florence, and was appointed vice-*Kapellmeister* to the Austrian court in 1666, remaining in Vienna until his death. He wrote chiefly for the stage.

Child, William (1606–97), organist and church composer, educated at Bristol Cathedral and appointed one of the organists at St. George's Chapel, Windsor, in 1632. At the Restoration he received a court appointment and in 1663 he took the D.Mus. degree at Oxford. He wrote a large number of anthems, services and psalms.

Clarke, Jeremiah (c. 1673–1707), composer, pupil of Blow at the Chapel Royal, organist at Winchester College in 1692–5 and of St. Paul's Cathedral from 1695. Sworn gentleman-extraordinary of the Chapel Royal in 1700 and organist in 1704. Wrote chiefly for the church and the stage.

Clifford, James (1622–98), divine and musician, chorister at Magdalen College, Oxford, 1632–42, and appointed minor canon at St. Paul's Cathedral in 1661. Published a collection of the words of *Divine Services and Anthems* in 1663.

Coleman, Charles (died 1664), chamber musician to Charles I and after the Civil War music teacher in London. Took the Mus.D. degree at Cambridge in 1651 and was appointed composer to Charles II in 1662. With Cooke (q.v.), Hudson (q.v.) and Lawes (q.v.) he contributed music to D'Avenant's entertainment at Rutland House in 1656. His son Charles (died c. 1694) was a member of the royal band in the latter half of the century.

Cooke, Henry (died 1672), musician and soldier, pupil at the Chapel Royal, captain in the Duke of Northumberland's army during the

Civil War. Appointed bass singer and master of the children at the Chapel Royal at the Restoration.

D'Avenant (or *Davenant*), *Sir William* (1606–68), poet and dramatist, son of an innkeeper at Oxford whose house was sometimes visited by Shakespeare, whose natural son D. claimed to be. Educated at Lincoln College, Oxford, he afterwards became involved in several political adventures and was twice imprisoned in the Tower of London. In 1656 he produced the English 'opera,' *The Siege of Rhodes*. Wrote numerous plays and succeeded Ben Jonson as Poet Laureate.

Draghi, Giovanni Battista (c. 1640–c. 1710), Italian harpsichord player and composer settled in London, music master to the princesses Mary and Anne and organist to Catherine of Braganza, wife of Charles II. Set Dryden's ode for St. Cecilia's Day in 1687 and contributed music to D'Urfey's *Wonders in the Sun* in 1706.

D'Urfey (or *Durfey*), *Thomas* (1653–1723), dramatist and collector of songs, published with verses of his own in *Wit and Mirth, or Pills to Purge Melancholy*.

Eccles, John (c. 1663–1735), composer, at first for the stage, member of the king's band from 1694 and appointed master in 1700.

Gay, John (1685–1732), poet and dramatist, left an orphan and apprenticed to a mercer in London, but began to write poetry and became a friend of Pope. He was most popular as a dramatic satirist and his greatest success was *The Beggar's Opera,* produced in 1728. He wrote the poem of *Acis and Galatea* for Handel.

Gibbons, Christopher (1615–76), organist and composer, son of Orlando Gibbons (1583–1625), became one of the children at the Chapel Royal, but is said to have been partly brought up by his uncle Edward Gibbons (c. 1570 – c. 1650) at Exeter. Became organist of Winchester Cathedral in 1638 and of the Chapel Royal and Westminster Abbey in 1660.

Gostling, John (c. 1650–1733), clergyman and bass singer, became gentleman of the Chapel Royal in 1679 and afterwards held various clerical posts in and out of London.

Grabu, Louis, French violinist and composer, appointed composer to the king in 1665 and master of the king's music in 1666. Produced an English adaptation of an opera, *Ariadne,* at the Theatre Royal in 1674 and wrote music for Shadwell's (q.v.) version of *Timon of*

Athens in 1678. He went back to France in 1679, but returned to London in 1683, where he composed music to Dryden's *Albion and Albanius* two years later.

Gregory, William (died *c.* 1688), singer, violist and composer, in the service of Cromwell, a private teacher during the Commonwealth, and subsequently one of Charles II's musicians.

Harris, Renatus, organ builder in London, who competed with Smith (q.v.) for the commission to build a new organ in Temple Church, enlarged the organ built by his grandfather at Magdalen College, Oxford, and built many other famous organs.

Hingston, John (died 1683), organist, violist and composer, pupil of Orlando Gibbons, in the service of Charles I and afterwards of Cromwell, whose daughters he instructed in music. Became violist in the king's band in 1660.

Howard, Sir Robert (1626–98), dramatist, son of the Earl of Berkshire and brother-in-law of Dryden, with whom he collaborated.

Hudson, George, violinist and composer, took part in the composition of a dramatic entertainment by D'Avenant (q.v.) given at Rutland House in 1656; was a member of the king's band in 1661 and composer to the king.

Humfrey, Pelham (1647–74), composer, entered the re-established Chapel Royal in 1660 as a chorister under Cooke (q.v.), joined Blow and Turner (q.v.) in the composition of the so-called *Club Anthem*, and was sent abroad for study by Charles II in 1664. Returned in 1667 and was sworn a gentleman of the Chapel Royal, where he succeeded Cooke as master of the children in 1672.

Hunt, Arabella (died 1705), singer and lutenist, music teacher of Princess (afterwards Queen) Anne and a favourite of Queen Mary. Purcell and Blow composed many songs for her and Congreve wrote an ode in her praise.

Killigrew, Thomas (1612–83), dramatist attached to the court of Charles II.

Lanier, Nicholas (1588–1666), English composer, singer and painter of French descent, wrote music for Ben Jonson's masque, *Lovers made Men*, in 1617, and not only sang in it but painted the scenery for it. Was sent to Italy in 1625 by Charles I to purchase pictures for the royal collection. Appointed master of the king's music in 1626. Lived in the Netherlands during the Commonwealth, but resumed his post at the Restoration.

Purcell

Lawes, Henry (1596–1662), composer and singer, became a gentleman of the Chapel Royal in 1626, wrote music for Milton's masque of *Comus,* performed at Ludlow Castle in 1634, and was the subject of a sonnet by Milton in 1646. Resumed court appointments on the Restoration and wrote an anthem for the coronation of Charles II.

Lee, Nathaniel (c. 1653–92), actor and dramatist, educated at Westminster and Cambridge, wrote tragedies and comedies and collaborated with Dryden. Spent four years in Bedlam, having been driven mad by drink, and died from an accident after a bout of drunkenness.

Locke, Matthew (1622–77), composer, chorister at Exeter Cathedral under Edward Gibbons (c. 1570–c. 1650), composed music for Shirley's masque, *Cupid and Death,* jointly with Christopher Gibbons (q.v.), in 1653, and for D'Avenant's (q.v.) *Siege of Rhodes* in 1656. Was appointed composer in ordinary to Charles II in 1661. He also contributed to Shadwell's (q.v.) *Psyche* in 1675 and to the same poet's adaptation of *The Tempest* in the previous year.

Lowe, Edward (c. 1610–82), organist and composer, was educated as chorister at Salisbury Cathedral and became organist of Christ Church, Oxford, about 1630. Appointed one of the organists at the Chapel Royal in 1660.

Mace, Thomas (born c. 1619), writer on music, clerk of Trinity College, Cambridge, published *Musick's Monument* in 1676.

Matteis, Nicola, Italian violinist who came to England about 1672. He published three collections of violin music, one of songs and a treatise, *The False Consonances of Musick.*

Mell, Davis (1604–62), violinist and clockmaker, at the Restoration became a member of the king's band and joint director.

Merula, Tarquinio, Italian composer, held appointments alternately at Bergamo and Cremona, and was court and church organist at Warsaw in 1624. He published several collections of vocal and instrumental music.

North, Roger (1653–1734), lawyer and amateur musician, brother of Lord Guilford, author of several works, including *Memoirs of Musick* and *The Musicall Gramarian.*

Paisible (or *Peasable*), *James* (died 1721), member of the king's band in London, probably of French extraction, composed incidental music for a number of plays as well as duets, sonatas and pieces for flute.

Appendix C—Personalia

Playford, Henry (born 1657), bookseller and music-publisher, son of the following, to whose business he succeeded in 1684. He established regular concerts, held three times a week at a London coffee-house from 1699 onwards, and another series at Oxford in 1701.

Playford, John (1623 – *c.* 1686), bookseller and music-publisher, established in London about 1648. His first musical publication, *The English Dancing Master,* appeared in 1650, dated 1651.

Reggio, Pietro (died 1685), Italian singer and lutenist to Queen Christina of Sweden, later settled at Oxford, where he published *A Treatise to sing well any Song whatsoever* in 1677. He also distinguished himself as a vocal composer.

Roseingrave, Thomas (1690–1766), English or Irish composer and organist, son of Daniel Roseingrave (*c.* 1650–1727). Organist of St. George's Church, Hanover Square, 1725–38.

Rossi, Luigi (1598–1653), Italian singer and composer, in the service of Cardinal Barberini in Rome about 1620. Invited to Paris by Cardinal Mazarin in 1647, when he produced the first Italian opera commissioned for France.

Rossi, Michele Angelo (*c.* 1600–*c.* 1660), Italian organist and composer, pupil of Frescobaldi, produced an opera, *Erminia sul Giordano,* in 1633, but wrote chiefly keyboard music.

Salmon, Thomas (1648–1706), clergyman and writer on music, published *An Essay to the Advancement of Musick* in 1672, which involved him in a controversy with Locke (q.v.).

Sedley, Sir Charles (*c.* 1639–1701), poet and dramatist at the court of Charles II, father of Catherine Sedley, a mistress of James II, who created her Countess of Dorset. S. was also a pamphleteer and essayist.

Settle, Elkanah (1648–1724), poet and dramatist, educated at Oxford, appointed City Poet of London.

Shadwell, Thomas (1640 *or* 1642–92), poet and dramatist, educated at Cambridge, travelled abroad and afterwards became a successful playwright in London. He was lampooned by Dryden, whom he had attacked. Succeeded Dryden as Poet Laureate.

Shore, Catherine (*c.* 1668 – *c.* 1730), singer and harpsichord player, daughter of Matthew Shore (q.v.), married Colley Cibber in 1693.

Shore, John (died 1752), trumpeter, son of Matthew Shore (q.v.), succeeded to the post of sergeant trumpeter on the death of his brother William in 1707.

Shore, Matthew (died 1700), trumpeter at the court of James II and William III.

Siface (Giovanni Francesco Grossi) (1653–97), Italian male soprano, became singer at the Papal Chapel in Rome in 1675 and came to England about 1679. Sang at the court of James II, but returned to Italy before long. D'Urfey mentions him in A Fool's Preferment of 1688. He was murdered by the brothers of the Marchesa Marsili.

Smith, Bernard (Bernhard Schmidt) (c. 1630–1708), German organ builder settled in England from 1660. His first English organ was that at the Chapel Royal at Whitehall. Having built the organ at St. Margaret's, Westminster, in 1675, he was appointed organist there. Competed with Harris (q.v.) for the commission to build a new organ for the Temple Church, also built instruments for Durham and St. Paul's Cathedrals.

Smith, Robert (c. 1648–75), composer, chorister at the Chapel Royal under Cooke (q.v.), became a musician in ordinary to the king on the death of Humfrey (q.v.) in 1674.

Southerne, Thomas (1660–1746), dramatist, educated at Trinity College, Dublin, afterwards studied law in London. Later became successively a soldier and a theatre manager.

Staggins, Nicholas (died 1705), violinist and composer, appointed master of the king's music by Charles II in 1674, appointed professor of music by the University of Cambridge in 1684.

Stradella, Alessandro (c. 1645–82), Italian composer of noble birth who appears to have held no regular musical appointment. Wrote operas, oratorios and cantatas.

Tate, Nahum (1652–1715), poet and dramatist, educated at Trinity College, Dublin, succeeded Shadwell (q.v.) as Poet Laureate in 1690 and published a metrical version of the Psalms with Nicholas Brady (1659–1726) in 1696. Made two adaptations of Shakespeare, according to the fashion of his time.

Tucker, William (died 1679), church composer, gentleman of the Chapel Royal and minor canon of Westminster Abbey.

Tudway, Thomas (died 1726), composer, organist and musical editor, became chorister in the Chapel Royal soon after the Restoration and lay vicar at Windsor in 1664. Elected organist of King's College, Cambridge, in 1670 and professor of music at the university there in 1705 in succession to Staggins (q.v.). In 1714–20 he compiled a large collection of English cathedral music in six volumes.

Appendix C—Personalia

Turner, William (1651–1740), singer and composer, chorister at Christ Church, Oxford, and later at the Chapel Royal, where he joined Blow and Humfrey (q.v.) in the composition of the so-called *Club Anthem*. Afterwards became a singer successively at Lincoln Cathedral, at St. Paul's and at Westminster Abbey. Graduated Mus.D. at Cambridge in 1696.

Wilson, John (1595–1674), composer, contributed music to *The Maske of Flowers* performed at Whitehall in 1614, became one of the king's musicians in 1635. Lived at Oxford during the Civil War and took the degree of D.Mus. there in 1645, and soon afterwards was in private service in Oxfordshire. After the Restoration he returned to London and became a gentleman of the Chapel Royal in 1662 in succession to Lawes (q.v.)

Wise, Michael (c. 1648–87), composer and singer, chorister in the Chapel Royal in 1660. Appointed organist and choirmaster at Salisbury Cathedral in 1668, but returned to the Chapel Royal as one of the gentlemen in 1676.

Wood, Anthony (1632–95), antiquary and musical historian at Oxford. His *History and Antiquities of the University of Oxford* contains many musical references.

Ziani, Marc' Antonio (1653–1715), Italian composer, became vice-*Kapellmeister* at Vienna in 1700 and first *Kapellmeister* in 1712.

APPENDIX D

BIBLIOGRAPHY

Akerman, John Yonge, 'Moneys received and paid for Secret Services of Charles II and James II.' (London, 1851.)

Arkwright, G. E. P., 'Purcell's Church Music.' (*Musical Antiquary,* i, pp. 63–72, 234–48.)

Arundell, Dennis, 'Henry Purcell.' (Oxford and London, 1927.)

Bridge, J. C., 'A Great English Choir-Trainer: Captain Cooke.' (*Musical Antiquary,* ii, pp. 61–79.)

Bridge, J. Frederick, 'Purcell's Birthplace and Residences.' (*Musical Times,* November 1895.)

—— 'Twelve Good Musicians.' (London, 1920.)

Burney, Charles, 'A General History of Music,' Vol. III. (London, 1789.)

Buttrey, J., 'Dating Purcell's "Dido and Aeneas",' in 'Proceedings of the Royal Musical Association,' 1967–8. (London, 1968.)

Chester, J. L., 'The Marriage, Baptismal, and Burial Registers of the Collegiate Church or Abbey of St. Peter, Westminster.' (London, 1876.)

Colles, H. C., 'Voice and Verse: a Study in English Song.' (London, 1928.)

—— 'Some Musical Instruction Books of the Seventeenth Century,' in 'Proceedings of the Musical Assocation,' 1928–9. (Leeds, 1929.)

Cooper, Gerald M., 'The Chronology of Purcell's Works.' (*Musical Times,* July–December 1943.)

Cummings, William H., 'Purcell.' (London, 1881.)

Dart, Thurston, 'Purcell's Chamber Music,' in 'Proceedings of the Royal Musical Association,' 1958–9. (London, 1959.)

Day, Cyrus Lawrence, & Murrie, Eleanor Boswell, 'English Song-Books, 1651–1702.' (London, 1940.)

Demarquez, S., 'Purcell: la vie, l'œuvre.' (Paris, 1951.)

Dent, E. J., 'Foundations of English Opera.' (Cambridge, 1928.)

Downes, John, 'Roscius Anglicanus.' Edited by Montague Summers. (London, 1928.)

Dupré, Henri, 'Purcell.' (Paris, 1927.)

E[dwards], F. G., 'A Master Organ Builder: Father Smith.' (*Musical Times,* August 1905.)

Appendix D—Bibliography

Evelyn, John, 'Diary.' Edited by E. S. de Beer. 6 vols. (Oxford, 1955.)

Favre-Lingorow, S., 'Der Instrumentalstil von Purcell.' (Berne, 1950.)

Fuller-Maitland, J. A., 'Foreign Influences on Henry Purcell.' (*Musical Times*, January 1896.)

Hawkins, John, 'A General History of the Science and Practice of Music.' New edition, Vol. II. (London, 1875.)

Hayes, Gerald R., 'Musical Instruments and their Music, 1500–1750,' Vol. II, 'The Viols, and other Bowed Instruments.' (Oxford, 1930.)

Holland, A. K., 'Henry Purcell: The English Musical Tradition.' (London, 1932.)

Holst, Gustav, 'Henry Purcell,' in 'The Heritage of Music,' Vol. I. (Oxford, 1927.)

Holst, Imogen, ed., 'Henry Purcell (1659–1695): Essays on his Music.' (London, 1959.)

Hughes-Hughes, A., 'Henry Purcell's Handwriting.' (*Musical Times*, February 1896.)

Husk, William H., 'An Account of the Musical Celebrations on St. Cecilia's Day.' (London, 1857.)

Lafontaine, Henry Cart de, 'The King's Musick.' (London, 1909.)

Laurie, Margaret, 'Did Purcell set "The Tempest"?,' in 'Proceedings of the Royal Musical Association,' 1963–4. (London, 1964.)

Lawrence, W. J., 'Foreign Singers and Musicians at the Court of Charles II.' (*Musical Quarterly*, 1923, pp. 217–25.)

—— 'The Elizabethan Playhouse and other Studies.' 2 vols. (Stratford-upon-Avon, 1912–13.)

—— 'The French Opera in London.' (*The Times Literary Supplement*, 28th March 1936.)

Luttrell, Narcissus, 'A Brief Relation of State Affairs from September 1678 to April 1714.' 6 vols. (Oxford, 1857.)

Mace, Thomas, 'Musick's Monument.' (London, 1676.)

Macrory, Edmund, 'Notes on the Temple Organ.' (3rd edition, London, 1911.)

McGuinness, Rosamond, 'English Court Odes, 1660–1820.' (Oxford, 1971.)

Meyer, Ernst Hermann, 'Die mehrstimmige Spielmusik des 17. Jahrhunderts in Nord- und Mitteleuropa.' (Cassel, 1934.)

Moore, R. E., 'Henry Purcell and the Restoration Theatre.' (London, 1961.)

Nicoll, Allardyce, 'A History of Restoration Drama, 1660–1700.' (4th edition, Cambridge, 1952.)

North, Roger, 'Autobiography.' Edited by Augustus Jessopp. (London, 1887.)

—— 'The Life of the Right Honourable Francis North.' (London, 1742.)

—— 'Memoirs of Musick.' Edited by Edward F. Rimbault (London, 1846.)

—— 'The Musicall Gramarian.' Edited by Hilda Andrews. (London, 1925.)

—— 'Roger North on Music.' Edited by John Wilson. (London, 1959.)

Parry, C. Hubert H., 'The Oxford History of Music,' Vol. III, 'The Music of the Seventeenth Century.' (2nd edition, Oxford, 1938.)

Pepys, Samuel, 'Diary.' Edited by R. Latham & W. Matthews. 11 vols. (London, 1970–.)

Prunières, Henry, 'L'Opéra italien en France avant Lulli.' (Paris, 1913.)

Pulver, Jeffrey, 'A Biographical Dictionary of Old English Music.' (London, 1927.)

Quervain, Fritz de, 'Der Chorstil Henry Purcell's.' (Berne, 1935.)

Ravenzwaaij, G. van, 'Purcell.' (Haarlem & Antwerp, 1954.)

Rimbault, E. F., 'The Old Cheque-book, or Book of Remembrance, of the Chapel Royal, from 1561 to 1744.' (London, 1872.)

Rolland, Romain, 'L'Opéra anglais au XVIIe siècle.' In 'Encyclopédie de la Musique.' 1re partie. (Paris, 1913.)

Runciman, John F., 'Purcell.' (London, 1909.)

Sandford, Francis, 'The History of the Coronation of James II and Queen Mary.' (London, 1687.)

Schjelderup-Ebbe, Dag, 'Purcell's Cadences.' (Oslo, 1962.)

Scholes, Percy A., 'The Puritans and Music in England and New England.' (London, 1934.)

Sietz, R., 'Henry Purcell: Zeit, Leben, Werk.' (Leipzig, 1956.)

Squire, W. B., 'Purcell as Theorist.' (*Sammelbände der Internationalen Musikgesellschaft*, vi, pp. 521–67.)

—— 'Purcell's "Dido and Æneas."' (*Musical Times*, June 1918.)

—— 'Purcell's Dramatic Music.' (*S.I.M.G.*, v, pp. 489–564.)

Squire, W. B., 'Purcell's "Fairy Queen."' (*Musical Times*, January 1920.)
—— 'Purcell's Music for the Funeral of Mary II.' (*S.I.M.G.*, iv, pp. 225–33.)
—— 'The Music of Shadwell's "Tempest."' (*Musical Quarterly*, 1921, pp. 565–78.)
Svanepol, P. E., 'Das dramatische Schaffen Purcells.' (Vienna, 1926.)

Tilmouth, Michael, 'The Technique and Forms of Purcell's Sonatas.' (*Music & Letters*, April 1959, pp. 109–21.)

Walker, Ernest, 'A History of Music in England.' (3rd edition, Oxford, 1952.)
Walker, F. H., 'Purcell's Handwriting.' (*Monthly Musical Record*, September 1942.)
Wessely-Kropik, Helene, 'Henry Purcell als Instrumentalkomponist.' (*Studien zur Musikwissenschaft*, xxii, pp. 85–141.)
West, John E., 'Cathedral Organists, Past and Present.' (2nd edition, London, 1921.)
Westrup, J. A., 'Fact and Fiction about Purcell,' in 'Proceedings of the Musical Association,' 1935–6. (Leeds, 1936.)
—— 'Purcell's Music for "Timon of Athens,"' in 'Festschrift Karl Gustav Fellerer.' (Regensburg, 1962.)
—— 'Purcell's Parentage.' (*Music Review*, 1964, pp. 100–3.)
Whittaker, W. G., 'Some Observations on Purcell's Harmony.' (*Musical Times*, October 1934.)
Wood, Anthony, 'Life and Times.' Edited by Andrew Clark. 5 vols. (Oxford, 1891.)

Zimmerman, Franklin B., 'Henry Purcell, 1659–1695: an Analytical Catalogue of his Music.' (London, 1963.)
—— 'Henry Purcell, 1659–1695: his Life and Times.' (London, 1967.)
—— 'A Newly Discovered Anthem by Purcell.' (*Musical Quarterly*, 1959, pp. 302–11.)
—— 'Purcell and the Dean of Westminster—Some New Evidence.' (*Music & Letters*, 1962, pp. 7–15.)
—— 'Purcell's Family Circle Revisited and Revised.' (*Journal of the American Musicological Society*, 1963, pp. 373–9.)

The following abbreviations are used in the footnotes:

Abbey Registers.	See *Chester, J. L.*
Baker's *Chronicle.*	*Baker, Richard,* 'A Chronicle of the Kings of England.' 4th edition. (London, 1665.)
Cal. S. P. Dom.	'Calendar of State Papers, Domestic Series.'
Cal. Treas. Books.	'Calendar of Treasury Books.'
Cheque Book.	See *Rimbault, E. F.*
H.M.C.	'Historical Manuscripts Commission.'
King's Musick.	See *Lafontaine, Henry Cart de.*
P.C.C.	Prerogative Court of Canterbury.
P.C.West.	Peculiar Court of Westminster.
Secret Services.	See *Akerman, John Yonge.*
W.A.	Westminster Abbey.
W.A.M.	Westminster Abbey Muniments.
Westminster Records.	*Smith, John Edward,* 'A Catalogue of Westminster Records.' (London, 1900.)

APPENDIX E

RATHER than cumber the earlier pages of the book with controversy
I have reserved for this appendix a discussion of the evidence for Purcell's
parentage and family. The only primary source is a letter from Thomas
Purcell to the Reverend John Gostling, dated 8th February 1679, which
was once in the possession of Dr. W. H. Cummings and later in the
Nanki Music Library, Tokyo (facsimile between pp. 84 and 85.)

'S^r

'I have re^cd y^r fauor of yours of ye 4th wth ye Incloseds [1] for my sonne
Henry: I am sorry wee are Like to be w^thout you soe Long as yours
mentions: but tis very Likely you may have a summons to appeare
among us sooner then you Imagin: for my sonne is composing: wherin
you will be cheifly consern'd. Howeuer your ocations and tyes where
you are must be consider'd and your conueniencies euer comply'de
w^thall; in ye meane time assure your self I shall be carefull of your
consern's heir by minding and Refreshing our masters memory of his
Gratious promis when there is ocation: my wife Returns thanks for y^r
compliment wth her seruis: and pray Sr Giue both our Respects and
humble seruices to Dr Belk [2] and his Lady and beleeue euer that I am

> 'S^r
>
> 'your affectionatt and humble seruant
> 'T. Purcell.

'D^r perce [3] is in towne but
I haue not see'n him since.
I haue perform'd y^r
compliments to Dr Blow
Will Turner et:
  'F faut: and Double Elamy are preparing for you.' [4]

---

[1] i.e. 'enclosures.'

[2] Thomas Belke (1635–1712), prebendary of Canterbury.

[3] Thomas Pierce (1622–91), dean of Salisbury and chaplain in
ordinary to Charles II.

[4] The letter is addressed: 'This for Mr. John Gostling, Chaunter of
the quire of Canterbury Cathedral.' Gostling became a gentleman of

This letter makes it quite plain that 'my sonne Henry' is the composer, who has, in fact, left abundant testimony of his respect for Gostling's low notes.

Hawkins, however, in his history (page 743), says that the composer was the son of Henry Purcell and the nephew of Thomas Purcell; and not only Burney but every other subsequent writer has followed him. It is obvious that Hawkins himself is not sufficient authority; his history was published in 1776, more than eighty years after Purcell's death, and has been proved to be unreliable in a large number of other particulars. Unless, therefore, he has some further authority behind him, his statement cannot be accepted in face of the plain evidence of Thomas Purcell's own letter. The authority that Hawkins gives is 'Ashmolean MS.,' which, as he explains elsewhere (page 455), consists of Anthony Wood's manuscript notes on the lives of English musicians, now in the Bodleian Library under the press-mark 'Wood D 19 (4).' Unfortunately Wood's note on Purcell contains no justification for saying that Henry Purcell was the composer's father. Wood says simply:

'*Purcell* Henry, originally one of the children in the Kings chap. or bred under Dr. Chr. Gibbons   I think afterwards Organist to K. Ch. 2 & K. Will. 3 & Organist of S. peters ch. at Westm.'

adding above:

'Borne in Lond.—He, Dr. Child & Dr. Blow are organists to K. Will. & Qu. Mary.'

The rest of his note consists of a list of compositions. The source of Hawkins's statement may have been Wood's note on Daniel Purcell, which originally read:

'*Purcell* Daniel, Organist of Magd. Coll. in Oxon. son of Hen. Purcell,'

but was corrected by Wood himself to 'brother to Hen. Purcell.'

The acceptance of Hawkins's statement by subsequent writers has had mischievous results. Cummings, who appears to have been the first to see Thomas Purcell's letter, was forced to adopt an airy hypothesis in order to reconcile it with Hawkins. Since one child cannot have

---

the Chapel Royal on 25th February 1679 (*Cheque Book*, p. 16). The references in the postscript are to his exceptional low notes. 'F fa ut' and 'E la mi' were the old names for F and E in the hexachordal system.

two fathers, he explained the contradiction by saying that on the death of the elder Henry Purcell in 1664 the boy was left to the care of Thomas, who adopted him as his son. This explanation has been borrowed by other writers, but there is not a scrap of evidence for it. Indeed, Henry Purcell did not make a will; his estate was administered by his widow Elizabeth.[1] The only proved offspring of Henry Purcell is a daughter, Katherine, who was baptized on 13th March 1662.[2] In 1691 she married by licence (Vicar-General) the Reverend William Sale of Sheldwich, Kent,[3] and in 1699 she administered the estate of her mother, Elizabeth Purcell, who was buried in St. Margaret's, Westminster, on 26th August.[4]

It will be seen that Thomas Purcell's letter is quite sufficient evidence in itself. When a man speaks of someone as his son, it is natural to suppose that he is using a common English word in its ordinary significance. But it is interesting to see what confirmation can be found for this perfectly natural and obvious interpretation. The inscription on Edward Purcell's tombstone at Wytham, near Oxford, does not give us any precise information. It begins:

HERE lieth the body of EDWARD PURCEL, eldest son of M.R PURCEL, gentleman of the ROYAL CHAPEL, and BROTHER to M.R HENRY PURCEL, so much renown'd for his skill in MUSICK.

But even the fact that no Christian name is given for the father is significant. The elder Henry Purcell died in 1664, after four years in the royal chapel. Thomas Purcell died in 1682, after twenty-two years in the king's service, and, as I have shown, held a number of important and responsible positions. 'Mr. Purcell,' without any qualification, would most naturally refer to Thomas. Consider, too, the evidence we should expect to find if the composer and his brothers were the

---

[1] P.C. West., Admon., 7th October 1664.

[2] *Abbey Registers*, p. 67.

[3] Registers of St. Mary Magdalen, Old Fish Street (typescript copy by W. H. Challen in the Guildhall Library), 18th June 1691; *Abbey Registers*, p. 67, n.

[4] Churchwarden's accounts of St. Margaret's, Westminster (now at the Westminster City Hall), vol. 80 (1699–1700), 22nd August 1699; *Abbey Registers*, p. 67; P.C. West., Admon., 7th September 1699.

[5] The transcription in Hawkins, p. 749 n., is inaccurate in detail.

children of Henry Purcell. Since Katherine Purcell was baptized in Westminster Abbey, why not Daniel, who can hardly have been born before 1663? Again, if Edward and Daniel were the sons of Henry Purcell, why was it left to Katherine to administer Elizabeth Purcell's estate in 1699? Edward and Daniel were both alive then.

Not only must Edward, Henry and Daniel be the sons of Thomas Purcell but also Joseph, who administered the estate of his brother Daniel in January 1718,[1] and Matthew, who is mentioned as Thomas's son in a power of attorney dated 1681.[2] Further, there is a Charles Purcell, who went to sea on board a sloop called *Le George* and died a bachelor 'in partibus Guineae' in 1686. Letters of administration were at first granted to his brother Matthew, but these were renounced when a will was discovered and proved two months later. In the will, which is dated 4th June 1682, Charles Purcell names his mother Katherine Purcell and his sisters Elizabeth and Katherine, and appoints his brother Edward his executor.[3] Since Thomas Purcell's wife was called Katherine,[4] and since he had a son Matthew, it is very probable that Charles was also his son. Another son, Francis, is mentioned as a groom of the Privy Chamber in 1673 and as succeeding 'his father, Thomas Purcell, deceased' as groom of the robes in September 1682.[5]

It must be admitted that the relationships of the Purcell family are not always easy to disentangle. One reason is that there were several Purcells living in London at the time, and some of them had the same Christian names. For instance, a Henry Purcell, who cannot possibly have been the composer, was 'Bishop's Boy' at Westminster School from 1678 to 1680. A further difficulty is that what appears to be evidence has sometimes been misinterpreted or has led to uncertain conclusions. We read in J. R. Bloxam's *A Register of the Presidents, Fellows, Demies ... of Saint Mary Magdalen College* (Oxford, 1853-85), vol. ii, p. 203, that Daniel

---

[1] P.C.C., Admon., 17th January 1718.

[2] Cummings, p. 34, where the full text is quoted. This is possibly the Matthew Purcell whose will was proved on 12th October 1702 (P.C.C., 165 Hern).

[3] P.C.C., Admon., 2nd March 1686; 63 Lloyd, 20th May 1686.

[4] She is named in his will (P.C.C., 138 Cottle, 8th November 1682).

[5] Zimmerman, *Henry Purcell, 1659-1695: his Life and Times*, pp. 316-319.

Purcell was 'Son of Henry Purcell, Gentleman of the Chapel Royal'; but this is a note by the editor, not a quotation from the actual registers, which merely record the annual payments made to Daniel as organist. John Hingston's will, dated 12th December 1683, includes the following, in addition to various bequests to his family and to fellow musicians and pupils:

Item I give and bequeath unto my Godson Richard Graham the summe of ffifty pounds Item I give and bequeath unto my ever beloved friend Mr Thomas Blagrave one of the Gent. of his Ma^{ts} Chappell Ten pounds and also my best Chest of Vyolls also I give and bequeath unto Peter Hingeston my apprentice the summe of forty pounds to be paid unto him as my Executors shall direct Item I give and bequeath one moyety of all arreares which shall be due unto me from his Ma^{ty} at the tyme of my decease unto my said Godsonn Richard Graham and the other moyety to my Relations afforementioned to be equally divided amongst them Item I give unto George Wyatte[1] of Westm. five pounds Also to my Godson Henry Pursall (son of Elizabeth Pursall) five pounds And also to my Godson John Andrews in Harthorne Lane five pounds.

The description 'son of Elizabeth Pursall' would suggest that this 'Henry Pursall' was the son of Henry the elder, since she was his wife and had been a widow for many years. But if this is the composer it is curious that Hingston should give no further description of a man who had not only been his assistant for some years but was also by that time composer for the violins, organist of Westminster Abbey and one of the organists of the Chapel Royal.

Only two of Purcell's children are known to have survived him. His daughter Frances married Leonard Welsted at the age of 19. Welsted, who was equally young at the time, became a civil servant and wrote poetry. He published a satire on Pope, to which that poet retorted with some acrimony in *The Dunciad*. Purcell's son Edward was appointed organist of St. Margaret's, Westminster, in 1726 and died in 1740. Edward's son, Edward Henry, was a chorister in the Chapel Royal in 1737 and was organist of St. John's, Hackney, from 1753 till his death in 1765.

---

[1] Presumably the organ-blower mentioned on p. 58.

APPENDIX F

A thousand, thousand ways (*The Fairy Queen*).
Æolus, you must appear. See *While these pass o'er.*
Ah! Belinda (*Dido and Æneas*).
Ah! cruel, bloody fate (*Theodosius*).
Ah! how sweet it is to love (*Tyrannic Love*).
Ah me! to many deaths (*Regulus*).
All our days and our nights (*Dioclesian*).
Arise, ye subterranean winds (*The Tempest*).

Begone, curst fiends of hell (*The Indian Queen*).
Beneath the poplar's shadow (*Sophonisba*).
Blow, Boreas, blow (*Sir Barnaby Whigg*).
Britons, strike home (*Bonduca*).

Celia has a thousand charms (*The Rival Sisters*).
Celia, that I once was blest (*Amphitryon*).
Charon the peaceful shade invites (*Dioclesian*).
Come all to me (*Timon of Athens*).
Come, all ye songsters of the sky (*The Fairy Queen*).
Come away, do not stay (*Œdipus*).
Come away, fellow sailors (*Dido and Æneas*).
Come down, come down, my blusterers (*The Tempest*).
Come every demon who o'ersees (*Circe*).
Come if you dare (*King Arthur*).
Come unto these yellow sands (*The Tempest*).
Corinna, I excuse thy face (*The Wives' Excuse*).
Cynthia frowns whene'er I woo her (*The Double Dealer*).

---

[1] This list includes only solo songs. Songs with chorus are given, except those in which the chorus plays the most important part. Short solos or recitatives in continuous scenes have not been indexed.

Dear, pretty youth (*The Tempest*).
Dream no more of pleasures past (*Theodosius*)
Dry those eyes (*The Tempest*).

Fair and serene (*The Tempest*).
Fairest isle (*King Arthur*).
Fled is my love (*A Fool's Preferment*).
For Iris I sigh (*Amphitryon*).
From rosy bowers (*Don Quixote*, part iii).
Full fathom five (*The Tempest*).

Genius of England (*Don Quixote*, part ii).
Great Diocles the boar has killed (*Dioclesian*).
Great Love, I know thee now (*King Arthur*).

Hail to the myrtle shade (*Theodosius*).
Halcyon days (*The Tempest*).
Hang this whining way of wooing (*The Wives' Excuse*).
Hark, behold the heavenly choir (*Theodosius*).
Hark how all things (*The Fairy Queen*).
Hark, the ech'ing air (*The Fairy Queen*).
Hear, ye gods of Britain (*Bonduca*).
Hence with your trifling deity (*Timon of Athens*).
Here's the summer, sprightly, gay (*The Fairy Queen*).
Hither this way (*King Arthur*).
How blest are shepherds (*King Arthur*).
How happy is she (*The Rival Sisters*).
How happy's the husband (*Love Triumphant*).
Hush, no more (*The Fairy Queen*).

I am come to lock all fast (*The Fairy Queen*).
I attempt from love's sickness to fly (*The Indian Queen*).
I call you all to Woden's hall (*King Arthur*).
I come to sing great Zempoalla's story (*The Indian Queen*).
I looked and saw within the book of fate (*The Indian Emperor*).
I see she flies me (*Aureng-Zebe*).
I sighed and I pined (*A Fool's Preferment*).
I sighed and owned my love (*The Fatal Marriage*).
If love's a sweet passion (*The Fairy Queen*).
If thou wilt give me back my love (*A Fool's Preferment*).
I'll mount to yon blue coelum (*A Fool's Preferment*).

I'll sail upon the dog-star (*A Fool's Preferment*).
In vain, Clemene, you bestow (*Sir Anthony Love*).
In vain 'gainst love I strove (*Henry II*).
Ingrateful love (*The Wives' Excuse*).

Kind fortune smiles (*The Tempest*).

Lads and lasses, blithe and gay (*Don Quixote*, part ii).
Let monarchs fight (*Dioclesian*).
Let not a moon-born elf mislead ye (*King Arthur*).
Let the dreadful engines (*Don Quixote*, part i).
Let the graces and pleasures repair (*Dioclesian*).
Let the soldiers rejoice (*Dioclesian*).
Let us dance, let us sing (*Dioclesian*).
Love in their little veins (*Timon of Athens*).
Love quickly is pall'd (*Timon of Athens*).
Lucinda is bewitching fair (*Abdelazer*).

Man is for the woman made (*The Mock Marriage*).
Music for a while (*Œdipus*).

Next winter comes slowly (*The Fairy Queen*).
No, no, poor suffering heart (*Cleomenes*).
Now, now the fight's done (*Theodosius*).
Now the night is chas'd away (*The Fairy Queen*).
Nymphs and shepherds, come away (*The Libertine*).

O lead me to some peaceful gloom (*Bonduca*).
O let me weep (*The Fairy Queen*).
Oft she visits this lone mountain (*Dido and Æneas*).
Oh, how you protest (*The Mock Marriage*).
One charming night (*The Fairy Queen*).

Pluto, arise (*Circe*).
Pursue thy conquest, love (*Dido and Æneas*).
Pursuing beauty (*Sir Anthony Love*).

Retired from any mortal's sight (*King Richard II*).
Return, revolting rebels (*Timon of Athens*).

Sad as death at dead of night (*Theodosius*).
Saint George, the patron of our isle (*King Arthur*).
Say, cruel Amoret (*The Wives' Excuse*).

Appendix F—List of Songs in the Plays

See, even night herself is here (*The Fairy Queen*).
See, I obey (*The Fairy Queen*).
See my many colour'd fields (*The Fairy Queen*).
See, see the heavens smile (*The Tempest*).
See where repenting Celia lies (*The Married Beau*).
Seek not to know (*The Indian Queen*).
Shake the cloud from off your brow (*Dido and Æneas*).
Since from my dear (*Dioclesian*).
Since the toils and the hazards (*Dioclesian*).
Sing while we trip it (*The Fairy Queen*).
Sound, fame (*Dioclesian*).
Still I'm wishing (*Dioclesian*).
Sweeter than roses (*Pausanias*).

Take not a woman's anger ill (*The Rival Sisters*).
Tell me no more I am deceived (*The Maid's Last Prayer*).
Thanks to these lonesome vales (*Dido and Æneas*).
The air with music gently wound (*Circe*).
The cares of lovers (*Timon of Athens*).
The danger is over (*The Fatal Marriage*).
The gate to bliss does open stand (*Theodosius*).
There's not a swain (*Rule a Wife and Have a Wife*).
There's nothing so fatal as woman (*A Fool's Preferment*).
They tell us that you mighty powers above (*The Indian Queen*).
Thou doting fool (*King Arthur*).
Though you make no return to my passion (*The Maid's Last Prayer*).
Thrice happy lovers (*The Fairy Queen*).
Thus happy and free (*The Fairy Queen*).
Thus the ever grateful spring (*The Fairy Queen*).
Thus the gloomy world (*The Fairy Queen*).
Thus to a ripe consenting maid (*The Old Bachelor*).
Thy genius, lo! (two settings) (*The Massacre of Paris*).
'Tis death alone can give me ease (*A Fool's Preferment*).
'Tis I that have warmed ye (*King Arthur*).
To arms, heroic prince (*The Libertine*).
Trip it, trip it in a ring (*The Fairy Queen*).
'Twas within a furlong (*The Mock Marriage*).

Wake, Quivera (*The Indian Queen*).
What power art thou ? (*King Arthur*).

What shall I do to show ? (Dioclesian).
When a cruel long winter (The Fairy Queen).
When first I saw the bright Aurelia's eyes (Dioclesian).
When I am laid in earth (Dido and Æneas).
When I have often heard (The Fairy Queen).
When the world first knew creation (Don Quixote, part i).
While these pass o'er the deep (The Tempest).
Whilst I with grief (The Spanish Friar).
Why should men quarrel ? (The Indian Queen).

Ye blustering brethren (King Arthur).
Ye gentle spirits of the air (The Fairy Queen).
Ye twice ten hundred deities (The Indian Queen).
Yes, Xansi, in your looks I find (The Fairy Queen).
Your hay it is mowed (King Arthur).

INDEX

INDEX

Index

318

Index

Index